Literary Images of Ontario

There are Russians and Australians who think of Ontario the same way that Ontarians think of Samarcand or Baghdad, romantic, improbable.

Hugh Hood

When we said 'home' and meant Ontario, we had very different places in mind.

Alice Munro

W.J. KEITH

Literary Images of Ontario

A project of the
Ontario Historical Studies Series
for the Government of Ontario
Published by University of Toronto Press
Toronto Buffalo London

ISBN 0-8020-3470-5 (cloth)
ISBN 0-8020-3469-1 (paper)

Printed on acid-free paper

Canadian Cataloguing in Publication Data

Keith, W.J. (William John), 1934–
Literary images of Ontario

Includes bibliographical references and index.
ISBN 0-8020-3470-5 (bound) ISBN 0-8020-3469-1 (pbk.)

1. Ontario in literature. 2. Canadian poetry (English) –
History and criticism.* 3. Canadian fiction (English) –
History and criticism.* I. Title.

PS8101.05K43 1992   c811.009'32713   C92-093796-9
PR91985.5.05K3 1992

PICTURE CREDITS

Archives of Ontario:
watercolour by Elizabeth Simcoe, c. 1796
(Simcoe Sketches #135); portrait of Anna Jameson, c. 1837
(AC 2305 s4299); sketch by Anna Jameson (ACC 2725);
Toronto waterfront, 1840s (ACC 1696 s1156);
iceboating on Toronto Bay (s17290); Grey Owl, c. 1931
(ACC 6996 s12935)

Metropolitan Toronto Reference Library:
view of Niagara Falls (917.1.H26); sketch
of road in Orillia township, c. 1844 (T-14377)

This book has been published with the assistance of funds provided
by the Government of Ontario through the Ministry of Culture
and Communications.

Contents

The Ontario Historical Studies Series

For many years the principal theme in English-Canadian historical writing has been the emergence and the consolidation of the Canadian nation. This theme has been developed in uneasy awareness of the persistence and importance of regional interests and identities, but because of the central role of Ontario in the growth of Canada, Ontario has not been seen as a region. Almost unconsciously, historians have equated the history of the province with that of the nation and have often depicted the interests of other regions as obstacles to the unity and welfare of Canada.

The creation of the province of Ontario in 1867 was the visible embodiment of a formidable reality, the existence at the core of the new nation of a powerful if disjointed society whose traditions and characteristics differed in many respects from those of the other British North American colonies. The intervening century has not witnessed the assimilation of Ontario to the other regions in Canada; on the contrary it has become a more clearly articulated entity. Within the formal geographical and institutional framework defined so assiduously by Ontario's political leaders, an increasingly intricate web of economic and social interests has been woven and shaped by the dynamic interplay between Toronto and its hinterland. The character of this regional community has been formed in the tension between a rapid adaptation to the processes of modernization and industrialization in modern Western society and a reluctance to modify or discard traditional attitudes and values. Not surprisingly, the Ontario outlook has been, and in some measure still is, a compound of aggressiveness, conservatism, and the conviction that its values should be the model for the rest of Canada.

From the outset the objective of the Board of Trustees of the series has been to describe and analyse the historical development of Ontario as a distinct region within Canada. When completed, the series will include thirty-one volumes covering many aspects of the life and work of the province from its foundation in 1791 to our own time. Among these will be biographies of several premiers, and thematic works on the growth of the provincial economy, educational institutions, labour, welfare, the Franco-Ontarians, the Native Peoples, and the arts.

In planning this project, the editors and the board have endeavoured to maintain a reasonable balance between different kinds and areas of historical research, and to appoint authors ready to ask new questions about the past and to answer them in accordance with the canons of contemporary scholarship. *Literary Images of Ontario* is the ninth theme study to be published. In this volume, W.J. Keith has distilled from the writings of early observers of Ontario, and of our poets and novelists, a series of portraits of the land, and of our rural and urban communities in the past and the present. He has shown Ontario 'as she was seen to be' in the 'imaginative responses of writers in prose and verse,' ranging from the acerbic comments of Anna Jameson through the ambiguous conceptions of Leacock, to the finely tuned perceptions of Davies, Atwood, and Hood.

Literary Images of Ontario is a scholarly, perceptive, and often delightful account of the ways in which writers have depicted Ontario and Ontarians, and as such is a significant addition to the cultural history of this province. We hope that it will stimulate further exploration of the relationship between imaginative literature and Ontarians' understanding of their society and culture.

The editors and the Board of Trustees are grateful to W.J. Keith for undertaking this task.

Goldwin French
Peter Oliver
Jeanne Beck
Maurice Careless, Chairman of the Board of Trustees

Toronto
16 March 1992

Preface

This book is a somewhat unusual contribution to the series in which it appears. The traditional historians turn to formal records and reliable documents in an effort to produce as accurate an account as possible of what happened in the past. By contrast, in *Literary Images of Ontario* I have sifted the evidence of literature in an endeavour to find out how our perceptions of the past have been filtered down to us. I am less concerned with a complete or accurate picture than with the admittedly subjective impressions that have established themselves through the imaginative responses of writers in prose and verse. For some of the early impressions of Ontario, I have interpreted the word 'literary' quite broadly, and have leaned heavily on diaries, memoirs, and other (supposedly) non-fiction sources. But for the most part I have turned to the more prominent poets and writers of fiction. How have they seen Ontario and the people of Ontario? What have been the aspects of both province and inhabitants that have struck them as most typical or most memorable? How are our own assumptions and attitudes affected by what they have written? The emphasis, then, is not so much on Ontario as she was or is, but as she has been seen to be.

I have found this task exhilarating, though not without its complications. As I proceeded, it became abundantly clear that the literary evidence was neither constant nor comprehensive. Some areas of the province have attracted more literary attention than others; some segments of the population have expressed themselves more conspicuously in literary terms than others. Moreover, since I have confined my attention to literature in English, certain immigrant groups are less well represented than they deserve. However, I have hopes that my findings may even prove useful in drawing attention to these gaps in the imaginative record. As it is, I have tried to convey accurately what I have found. These are the terms in which, as I see it, writers have viewed Ontario and Ontarians, though my own cultural biases and predilections are clearly significant in my choice of images. Whether this constitutes a just and faithful picture is something individual readers must decide for themselves.

In a wide-ranging project of this kind, one is inevitably indebted to countless individuals who, through personal communication or the written word, have given invaluable hints. While I have doubtless committed many sins of omission and commission in the following pages, I realize that these are fewer in number than they would otherwise have been, thanks to the assistance of persons too numerous to be specified here. I am conscious, however, of two literary debts too prominent to go unacknowledged. William Kilbourn's compilation *The Toronto Book* was of considerable help in the early stages of my exploratory forays into the literary presentation of Toronto, and sent me scurrying to libraries to look up items I might otherwise have missed. And more recently, my colleague Linda Hutcheon helped to fill a bothersome gap by drawing my attention to the novels of F.G. Paci.

In addition, of course, there are more general debts. I am deeply grateful for the support and encouragement given to me by the officers of the Ontario Historical Studies Series, especially the editor-in-chief, Goldwin S. French, Peter Oliver, the associate editor, and the assistant editor and secretary-treasurer, Jeanne R. Beck. Over the years in which this book was being prepared, they have coped with the oddities and puzzlements of a non-historian with remarkable aplomb. And finally, a special thank-you to my wife Hiroko for being, as always, quietly supportive.

W.J. KEITH, University College, University of Toronto

Acknowledgments

Margaret Atwood. 'At the Tourist Centre in Boston' and 'A Bus along St. Clair: December' from *Selected Poems 1966–1984*, copyright © Margaret Atwood 1990. Reprinted by permission of Oxford University Press Canada.

Earle Birney. From *The Collected Poems* by Earle Birney. Used by permission of The Canadian Publishers, McClelland & Stewart, Toronto.

Christopher Dewdney. From *Predators of the Adoration* and *Radiant Inventory* by Christopher Dewdney. Used by permission of The Canadian Publishers, McClelland & Stewart, Toronto.

Mary di Michele. The quotations by Mary di Michele from *Bread and Chocolate* are reprinted by permission of Oberon Press. The quotations from *Mimosa and Other Poems* are reprinted by permission of Mosaic Press.

Joan Finnigan. Quotations from *Living Together* by permission of the author.

George Johnston. Passages on pp. 184–5 are from George Johnston's *Endeared by Dark*, published by The Porcupine's Quill, Erin, Ontario – reproduced here with their permission.

Dennis Lee. Quotations from *Civil Elegies and Other Poems* are reproduced with the permission of Stoddart Publishing Co. Limited, 34 Lesmill Rd., Don Mills, Ontario.

Douglas LePan. From *Weathering It* by Douglas LePan. Used by permission of The Canadian Publishers, McClelland & Stewart, Toronto.

Douglas Lochhead. Quotations from *The Full Furnace: Collected Poems* by permission of McGraw-Hill Ryerson.

E.J. Pratt. Quotations from *Complete Poems* by permission of University of Toronto Press.

Al Purdy. From *In Search of Owen Roblin* by Al Purdy. Used by permission of The Canadian Publishers, McClelland & Stewart, Toronto. From *Collected Poems* by permission of the author.

James Reaney. Quotations from *Poems* (ed. Germaine Warkentin, 1972) by permission of the author.

W.W.E. Ross. Quotations from *Shapes & Sounds* (ed. Raymond Souster and John Robert Colombo) by permission of John Robert Colombo.

Duncan Campbell Scott. Quotations from *Poems* and *The Green Cloister* by permission of John G. Aylen, QC.

F.R. Scott. From *The Collected Poems* by F.R. Scott. Used by permission of The Canadian Publishers, McClelland & Stewart, Toronto.

A.J.M. Smith. From *The Classic Shade* by A.J.M. Smith. Used by permission of The Canadian Publishers, McClelland & Stewart, Toronto.

Raymond Souster. The quotations by Raymond Souster from *Collected Poems* are reprinted by permission of Oberon Press. The quotations from *A Local Pride* are reprinted by permission of the author.

Miriam Waddington. 'Dead Lakes' from *Collected Poems*, copyright © Miriam Waddington 1986. Reprinted by permission of Oxford University Press Canada.

'The Simcoes left a ... mark on the nomenclature of Toronto by building a cabin for their son Francis on the eastern side and playfully but permanently christening the area Castle Frank' (p. 193). This romanticized water-colour was painted by Elizabeth Simcoe, c. 1796.

'... awfully grand, magnificent, and sublime' (George Heriot, qtd p. 21). Heriot
attempted to portray Niagara Falls in both words and pictures. This lithograph of the

view of the Falls of Niagara from the bank near Birch's Mills was executed for his book *Travels through the Canadas*, published in 1807.

OPPOSITE

The Dunsfords 'are bringing a carriage out with them [from England] ... I hope they do not forget to bring a good road too' (Anne Langton, qtd p. 20). Early roads were primitive, like this sketch of a corduroy road over a swamp in Orillia township by T.H. Ware, c. 1844.

Anna Jameson (1794–1860), the 'most intelligent as well as acid-tongued of the travellers in Upper Canada' (p. 195). This portrait, c. 1837, represents her at the time of her visit to Canada.

'On this [west] side of Toronto you are immediately in the pine forest, which extends
with little interruption ... for about fifty miles to Hamilton' (Jameson, qtd p. 26).
Sketch by Jameson of a journey from Toronto to Niagara in 1837. Note the 'boundless forest' (p. 26) and the blackened stumps.

Toronto waterfront, 1840s. For many early travellers, who arrived by water, this would be their first sight of the provincial capital.

'These ice-yachts, which seemed to consist of one huge white sail, flitted here and there at incredible speed' (Robert Barr, qtd p. 200). Iceboating on Toronto Bay

Grey Owl, or Wa-sha-quon-asin, nature writer who adopted an Indian lifestyle and became a spokesman for the preservation of the North American wilderness. Only after his death in 1938 was it discovered that he was not an Indian, but in fact an Englishman named Archie Belaney. Photo, c. 1931

Literary Images of Ontario

Introductory: Three Approaches to Ontario

1   Atlantic Crossing

This is a book about the way in which a region of North America is presented within the literature of a European language. Behind it lie countless stories of peoples coming to a new and seemingly alien land, adapting its physical features to their own needs, and ultimately learning to see it through new eyes and to recognize it as home. Because this is a process I have gone through myself, it would be foolish to lay false claim to an impossible objectivity. At the risk of egotism, therefore, I must begin with myself.

I was twenty-four years old when I emigrated from England to Ontario in August 1958 to embark upon graduate studies in English at the University of Toronto. I came by ship from Southampton. We had an extraordinarily smooth voyage, sighted a number of icebergs as our path crossed the Labrador Current, and soon approached the fog-bound coast of Newfoundland, encountering an impressive array of (to me) strange-looking fishing craft. We sailed through the Straits of Belle Isle, passed Anticosti, took on a pilot, and then gradually moved up the St Lawrence. I remember noticing on both shores small, almost toy-like French-Canadian communities, which looked decidedly foreign to my English eyes, especially the wooden churches with their tapering silver spires. Not long after, we came to Cape Diamond, the Plains of Abraham, and a curious reunion with history, a history that seemed to me, paradoxically, at once pressing and remote. We docked at last at Montreal (we did not yet feel obliged to call it Montréal); a few hours later, I took the night train to Toronto.

Looking back now, I realize how shockingly ignorant I was of the land that was to become my home. I had only the haziest notions of its history or even of its geography. While I must have been vaguely conscious of the fact that I was following in the footsteps of large numbers of European immigrants in the previous century and a half, this awareness made little emotional impression upon me at the time. Moreover, I was not in a position to realize that I belonged to that last generation for whom a passage by sea would be regarded as the normal way of coming to the New World. Nowadays, of course, the average immigrant catches some stray glimpses of land through high cloud-breaks at several thousand feet, and is then confronted by the standardized architecture of an international airport. In a curious, perhaps sentimental, but nonetheless, I am convinced, very real way, I now feel a bond with those earlier sea-going expatriates who set such a noticeable stamp upon the life and culture of what we now know as Ontario.

If I knew little of Canadian history and geography at that time, I knew even less of its literature. I had brought with me Ralph Gustafson's newly published *Penguin Book of Canadian Verse*, but found its contents disconcertingly uninspired and derivative. Because of my lack of a familiarizing literary background, I missed a dimension that could have given depth and meaning to the voyage. When we encountered the icebergs, for example, I thought of Thomas Hardy's poem 'The Convergence of the Twain,' but knew nothing of Charles G.D. Roberts's 'The Iceberg' or E.J. Pratt's *The Titanic*. When we caught our first glimpses of barren New-World rock, it seemed bleak, but I did not know that Jacques Cartier had mythologized it as 'the land God gave to Cain,' or that Northrop Frye (in whose graduate course I was about to enrol) had likened a ship journeying up the St Lawrence to 'a tiny Jonah entering an enormous whale' (10). I wish I had known that Stephen Leacock, at the tender age of six, had been impressed by the harshness of the Gaspé landscape in contrast to the greenness of the England he had left behind; 'there it was,' he remembered, 'a tall, hard coast of trees and rock, clear and bright in the sunshine, not a bit soft, like England' (*Boy* 28). I was not even aware that writers like Susanna Moodie and Catharine Parr Traill had made similar voyages (in, be it noted, decidedly more uncomfortable conditions), and so could not compare my own reactions with theirs. When I boarded the train for Toronto, it would have been comforting if I had been able to see my situation in relation to Phil Branden's equivalent journey as recounted in the second chapter of Frederick Philip Grove's *A Search for America*.

The term 'culture-shock' was not then in general currency, but I experienced a mild attack of the condition on my arrival at Ontario's capital, which still, in 1958, retained more than a faint aura of its earlier designation, 'Toronto the Good.' I remember being struck by the extraordinary proliferation of Union Jacks and portraits of royalty in shops and public places; a generation later, I still find it amazing (as, I now know, did Leacock over a century ago) that any country in the late twentieth century should celebrate Queen Victoria's birthday with a national holiday. On my first visit to the theatre, a production of Shaw's *Pygmalion* at the Crest, I was intrigued – in what I must now recognize as a somewhat condescending way – by the program's insistence that the action took place in 'London (England).' At that time, Toronto was still a relatively compact, rather dull, Anglo-Saxon-dominated city with a deep concern, even among the young, for 'respectability'; shortly after I arrived, a fellow student refused to go to a local snack-bar with me unless I changed into proper shoes, since in Toronto, he explained uncomfortably, open sandals were a sign of homosexuality. It was all very bewildering.

Yet the beginnings of the present cosmopolitan city were even then discernible. The era of downtown high-rise apartments and grandiose office buildings was being relentlessly ushered in. One morning, walking along a street close to the university, I heard a tuneful aria wafting down to me from the girders. That was an experience which would have been inconceivable in England, and a practical indication that the Italian impact on the city's construction industry was considerable. (Only while writing this book did I discover that Rupert Brooke had had a similar experience in 1913.) This may well have been my first exposure to what, a decade later, would be christened 'multiculturalism,' though a friend from Hong Kong soon introduced me to the inexpensive gastronomical exoticism of Toronto's Chinatown. I also remember how another graduate student from England who held a teaching fellowship (as I did not) was assigned a class divided in terms of alphabet; he received those whose surnames ranged from S to Z, and was dramatically alerted to the number of students from Oriental or Eastern European backgrounds. At university level this was, I think, a comparatively recent phenomenon. There had, of course, been various and varying 'ethnic' pockets in the city for decades – as will become evident in a later chapter – but it is important to remember that the multicultural blend that most young and even middle-aged Torontonians take for granted is a surprisingly recent development.

At the 1958 Thanksgiving Weekend (another new holiday so far as I was concerned), I was invited down to Windsor by a cousin whom I had only met briefly once before. She took me on a tour of the immediate area, and I shall never forget the personal shock of driving through Essex County. I came from the English county of Essex myself, and here, suddenly, were sign-posts with familiar place names on them – but the directions and distances (though still in miles then) all seemed awry.

There was something literally disorienting about this experience, but it taught me in an emphatic manner two lessons that I ought to have learned long before: first, that even a simple act of naming can reveal deep personal and psychological implications; second, that a profound historical movement, duly commemorated here, dramatically linked my own past and present.

A brief anthology of subsequent experiences needs to be recorded also. I spent two happy years as lodger in the home of a septuagenarian Canadian landlady, more English than the English, who had never travelled further west than Stratford (and then only to visit the Stratford Festival); she maintained – so far as I was concerned – some surprisingly old-fashioned rituals, and proved a feminine variant of the man in Irving Layton's poem 'Anglo-Canadian' (which, of course, I only discovered later), who made 'even Englishmen / wince, and feel / unspeakably colonial' (150). I remember, too, the amazingly solemn way in which the Toronto of that time endured its occasional bouts of culture. At another Crest Theatre performance, this time of Dylan Thomas's *Under Milk Wood*, the audience, overawed by the knowledge that the author was an esteemed poet, took half the play to wake up to the fact that there was humour to be enjoyed there. At about the same time, I came to realize something I would already have known had I been a reader of Robertson Davies's *alter ego* Samuel Marchbanks (see *Papers* 61): that, while Torontonians found my own accent either impressive or hilarious, I must on no account suggest that they spoke with accents themselves. Tronno, after all, *was* Tronno. Finally, a later image from the early 1970s: when at last becoming a Canadian citizen, I was required, by an official who epitomized the characteristics and features of a stage Italian, to renounce all former allegiances before taking an oath of loyalty to the Queen. Ontario in a nutshell.

This may seem a strange way to begin a volume in a scholarly historical series, but it is necessary, I think, to acknowledge the personal dimension that is inevitably involved. In many respects, it is ironic that someone who came to Ontario as an immigrant only a generation ago should attempt to write this book. Yet, on the other hand, we are a province as well as a nation of immigrants (even the Indians – as we automatically called them then – had their ultimate origins elsewhere), so there may be a curious appropriateness to the fact after all. Indeed, there is a sense in which this book represents the fruits of a continuous process. When I had spent a decade in Ontario as a student and teacher of English literature, I began to be conscious of an increasingly urgent imperative to explore the literature of the land which I was clearly recognizing as my (albeit adopted) home. As I did so, I was struck by the variety of life and terrain recorded in Canadian – and in 'Ontarian' – literature. We have, surely, a unique situation here: a vast country with a well-nigh incredible range of climate and scenery – a 'sleeping giant' in the phrase that the poet D.G. Jones has aptly Canadianized (*Butterfly* 13) – awaiting through countless centuries a language that evolved in a more temperate and confined geography. The tensions generated are both frustrating and exhilarating. Moreover, we have also a remarkable blend of peoples, many of them English-speaking but from diverse origins – not only English, Scots, Irish, but immigrants from India, Pakistan, the Caribbean, and elsewhere. And along with these, a blend of other peoples – eastern European, Oriental, South American, as well as the more expected minorities from central and western Europe. All these inhabiting, exploring, and dominating an area that had once been the sole domain of the tribes we now call, in a revealingly curious phrase, 'the Native Peoples.' A blend of customs, attitudes, religions, prejudices, as well as human beings. The result is a rich hoard of literary images expressed in an equally rich diversity of styles. As one contemplates all this, one realizes that the various jigsaw pieces of experience are gradually fitting into a larger design. It is not quite the design of a historian, but it has its own peculiarly human resonance.

2   *Imaginative Geology*

'When did you come from the old country?': a recurrent question. I remember being struck at first by the oddity of the phrase 'the old country.' It represented a way of thinking I had not encountered before. Here was just another indication that I was in the New World – but suddenly the phrase 'the New World' seemed equally strange. The words 'old' and 'new' had once seemed clear-cut, obvious; now they took on unexpected meanings in a mysteriously elusive context. How did countries and continents come to acquire such labels? It was years before some of the implications behind this linguistic puzzle began to clarify within my mind.

From 'the old country' – or, rather old countries, for we must belatedly acknowledge that they were many – to ' the New World' is now a familiar pattern; by the end of the nineteenth century it had already become a combination of cliché and dead metaphor. Yet, had they paused to think about it, these immigrants must have realized that the new world is not – could not be – any newer than the old. It so happens that in 1832, the year that Catharine Parr Traill and Susanna Moodie made their Atlantic crossings along with so many hundreds of others, Charles Lyell was in the process of publishing his *Principles of Geo-*

logy, a study that was to revolutionize prevalent notions about the age of the earth. Many of those who came to Upper Canada at that time were doubtless prepared to accept Archbishop Ussher's well-known calculation of 4004 BC as the date established by biblical chronology for the creation of the world. But even those who were content with the oddly contradictory opening chapters of Genesis should have realized that all the dry land that appeared at this primordial gathering-together of the waters shared the same divine birth-date.

The early settlers judged such matters, however, by the presence or absence of familiar signs from their own cultural past. Everyone knew that 'America' was not discovered until 1492. If the Indians were recognized as having any kind of past, it was not accepted as an authentic or knowable past. Those with anthropological interests might detect traces of a traditional mythology, but it was crude – and, even worse, pagan. The romanticism of the period (the 1830s was, after all, the decade that saw the rise to prominence of Thomas Carlyle) may have brooded enthusiastically over the Eternities and Immensities, especially when confronted by scenes of natural sublimity like Niagara Falls, but these emotions were suitably vague and unfocused. Geological time-schemes, as they seeped into the popular consciousness, boggled rather than stimulated the mind. The awesome past of the area that has been designated Ontario for so tiny a percentage of the span of its physical existence is inevitably elusive. Even when the scientific experts – geologists, palaeontologists, archaeologists – have made their cautious and empiric reports, it is left to the poets and visionaries to create these pasts imaginatively, to connect them in a realizable form with modern human experience. Dennis Lee, for example, in his *Civil Elegies* can think back from modern Toronto to

> the barren Shield, immortal scrubland and our own,
> where near the beginning the spasms of lava
> settled to bedrock schist,
> barbaric land, initial, our
> own, scoured bare under
> crush of the glacial recessions ...   (40)

Here cosmic processes are brought within the scope of human awareness. Significantly, perhaps, the writers who have communicated their visions of the primordial past most memorably have generally received their enlightenment in a magic and unforgettable childhood moment.

For Hugh Hood, expressing himself through the mouth of his fictional Matt Goderich, the seeds of this vision were sown during family excursions made at weekends. These were either 'Down to the docks,' a journey that led deeper and deeper into 'the essential Toronto of pickup and delivery and redistribution of wealth,' or 'Into the country,' exploratory forays that attempted to unearth 'the recoverable past of Upper Canada' (*Swing* 175). But these two kinds of excursion, which initially seemed to represent a radical contrast, like the alternative 'ways' in Marcel Proust's *A la recherche du temps perdu*, are, he finds in later life, profoundly complementary. This time-journey starts, in terms of the narrative, from Toronto Island:

For all of recorded North American history, Toronto has been 'the Carrying Place.' That narrow forefinger of sand curving out from Ashbridge's Bay and Cherry Beach, cut off from the mainland by the Eastern Gap – those two trickling streams now dirtied, damned, nearly destroyed, our Don and Humber – this excrement-laden bay, these polluted beaches, are the scenes of aboriginal commerce unimaginably ancient. Before historical time begins in North America the carrying place was and is. When I mounted our tall old family bicycle those long calm days in August 1939 and wheeled shakily and tentatively eastward towards the Gap, I was beginning to grasp at – to sense myself in time with – a system of living predating the Bronze Age, extending back perhaps to the Palaeolithic.   (*Swing* 176)

In a half-Proustian, half-Wordsworthian spot of time, the young Matt Goderich discerns faintly and as yet below the level of language what he describes later as a 'notion that there might be such a thing as an Ontario style' (*New Athens* 70), a local experience that provides for its inhabitants links with the larger world of time and process.

At about the same time, the speaker in Alice Munro's short story 'Walker Brothers Cowboy' is taken by her father along the street of their southwestern Ontario small town to 'see if the Lake's still there' (*Dance* 1). At other docks (very different from Toronto's) where the grain boats wait, he offers her a glimpse of the even older forces of geology:

He tells me how the Great Lakes came to be. All where Lake Huron is now, he says, used to be flat land, a wide flat plain. Then came the ice, creeping down from the north, pushing down into the low places ... And then the ice went back, shrank back towards the North Pole where it came from, and left its fingers of ice in the deep places it had gouged, and ice turned to lakes and there they were today. They were *now*, as time went. I try to see that plain before me, dinosaurs walking on it, but I am not able even to imagine the shore of the Lake when the Indians were there, before Tuppertown. The tiny share we have of time appalls me, though my father seems to regard it with tranquillity.   (*Dance* 3)

A new, troubling, but mind-expanding horizon opens up for the sensitive child, who will for the rest of her life see her locality with new eyes.

But it is the poet Christopher Dewdney who has responded most acutely to the imaginative implications of local prehistory and geology. The son of novelist and antiquarian Selwyn Dewdney (co-author of a pioneering book on Indian rock-paintings in Ontario, some of which he was the first to discover), he may be said to have made geology the cornerstone of his poetic temple. In the preface to his selected poems, *Predators of the Adoration*, he records an early childhood experience that took place in the mid-to-late 1950s and is remarkably similar in essence to those of Hood's and Munro's protagonists:

I have been fascinated by limestone ever since my father first pointed it out to me when I was 5 or 6 years old. On a summer evening as we drove down into the Grand River valley near Paris, Ontario, he explained that the limestone was almost entirely composed of the shells & skeletons of underwater creatures, millions of years old, compacted and turned to rock. His explanation transformed the rock into a miraculous substance, which, as I elaborated my passion over the next few years, became a slow oracular fountain of compressed millennia. (7)

Science and imaginative vision blend here. The area of London, where the Dewdneys lived, underwent for the young boy a miraculous metamorphosis, revealing within itself 'exotic tropical landscapes and fabulous creatures, themselves steeped in the diffuse light of shallow equatorial oceans' (7). He made the momentous discovery that he could 'travel millions of years forward and backward in prehistory merely by traversing the strata which underlay Southwestern Ontario' (7).

Out of this experience has come a series of books with, for poetry, unlikely titles such as *A Palaeozoic Geology of London, Ontario* and *The Cenozoic Asylum*, seen as part of an ambitious work in progress entitled *A Natural History of Southwestern Ontario*. Dewdney identifies certain key spots in the area that become, as it were, local entrance points to a vast cosmological understanding. I select a few representative examples:

And on the sandbanks of Greenway park, pebbles of edible beige limestone, frosted with ossicles. (*Predators* 57)

At Bayfield the White Sands testing blue sky with the clarity of aerospace ... (58)

St. Mary's quarry at night and the unearthly fish that surface there. (66)

Petrolia bathed in a neo-carboniferous glow.   (68)

Jewelled sundews at Byron Bog.   (68)

Peripheral glimpse of trilobites scuttling into murky water at the edge of the Ausable.   (139)

Dewdney's vision is important not only because it reveals a so-called new world to be primordial, but also because, while glorying in the uniquely local, it simultaneously transforms it into an unbounded universal. Northrop Frye's famous Canadian question 'Where is here?' is transcended by Dewdney's implicit answer: 'Here is everywhere, at all times.' Or, in Dewdney's own words: 'Southwestern Ontario, through its extensions, became continuous with the world system at large' (8).

In a more recent volume, *Radiant Inventory*, Dewdney has further explored the interrelations of the regional and the cosmic in a prose-poem entitled 'Elora Gorge.' Here, he maintains, is an entry into the prehistoric past: 'The gorge is an erotic slash into the memory-soaked depths of the Silurian era' (96). For some it may seem no more than a geographical and geological phenomenon, but for Dewdney there is 'something deeper in this geography, stirring ancient racial memories' (105). As 'prehistoric light begins to glow through the rock' (102), the Elora landscape is recognized as a sacred place; this is indicated by a subtitle, 'The Stations of the Gorge' (104). The combination of scientific understanding and imaginative vision is nowhere better exemplified than in this almost mystical paragraph:

The gorge white in the noonday sun, the faces of limestone cliffs pale coffee and white, alternately brilliant with crystal facets and dark with moss in the damp elbows of the river. The sound of the rapids never far away. The river slowly cutting through limestone over thousands of years, eventually slicing through five million years of rock.   (102)

Dewdney is intent, like William Blake, on altering our consciousness, the way we see. He offers an instance when he listens to the dawn chorus in the gorge and visualizes it through the transforming lens of prehistoric awareness:

The morning chorus of birds is as alien as the first croaking of amphibians around coal-age swamps. A cacophony of reptilian twittering so refined it has taken on melodies, fragments of broken symphonies.   (94)

The ultimate confrontation is between primordial rock and the human mind. Two poets have articulated this confrontation in passages that, when juxtaposed, profoundly illuminate the possible relation between contemporary human beings and the awesome Ontario past. Dewdney is one of them, in the following prose extract:

It is a warm grey afternoon in August. You are in the country, in a deserted quarry of light grey devonian limestone in Southern Ontario ...

  You ... lean over and pick up a flat piece of layered stone. It is a rough triangle about one foot across. Prying at the stone you find the layers come apart easily in large flat pieces. Pale grey moths are pressed between the layers of stone. Freed, they flutter up like pieces of ash caught in a dust-devil. You are splashed by the other children but move not.   (*Predators* 105)

The other is Douglas LePan brooding on his connection with and separation from 'rock that is older than time':

> Rock, moss, lichen, and lichen over the moss,
> give me grounds for staring quartz in the eye,
> and feldspar, and mica, and boulder-beds teetering on granite,
> ice-ages forgotten at last and glaciers,
> and my own full share of fury and fire ...   (199-200)

If we are prepared to follow Dewdney and LePan's lead, our view of what was once thought of as 'prosaic Ontario' (Bourinot 24) will never be the same again.

3   Region at the Centre

At this point it may seem as if I have entangled myself in a hopeless contradiction. A book with the title 'Literary Images of Ontario' ought, surely, to concern itself with a local cohesiveness and sense of shared identity, yet I have been emphasizing 'rich diversity' and 'variety of life and terrain,' geological immensities which the area shares with the rest of the globe. How can these be reconciled? Ultimately, perhaps, they cannot, but we confront here a paradox that is at the heart of the Ontario experience. What makes Ontario Ontario? How is this subdivision of land and population within the larger entity of Canada (itself a part of the even larger entity of North America) to be recognized? Any account of the literary images of Ontario must therefore, sooner or later, face up to the thorny question not only of regionalism but more particularly of regionalism in the contemporary world. It is, of course, a well-known fact that Canada, even in the closing decade of the twentieth century, an age that has seen so much standardization and obliteration of local characteristics, is still remarkable for its regional differentiations. Canada remains, by world standards, a vast country in terms of geographical area (most of it, to be sure, barely habitable) with a decidedly small population scattered over dramatically varied geological terrain. Distances still constitute a problem, and individual isolated communities still depend for their survival (let alone growth) upon an extraordinary variety of physical conditions. Thus regionalism, although threatened in so many parts of the world, remains a fact of life in Canada.

Canada is generally divided into six or seven regions, depending upon whether one counts Newfoundland as separate or includes it with the previously established historical area known as the Maritimes. Here, for simplicity and convenience, I shall treat them as one, as 'the Atlantic Provinces.' The special features of five out of these six regions are immediately obvious. The Atlantic Provinces are distinctive by virtue of their seaboard culture and economy; Québec is clearly identified because of its French language and its Catholic historical traditions; the Prairies are known for their geography and environment; British Columbia is special as a result of its west-of-the-Rockies climate, ecology, and history; the North (though parts of it belong in a political sense to other regions) is obviously in a category by itself on account of its unique climate and geography.

But what about Ontario, the sixth region? Here is a diverse area, split geographically and geologically into the Canadian Shield on the one hand and the fertile area of the St Lawrence / Great Lakes lowlands on the other. It contains a bewildering array of urban / industrial and rural / agricultural societies; it has been settled by a diversity of peoples (although in the nineteenth century those of British origin were conspicuous in influence, the province was never as predominantly 'British' as is sometimes assumed). In many respects, the idea of Ontario as a distinct region fails to make sense. As Randall White, author of *Ontario 1610-1985: A Political and Economic History*, points out, southwest Ontario (that is, west of the Bruce / Niagara escarpment) would better be seen as an 'extension of the adjacent geography of the midwest United States' (27) just as southeast Ontario is in reality 'an extension of the adjacent geography of Quebec' (26). Above all, the province has a dauntingly centralist reputation. George Woodcock's descriptive assessment seems to me just:

Ontario, the heir to Upper Canada, with its Loyalist and Regency English traditions, its memories of the war of 1812 that shaped its special self-aware-

ness, its old communities of German sectarians and its sharp geographical
definition by lakefront and Shield, remains a distinct region even though its two
greatest cities, Ottawa and Toronto, have become the foci of a political, economic
and cultural centralism that goes entirely against the Canadian grain.   (25)

Ontario, one might say, is a region that sees itself as a centre – or even,
perhaps, *the* centre – and is reluctant to acknowledge its position within
regionalist categories.

It is certainly a region that hesitates to admit that it has a regional
literature. Is it possible, in the modern world, to imagine oneself exclusively in regional terms – 'Ontarian' or any other? How can such a
concept be defined or expressed? One of the best known of Ontario
writers, Margaret Atwood, has herself addressed these questions in a
poem entitled 'At the Tourist Centre in Boston.' Here, looking at her
country as seen (significantly) from outside, she notes the difficulty of
summing up the Canadian provinces in pictorial, imagistic terms. The
attempt seems to turn inevitably into parody. Ontario, interestingly, is
represented by 'the empty / interior of the parliament buildings' (*Animals*
18) – where the line-break speaks volumes. Not, certainly, an inspiring
picture. (In one of Atwood's later novels, *Life before Man*, these same
Parliament Buildings – assuming that the provincial parliament was
intended in the poem – are described as the 'squat pinkish heart of a
squat province' [40]). Do our writers think of themselves as 'Ontarian'?
With the probable exception of James Reaney, surely not. It is even
worth noting that the adjective itself is comparatively rare, and looks
somewhat odd when one encounters it. (Personally, I have only got used
to it in the course of writing this book.) When Sara Jeannette Duncan, in
her early Canadian and 'Ontarian' novel *The Imperialist* (1904), explored the sociopolitical tensions and awkwardnesses of her time, she
wrote eloquently: 'Any process of blending implies confusion to begin
with; we are here at the making of a nation' (47). Not a 'region,' not a
'province,' but a 'nation.' Henry Kreisel, an Austrian immigrant who
made his home in Alberta, described the Prairies in a famous essay as 'a
state of mind.' Perhaps the same can be said of Ontario, though whether
it is a regional state of mind remains a moot point.

Writers themselves, of course, almost always sheer away from regionalist identification because it seems unduly limiting. Naturally
enough, they want to be read by as many people as possible, throughout
the world. A number of the best-known Canadian writers – Mavis
Gallant and Mordecai Richler, among others – are even reluctant to be
seen as too obviously Canadian; they have no wish to be large fishes
within (literature in English ultimately being in question) a small pond.

To be associated with a mere province would be even more reductive. Certainly, to see Margaret Atwood or Robertson Davies, say, as Ontario writers *rather than* Canadian or North American or even world writers would be absurd. At the same time, one of the paradoxes of regionalism, continually rediscovered and reiterated in all times and places, is the realization that all literature of any interest invariably arises out of a local matrix. The finest regional writers – Thomas Hardy in England, William Faulkner in the United States, Alice Munro in Ontario – become universal by writing about, and out of, what they know best, which is generally their own back-yards.

If, however, we look back to the earliest Ontarian writers – technically pre-Ontarian, since the area was then called either Upper Canada or Canada West – we see a complication which is clearly a factor in most New World cultures. Literary regions – and many physical regions – develop their characteristic qualities through the gradual processes of history. Geographical determinants (climate, geological structure, fertility of soil, amount of water supply) affect the main work of the people, the life-styles they evolve and adopt, the food they eat, the architecture under which they live, and so on. Slowly but relentlessly, historical traditions become established. But what happens when immigrants come to a land that (so far as they can see) has no past, in which the past they themselves recognize is a past that exists elsewhere? This book attempts to provide one plausible answer to that question.

Part One:
The Emerging Province

1 Old-World Perspectives

Although 'Ontario' is said to be derived from an Indian word variously translated as 'beautiful water' or 'rocks standing by water,' the dominant image that comes down to us from early explorers, travellers, and settlers is one of almost interminable forest. At the end of the eighteenth century, one suspects, a marathon-minded squirrel could have crossed virtually the whole of the future province without ever touching ground. Occasional settlements had already established themselves by this time in suitable places, but they were surrounded by the all-encompassing woods. To a historically informed European, venturing into this land was like returning to the way of life of the 'dark-age' Anglo-Saxon world, a pattern of isolated communities encircled by wilderness that was unknown and almost certainly dangerous. As soon as we have said this, however, we have introduced an extraneous element into the picture: a basis of comparison derived from outside, something imposed upon the landscape rather than wholly endemic to it. This is, nevertheless, a precise reflection of early pioneer practice. It will be as well to begin, then, not with what the first immigrants or visitors saw when they arrived, but with the preconceptions – even the prejudices – which they brought with them and which unconsciously affected what they saw.

'I have estimated the luggage [for an average family] at 20 cwts. Ours was 7 tons, 3 cwts.!!!' This is Thomas William Magrath writing back to Ireland in a letter reproduced by Thomas Radcliff in *Authentic Letters from Upper Canada* (1833); he goes on to report that this was the 'largest quantity ever landed by a single family on the Wharf at York [i.e., Toronto]' (3). But every settler, however poor, was necessarily concerned with what to bring to the new land. All writers, especially those who produced emigration handbooks, devoted attention to this matter. One of the subsections, for instance, of the eleventh letter in Catharine Parr Traill's *The Backwoods of Canada* (1836) reads: 'Useful Articles to be brought out.' She recommends tools, good clothes, shoes and bedding, garden seeds, but not furniture or hardware. Some newcomers, of course, had their own ideas about what was necessary. Anne Langton, who emigrated like Traill in the 1830s, records in her diary that the Dunsfords 'are bringing a carriage out with them' and adds in her characteristically dry manner: 'I hope they do not forget to bring a good road too' (72). Since road conditions in Upper Canada at this time were notorious, we may reasonably assume that the Dunsfords' response on arrival was directed not so much at what they found as at what was conspicuously lacking.

It is clear, then, that besides material possessions (necessary or otherwise) immigrants and travellers brought with them built-in cultural attitudes and assumptions, set ways of looking at the land and 'landscape,' and above all established patterns of language that originated in a very different locale and had been developed and refined for very different purposes. Moreover, the earliest accounts of the future province of Ontario that can legitimately be described as literature rather than practical jottings and statistical notes occur at the time when eighteenth-century notions of human order and rationality were being complicated by a 'Romantic' interest in the primitive, the wild, and the imaginatively stimulating. Interest in 'the Picturesque' – the aesthetics of landscape that advocated observing a natural scene as though it were an artistically composed picture – was at its height. Artists like George Heriot, author of the generously illustrated *Travels through the Canadas* (1807), and William Henry Bartlett, who published *Canadian Scenery* in 1842, had been trained as topographical artists in England and brought with them their aesthetic assumptions about European landscape painting. In both we can readily see the use of framing devices (in Canada generally trees rather than ruins) derived ultimately from the practice of such European masters as Nicholas Poussin and Claude Lorraine. What is new in Canadian visual images (dramatic waterfalls, Indian encampments, and the like) is filtered through imported techniques and interests that radically affect the ultimate impression of the scene presented.

Similar conventions had evolved for descriptive prose. A whole vocabulary had arisen to communicate gradations of the sublime and the beautiful. Heriot's account of the approach to Niagara Falls provides a typical and convenient instance of the union of these related traditions in what might be called the verbal picturesque. He follows a conventional pattern worked out in the great estates of eighteenth-century England where vistas and sudden prospects seen over ha-has were intricately planned to provoke the maximum of pleasure and astonishment: 'the traveller proceeds through a forest of oak-trees, until he becomes surprised, and his attention is arrested by the falls presented to the eye through openings now cut in the woods' (1.156–7). The artist has noticed how, even at this primitive stage in the history of North American tourism, the visitor is as it were manipulated into seeing the Falls to best advantage.

Unfortunately, Heriot's literary talents are decidedly inferior to his artistic ones; in prose, he can do no more than offer an anthology of the sanctioned 'picturesque' terms. He notes 'the beauty and grandeur' of Queenstown's situation (1.157), the 'profound and rugged channel' of the Niagara River and its 'wide and stupendous flood,' the 'many singular and romantic scenes' such as the whirlpool (1.158), until, arriving at the Falls themselves, he describes the effect as 'awfully grand, magnificent, and sublime' (1.160). There then follows a paragraph that unwittingly illustrates to perfection the strain that Niagara places upon the available language:

The lofty banks and immense woods which environ this stupendous scene, the irresistible force, the rapidity of motion displayed by the rolling clouds of foam, the uncommon brilliancy and variety of colours and of shades, the ceaseless intumessence [sic], and swift agitation of the dashing waves below, the solemn and tremendous noise, with the volumes of vapour darting upwards into the air, which the simultaneous report and smoke of a thousand cannon could scarcely equal, irresistibly tend to impress the imagination with such a train of sublime sensations, as few other combinations of natural objects are capable of producing, and which terror lest the treacherous rock crumble beneath the feet by no means contributes to diminish.   (1.160–1)

I am, of course, being a little unfair in quoting from a description of Niagara Falls, which virtually every writer (Heriot included) insists is beyond the capacity of words to convey. But the same words –'grandeur,' 'sublime,' 'vast,' 'rugged,' 'picturesque,' 'solemn,' 'stupendous'– are repeated again and again by writer after writer; they fail, inevitably, because they are old, tired words continually reapplied to a landscape for which an appropriate language has not yet been evolved. Small wonder that a law of diminishing emotional returns operates as we read. The problem is compounded, of course, by the fact that those writers who came to Canada at this time were rarely experienced in their craft, and so reproduced, seemingly by rote, the standard epithets and responses. We always need to remember that it is through these linguistic and conventional filters that the first literary images of Ontario are presented to us.

One of the most readily understandable characteristics that we detect in these early writers is their search, often (one suspects) with a sense of desperation, for aspects of the new land that reminded them in some way of 'the old country' and so of home. Elizabeth Simcoe, wife of the first lieutenant-governor of Upper Canada and the founder of Toronto, offers a typical illustration when she writes in her diary in July 1793: 'we were struck by the similarity between these Hills & Banks [along the Niagara River] & those of the Wye above Symond's Gate' (76). In similar fashion, Frances Stewart, recently arrived from Ireland in 1822, found Rice Lake comparable to Killarney without the mountains and described the Otonabee River as 'wide as the Liffey' (20). Surprisingly often, the standard of natural beauty seems to be found in a gentleman's park as laid out by Capability Brown. As early as 1819, the future Bishop of Toronto, John Strachan, writing under the name of his brother James, would comment on the oak plains of what would later be southwest Ontario (an exception to the more usual pattern of thick woodland) as 'so open that you may ride in any direction, as in a royal park' (37).

In 1832, Catharine Parr Traill had got no further than Crane Island in the St Lawrence before she noticed 'smooth lawns and meadows of emerald verdure' (*Backwoods* 19) that must have seemed comfortingly familiar; a little later, her reference to 'clumps of trees here and there to break the monotony of the clearing' (30) is based on the same premise, and this becomes explicit in her description of the plains around Rice Lake: 'The trees ... though inferior in size to those in the forests, are more picturesque, growing in groups or singly, at considerable intervals, giving a sort of park-like appearance to this portion of the country' (61). Her sister, Susanna Moodie, en route to her bush home, is similarly comforted by finding the plains near Peterborough 'thinly wooded with picturesque groups of oak and pine, and very much resembl[ing] a gentleman's park at home' (*Roughing It* 284). It should be remembered, of course, that such descriptions were being written for English readers, and that these connections may have been made, at least in part, to assist them in understanding, but the writers' own need for familiar comparisons is also evident, as is a sense of visual conditioning. Moodie significantly recalls the reason for the eighteenth-century landscape gardener's famous nickname when she alludes to a man who had been employed 'to visit Canada, and report the capabilities of the country' (51).

All these characteristics come together in a crucial passage from Traill's *Backwoods* that deserves quotation at length. She is describing the countryside between Amherst and the Rice Lake area:

The outline of the country reminded me of the hilly part of Gloucestershire; you want, however, the charm with which civilization has so eminently adorned that fine county, with all its romantic villages, flourishing towns, cultivated farms, and extensive downs, so thickly covered with flocks and herds. Here the bold forests of oak, beech, maple, and bass-wood, with now and then a grove of dark pine, cover the hills, only enlivened by an occasional settlement, with its log-house and zig-zag fences of split timber: these fences are very offensive to my eye. I look in vain for the rich hedge-rows of my native country. Even the stone fences in the north and west of England, cold and bare as they are, are less unsightly. The settlers, however, invariably adopt whatever plan saves time, labour, and money.   (56)

The passage is typical because it combines so many of the standard reactions: the comparisons with parts of England, the faithful representation of comparisons and contrasts, the careful delineation of species so typical of Traill, who was later to make amateur but nonetheless valuable contributions to Canadian botany. But most significant, perhaps, is the automatic rejection of the unfamiliar zigzag fences, features which, a century and a half later, have come to be recognized as a characteristic, distinctive, and aesthetically pleasing part of the now traditional landscape. Traill is by no means unusual in this. John Howison, over a decade earlier, had made a similar observation in *Sketches of Upper Canada* (1821): 'the fields, though smooth, had no regularity of form, and were divided by wooden fences. This is annoying to the eyes of a British traveller, who has been accustomed to see lands enclosed with thorn hedges' (13–14).

   Both Howison and Traill were perceptive and talented people; their responses demonstrate dramatically that we see what we have been taught to see, that aesthetic ways of seeing, like practical methods of survival in a new environment, have to be learned. The point, so far as the vexed question of zigzag fences is concerned, is conveniently discussed by John Strachan:

Fences, through the whole country ... are the ugliest feature that strikes your eyes: even worse than the stumps of trees, with which the fields are full ...
   Englishmen are more offended with the fences than with any thing they see in the new country; and certainly, when compared to walls and hedges, they have but a slovenly appearance. They are soon, however, reconciled to them.   (85)

That final sentence is shrewd. Even Susanna Moodie is (ultimately) reconciled. When, at the end of *Roughing It in the Bush*, she bade adieu to the backwoods, among those objects which 'had become endeared to me during my long exile from civilized life,' she included her garden, 'with its rugged snake-fence which I had helped Jenny to place with my own hands' (507–8). Shared labour, then, can produce startling aesthetic transformations.

With all this in mind, we can now return to the fact of the omnipresent forest with a subtler awareness of the variety of responses that become possible. Howison is of particular interest here, because his book covers a remarkably broad spectrum of such responses. Although it appeared as early as 1821, and records travels undertaken two years earlier, *Sketches of Upper Canada* is late enough for him to be impressed, like Strachan, not merely by the expanses of forest and bush but by the extent of the clearing that had already been achieved: 'instead of being immured among forests, as I had anticipated, I saw extensive tracts of land waving in all the gayety and loveliness of harvest' (7). Nonetheless, the woods necessarily occupy his attention, and he responds to them in a variety of ways. On the one hand, he can report: 'I had never before experienced the sublimity of a *real* forest, nor witnessed a succession of trees of such magnitude and beauty' (11). On the other, he can refer to 'the appalling loneliness and depressing monotony of the boundless forest' (186).

This variety is also well caught by Moodie's Tom Wilson in *Roughing It in the Bush*, who highlights the contrast between what an enthusiast had led him to expect and what he actually encountered:

'Most of the wise men of Gotham we met on the road were bound to the woods; so I felt happy that I was, at least, in the fashion. Mr. —— was very kind, and spoke in raptures of the woods, which formed the theme of conversation during our journey; their beauty, their vastness, the comfort and independence enjoyed by those who settled in them; and he so inspired me with the subject that I did nothing all day but sing as we rode along –
    "A life in the woods for me;"
until we came to the woods, and then I soon learned to sing that same, as the Irishman says, on the other side of my mouth.'   (71)

Moodie has here built the varied responses into her book at the point immediately prior to her own journey into the bush (Tom Wilson may well be a fabricated character; Moodie's account is far more imaginative than its official library-classification as 'non-fiction' warrants). Her own response runs the gamut from romantic appreciation of natural sublimity to an appalled culture-shock.

Roughing It in the Bush contrasts dramatically with her sister's *Backwoods of Canada*, since they represent diametrically opposed psychological approaches to a life of isolation in a foreign environment. Traill was the more accomplished (though not necessarily the more interesting)

writer of the two. Her description of her first close encounter with a
forest landscape, on the journey from Peterborough to the home of her
brother, is richly evocative:

We soon lost sight entirely of the [Otonabee] river, and struck into the deep
solitude of the forest, where not a sound disturbed the almost awful stillness
that reigned around us. Scarcely a leaf or bough was in motion, excepting at
intervals we caught the sound of the breeze stirring the lofty heads of the pine-
trees, and wakening a hoarse and mournful cadence. This, with the tapping of
the red-headed and grey woodpeckers on the trunk of the decaying trees, or the
shrill whistling cry of the little striped squirrel, called by the natives 'chitmunk,'
was every sound that broke the stillness of the wild ...   (111–12)

Traill goes on to offer more generalized conclusions about her attitudes
to her new country, but what strikes us here is the immediacy and
specificity of her response, appropriate in one who is later to write so
perceptively about the flora and fauna of eastern Canada. Where Howison
tended to use description as setting for ponderous thoughts about the
Creator of the Universe, Traill reproduces her experience of the sound
of the breeze, and the sight and sound of the birds and animals.
    Both aspects are combined in the almost contemporaneous report by
Anna Jameson, writing of a drive from Hamilton to Woodstock:

No one who has a single atom of imagination, can travel through these forest
roads of Canada without being strongly impressed and excited. The seemingly
interminable line of trees before you; the boundless wilderness around; the
mysterious depths amid the multitudinous foliage, where foot of man hath
never penetrated, – and which partial gleams of the noontide sun, now seen,
now lost, lit up with a changeful, magical beauty – the wondrous splendour and
novelty of the flowers, – the silence, unbroken but by the low cry of a bird, or
hum of insect, or the splash and croak of some huge bull-frog, – the solitude in
which we proceeded mile after mile, no human being, no human dwelling
within sight, – are all either exciting to the fancy, or oppressive to the spirits,
according to the mood one may be in.   (2.113–14)

Jameson is the unabashed tourist *par excellence*. If one has read exten-
sively in the travel literature of the period, this passage reads like an
anthology of stock responses, but its comprehensiveness is impressive.
Elsewhere, she is especially adept at conveying a sense of the closeness
of the woods as they impinge upon the human settlements. When passing through Erindale (where, incidentally, she visited the Magraths of
Authentic Letters from Upper Canada), she observes:

a few log-houses and a saw-mill on the river-bank, and a little wooden church crowning the opposite height, formed the chief features of the scene. The boundless forest spread all around us.   (1.301)

Similarly, she reports of the newly incorporated Toronto: 'On this [west] side of Toronto you are immediately in the pine forest, which extends with little interruption (except a new settlement rising here and there) for about fifty miles to Hamilton' (2.7). It was this 'boundless forest' with which the original settlers had to contend. The warlike image is apt, as will be seen in the next chapter.

2 *The Battle of the Trees*

Trees, then, supplied the frame for every early Ontarian view; they
constituted the setting for every community, and had to be accepted as a
basic fact of the Upper Canadian life. Indeed, it is in terms of individual
responses to the ever-present woodland that so many of the main attitudes
to life in the new land were expressed. Once again, of course, Old-
World assumptions were prominent, and once again Catharine Parr
Traill provides a convenient starting point. She had expected a romantic
sense of antiquity from the prospect of age-old virgin forest, and this
was not forthcoming:

I was disappointed in the forest trees, having pictured to myself hoary giants
almost primeval with the country itself ...

  There is no appearance of venerable antiquity in the Canadian woods. There
are no ancient spreading oaks that might be called the patriarchs of the forest. A
premature decay seems to be their doom. They are uprooted by the storm, and
sink in their first maturity, to give place to a new generation that is ready to fill
their places. (*Backwoods* 112–13)

There is something at one and the same time challenging and troubling
about that final image, both to the reader and, one suspects, to Traill
herself. At first, it seems an appropriate image for a young country,
providing suggestions of youthful challenge and manifold opportunity,
yet, though the full flowering of Darwinism and the struggle for existence
was still a generation in the future (the young Darwin was assembling
evidence on the voyage of the *Beagle* at the very time that Traill was
writing), a hint of conflict and 'premature decay' even within 'first
maturity' is conspicuous and troubling.

  The forest that was expected to provide an image of continuity has
instead offered an elusive emblem of continual change. Perhaps inevita-

bly, descriptions by settlers tend to be preoccupied with trees falling, whether naturally or as a result of human action. Few have described such an event more skilfully, or more vividly, than Frances Stewart:

It is quite a sublime sight when a great hemlock nearly a hundred feet in height begins to shake its dark head, then to fall, slowly at first, then as it comes lower increasing in rapidity, tearing branches off its neighbours and shaking all the trees around; coming down at last with such a crash that the whole forest re-echoes the sound.   (31)

George Head, whose *Forest Scenes and Incidents in the Wilds of North America* was published in 1829, observes the same phenomenon but creates an eerie effect by emphasizing it as a natural and continual process:

the dead branches were tumbling about my ears from the tops of the trees so frequently, that I had great difficulty to avoid them ... The crash of trees falling around was so frequent as to be to me really astonishing ... Even in the finest weather, hardly a quarter of an hour ever passes in a North American forest, when, if one listens, a tree is not heard to fall to the ground.   (225–6)

Traill was, however, a perceptive observer of herself and of those about her. She admits that her yearning for the primeval forest is an educated, genteel, minority viewpoint, and shrewdly communicates a decidedly opposed attitude which is of considerable importance to our understanding of the basic sentiments of this period:

the class of people to whom this country is so admirably adapted are formed of the unlettered and industrious labourers and artisans ... They would not spare the ancient oak from feelings of veneration, nor look upon it with regard for any thing but its use as timber. They have no time, even if they possessed the taste, to gaze abroad on the beauties of Nature, but their ignorance is bliss.   (*Backwoods* 154)

Traill is characteristically balanced and practical, but the tone of regret that is evident here was destined to increase in intensity as the years passed and the forests fell. The whole process was doubtless inevitable. The point has been made succinctly by Edith Fowke, who has done so much to preserve the oral culture of the men who cut down the forests: 'The first settlers were also the first lumbermen: the land had to be cleared before it could be planted' (*Lumbering Songs* 4). Moreover, political and economic factors, notably the need to supply Britain with desperately needed timber at the time of the Napoleonic Wars, had already created an industry that could hardly be interrupted by vaguely romantic sentiment. At the same time, the relentless development as the decades passed from clearing in the interests of personal living space to wholesale destruction for commercial profit is awesome.

We can appreciate something of the complexity by juxtaposing the attitudes of Mary O'Brien and Anna Jameson. O'Brien, newly arrived in 1829, could paint an enthusiastic verbal picture of 'magnificent pines in all their wildness, with their dark foliage contrasted against the sky and their trunks rising like shafts of pillars' (37). Jameson, in the next decade, agrees with her but is well aware that this is not an undisputed sentiment: 'A Canadian settler *hates* a tree,' she reports (1.96), and her brutal phrasing in discussing the 'two principal methods of killing trees in this country' (1.97) sufficiently indicates her distaste. It is a phrasing that, as we shall see, resonates through the century. She realizes, however, that, as a traveller rather than a settler, she has no need to develop the kind of understanding that Traill expresses. Jameson remarks later: 'The pity I have for the trees in Canada, shows how far I am yet from being a true Canadian' (2.102). I labour the point because it draws attention to an extremely important factor in the literary presentation of early Canada, and particularly Upper Canada (or Canada West as it was soon to become).

This attitude receives forceful if rough expression in *The Emigrant* (1861), a long poem by Alexander McLachlan, who himself emigrated from Scotland and cleared land for some years before settling down to combine the roles of tailor and (in David Latham's words) 'poet of the backwoods pioneers' (489). McLachlan's is essentially a poetry of the people; one of his best-known songs employs the radical refrain 'Jack's as good's his master!' (207) – a sentiment that would have shocked Susanna Moodie to the core. As might be forecast, he reflected the attitudes of Traill's 'unlettered and industrious labourers and artisans.' One of the sections of *The Emigrant* is entitled 'Cutting the First Tree,' an event which is represented as a signal victory over the oppressive forces of nature. When the 'sturdy elm' in question finally crashes down 'as loud as thunder / Crushing limbs and brushwood under,' the settlers rejoice in triumph:

> Then we gazed upon the sight
> With the consciousness of might,
> And we cheer'd, as when a foe
> Or a tyrant is laid low ...

No regrets here. Indeed, the process is seen as part of God's design:

> We are God-commission'd here,
> This rough wilderness to clear.   (227, 229)

In another poem, 'Fire in the Woods,' the settler-narrator states specifically: 'The forest was my foe' (274).

This side of the settlers' attitude to the Ontario woods is clearly displayed in the narrative poem 'Malcolm's Katie' by Isabella Valancy Crawford, a decidedly more polished poet than McLachlan. Here the hero, Max, described as a 'soldier of the axe' (193), has no compunction about felling the ancient trees in order to found his own settlement:

> The mighty Morn strode laughing up the land,
> And Max, the lab'rer and the lover, stood
> Within the forest's edge beside a tree –
> The mossy king of all the woody tribes –
> Whose chatt'ring branches rattled, shuddering,
> As the bright axe cleaved moon-like thro' the air,
> Waking strange thunders, rousing echoes linked,
> From the full lion-throated roar to sighs
> Stealing on dove-wings thro' the distant isles.
> Swift fell the axe, swift followed roar on roar,
> Till the bare woodland bellowed in its rage
> As the first-slain slow toppled to his fall.
> 'O King of Desolation, art thou dead?'
> Cried Max, and laughing, heart and lips, leaped on
> The vast prone trunk. 'And have I slain the king?
> Above his ashes will I build my house;
> No slave beneath its pillars, but – a king!'   (202)

The forest wilderness is seen unequivocally as a 'battle-field high strewn with tangled dead' upon which Max 'slew the trees' (203). The emphasis throughout is on 'the axe-stirred waste' (203) and 'blackened stumps' (204). Katie's father, Malcolm Graeme, had made 'riches' (209) out of his 'forests' (211). Katie herself has a love of flowers but not a love of trees, and it is while attempting to reach an island over a log-jam to gather lilies that she almost drowns. This is offered, however, as part of the melodramatic love-plot; there seems to be only the faintest suggestion of irony when, at the moment of near-tragedy, Crawford remarks that 'the rich man's chiefest treasure sank / Under his wooden wealth' (212).

Although 'Malcolm's Katie' is usually praised for other qualities, to

be discussed later, it is important as one of the few examples of imaginative art that emphasizes the settlers' viewpoint to the exclusion of all
others. Max's vision of 'our home / On yonder slope, with vines about
the door' (205) is a paean to progress. Out of the destruction of the
forest comes the prospect of human domesticity:

> And the black slope all bristling with burnt stumps
> Was known amongst them all as 'Max's house.'   (205)

It is difficult to imagine a clearer image of the process of development
in the Ontario backwoods than the following passage:

> Then came smooth-coated men with eager eyes
> And talked of steamers on the cliff-bound lakes,
> And iron tracks across the prairie lands,
> And mills to crush the quartz of wealthy hills,
> And mills to saw the great wide-armed trees,
> And mills to grind the singing stream of grain.
> And with such busy clamour mingled still
> The throbbing music of the bold, bright Axe –
> The steel tongue of the present; and the wall
> Of falling forests – voices of the past.   (205)

These are the men who, for good or ill, have created the modern Ontario.

The historical gap between primeval forest and twentieth-century Ontario
is also bridged, so far as popular fiction is concerned, by Ralph Connor's
stories of Glengarry, one of the easternmost counties in the province,
traditionally well known not merely for the high incidence of Scots
immigrants but also for their dogged traditionalism in terms of dress and
language. They had arrived in 1786, and only six years later the Simcoes
passed through the township and Elizabeth Simcoe noted the 'Highlanders
in their national dress' (67). To John Howison they were 'blunt and
uncultivated' (18). Connor (or, to give him his real name, Charles William Gordon) was born there in 1860, at which time, if *Glengarry School
Days* (1902) can be trusted, it was still 'this wild, woody land' (266). But
the preface to *The Man from Glengarry* (1901) begins: 'The solid forests
of Glengarry have vanished, and with the forests the men who conquered
them.' There is, then, an elegiac quality to this novel, but it does its best
to provide a written record of a lost way of life. Many of the scenes
verge on cliché – the rivalry between logging-gangs, the various mani-
festations of anti-French and anti-Catholic sentiment, the night ride

through the forest pursued by wolves – but a vivid picture of a society maintaining itself within the all-surrounding woods, a Highland Presbyterian society around the time of Confederation, is impressive:

There is forest everywhere. It lines up close and thick along the road, and here and there quite overshadows it. It crowds in upon the little farms and shuts them off from one another and from the world outside, and peers in through the little windows of the log houses ...   (20)

Both *The Man from Glengarry* and *Glengarry School Days* chronicle a significant development in human attitudes towards forest scenery. For the original settlers there, as elsewhere, 'the forest was dreaded and hated, but the sons, with rifles in hand, trod its pathless stretches without fear,' though it is still 'their ancient foe' (*Man* 4). They came to recognize 'square-timber,' however, as 'their only source of wealth' (4), so 'their common life-long conflict with the forest' becomes a 'heroic struggle with stern nature' (3). But for women like Mrs Murray, who comes like Susanna Moodie to rough it in the bush but does so with all the zeal and determination of a minister's wife, there is beauty in the scene, and an appreciation of this beauty is duly passed on to her son Hughie: 'Into the forest in the west the sun was descending in gorgeous robes of glory' (22). Hughie, a minor figure in *The Man from Glengarry*, becomes the hero of the later book, and by this time the forest has become 'an enchanted land' (*School Days* 13). He responds to the 'mystery and wonder of the forest,' as well as to 'the majesty of its beauty and silence' (109). Later, the attitudes approach the Wordsworthian:

It is hard to resist the ministry of the woods. The sympathetic silence of the trees, the aromatic airs that breathe through the shady spaces, the soft mingling of broken lights – these all combine to lay upon the spirit a soothing balm, and bring to the heart peace.   (194)

These sentiments, though compatible with those of early cultured settlers like Traill, are far removed from the general responses of the pioneers. Connor represents a significant link.

As a writer of fiction, unfortunately, Connor never rises above the second-rate. Nonetheless, he is skilful in creating suspense, and even his tear-jerking religious death scenes can often provoke a somewhat reluctant response in modern readers. But his too easy juxtaposition of romantic violence with Presbyterian piety (the 'battle' or 'game' of life is his centralizing metaphor) tends to grate upon contemporary sensibilities. His plots have all the subtlety of the average in-flight movie, and few of us now find them redeemed by the naively uplifting message. At the same time, Connor records some notable aspects of Ontario life that might otherwise be forgotten – most notably the customary use of Gaelic in Scots communities during the nineteenth century. (Gaelic was the third commonest language in early Canada.) Thus we see in *The Man from Glengarry* the Gaelic service following that given in English on the sabbath, the singing of Gaelic shanties, and the habitual reading of the Gaelic Bible. Above all, whatever exaggeration may be involved (a religious revival is said to have continued 'night after night, every night in the week except Saturday' for eighteen months [157]), the church-centred society presented here is as impressive as it must, to some, have been oppressive. Similarly, the story of Ronald MacDonald, his dazzling growth from 'a half-savage life' (40) to the status of a famous Canadian, serves (perhaps intentionally) as a sort of paradigm of the foreshortened quality – by Old-World standards – of Canadian and Ontarian history. We may also recognize in Connor's otherwise puzzling blend of violent pugnacity and sentimental regret an almost emblematic presentation of the split in nineteenth-century attitudes towards the vanishing forest.

In terms of landscape, we begin to discern at this time a new ingredient in the nineteenth-century Ontarian scene. As the trees were felled, their rotting stumps became conspicuous features. After several months' residence in the woods in the 1820s, George Head returned from Lake Simcoe to York (Toronto) 'along a wide earthy road' and observed that, 'in the short space between the road and the forest, the naked stumps of trees standing in the ground gave a desolate appearance to the fields on either side' (328, 329). The newly arrived Mary O'Brien, responsive to the varieties of texture favoured by Picturesque theory, could be more positive:

The country for two miles on the York side of us, which I saw today for the first time by daylight, is much more pleasing in its appearance than I had supposed. You have now a field or two quite cleared and almost level; now seven or eight more or less dotted with stumps from four to five feet high; now a field or a strip of land thickly set with high tapering poles. The fences are universally zig zag walls which are generally untidy, and at all times perhaps more picturesque than neat. (21)

In the main, the more literate and creative of the settlers, though themselves responsible for the development, tended to share Head's distaste. Anne Langton takes up O'Brien's details, but favours neatness and smoothness over picturesque variety: 'The stumps must give every place a rubbishy appearance, and the spreading roots prevent anything like a smooth pathway' (38). Herself a minor though talented artist, she is here stressing everyday realities. Others, however, found the stumps aesthetically displeasing. Traill, in the early stages of settlement, looks forward to a time when 'horrid black stumps' will be removed (*Back-woods* 126). Her sister Susanna Moodie, though employing the current aesthetic jargon, brought very different perceptions to the terms. For her, the 'charred and blackened stumps ... were everything but pictur-esque' and she concluded in a moment of depression and disgust 'that there was very little beauty to be found in the backwoods' (*Roughing It,* 293). Physical traces of the stumps remained visible for a surprisingly long time. Well into the twentieth century we find Frederick Philip Grove recording what happened to some of them. In *Two Generations* (1939), his novel about settled ex-pioneers in southwest Ontario, he writes:

The fields to the south and the west were separated from each other and from the copses of bush by enormous root fences, the stumps of the huge pines that had covered them being simply upended in long rows marking their margins as strip after strip had been wrested from the ancient forest.   (29–30)

If the trees possessed either immediate or commercial value, they were felled; otherwise they were burnt. Peter McArthur and Stephen Leacock, elder contemporaries of Grove and important witnesses to the later processes of settlement, shared similar memories of growing up in a land that had already been cleared but in which occasional hints of wilderness persisted. And they also shared faint memories of the last stages of clearing. Here is McArthur:

It is so long since this part of Canada was cleared, and cleared altogether too thoroughly, that it is a little hard to realize that not so many years ago you could see the glare of great clearing fires every night and be blinded by the smoke of them every day.   (9–10)

And here is Leacock:

of course in 1876 a lot of old primeval trees, towering hemlocks and birch, were still standing. The last of the great bush fires that burned them out was in the summer when we came.   (*Boy* 41)

They were alike, too, in the force of their bitterness. With the gift of hindsight we can see them looking back to Anna Jameson (and even echoing her in choice of metaphor, as did the historian A.R.M. Lower in a book title, *The North American Assault on the Canadian Forest*) but also looking forward to our own environmentalist awareness. McArthur records: 'when I was a boy trees were regarded almost as enemies ... In those far days trees were things to be destroyed' (8). Leacock echoes: 'For the earlier settler trees, to a great extent, were the enemy. The Upper Canada forest was slaughtered by the lumber companies without regard for the future' (*Boy* 55).

The battle of the trees was over, and the forests were vanquished. Traces still remain, in Algonquin Park and elsewhere, but for an appreciation of the extent of this continuous woodland and its effect on those who tried to live within it, we now have to rely on the memory embodied in literature. Also preserved there are imaginative, elegiac responses to the passing of the forest. McArthur, once again, serves as an eloquent witness in this recollection of a symbolic representative of the old, uncleared bush. What he presents, significantly, is not nostalgia but a sense of almost chilling otherness:

But there is one tree in the place with which I can never establish a feeling of intimacy. It is the one remaining specimen of the original forest – a great maple over three feet in diameter, whose spreading top rises far above the other trees in the woodlot. Even though it stands beside the public road, it seem to retain some touch of the shyness of the wilderness, and does not invite the fellowship of man.   (8)

The equivalent poetic response is to be found in Al Purdy. His poem 'Boundaries' begins with an elegy for lost forest:

> In all these southern counties
> with English names
> York   Dufferin   Hastings   Northumberland
> stood the great trees
> gone for a hundred years now   (*Poems* 134)

His historical inquiries into the origins of Ameliasburg, recorded in *In Search of Owen Roblin*, forcefully present the two sides of the process. Roblin

> built a gristmill   and a village gradually
> grew round it   and the deep woods vanished.   (n pag)

But this leads Purdy to brood upon the extraordinary continuity (within the natural process of perpetual change) that the trees represented; he writes with feeling of

> the great pine forests
> once blanketing Prince Edward County
> 19th-century forests seemingly
> nearer the last ice age
> than the birth date of any man living.

Roblin and Purdy's own grandfather act as transitional figures linking that primordial forest past with the modern Canadian present. In 'My Grandfather Talking – 30 Years Ago' (which was incorporated into *In Search of Owen Roblin*) the grandfather is himself the medium for passing on recollections going back perhaps to the early 1870s. One day, he promises, he will tell

> what it was like
> the way it was
> without no streets
> or names of places here
> nothin but moonlight boy
> nothin but woods   (*Poems* 72–3)

He never fulfils the promise, but Purdy preserves for ever a child's keen anticipation, a dream of forest.

3 *Ambivalent Indians*

Ever since the beginnings of exploration and colonization out of Europe, the question of indigenous peoples – their nature, their behaviour, their disposition – had been a pressing matter, and this was nowhere more critical than on the North American continent. White explorers, benefiting from their recently acquired mastery of technical skills, had no doubts about their superiority to peoples who lacked such inventions as the wheel, had developed no obvious written language, and possessed only the most rudimentary knowledge of agriculture and human organization; nor did they see anything dubious about laying claim to uninhabited or at least only occasionally inhabited land that had not – according to their own accepted practice – been claimed formally as territory by the native tribes. In differing circumstances, these confrontations of sophisticate and primitive (the terms are, of course, white terms and perhaps more relative than their inventors would admit) could result in peaceful coexistence or violent hostility. Moreover, as years went by, two basically opposed political-philosophical attitudes about the indigenous peoples began to develop. Briefly stated, there was, on the one hand, the Hobbesian view that this life in nature was essentially nasty, brutish, and short, and that human progress depended upon the creation of mutually desirable practices and contracts; on the other, the view popularized by Rousseau regarded a simple life close to nature as the ideal and any form of social complication as a step away from perfection. At this point, the foundations for the two radically opposed literary archetypes representing the North American Indian – bloodthirsty savage and noble primitive – were firmly set.

It will be noted at this point that the two verbal components of the best-known phrase for any Rousseauistic attitude, 'noble savage,' have been assigned here to different sides of the division. I have done this deliberately to draw attention to the ambiguity within the word 'savage.'

Writers on early white/Indian contacts have recognized that this is the word most often recurring in both the historical and the literary accounts, but they have sometimes assumed that it conveys an implication of barbarity and ferocity. This may indeed be so, but the *Oxford English Dictionary* lists a multiplicity of possible meanings for 'savage,' including the following: 'Uncivilized; existing in the lower state of culture'; 'a human figure naked or enveloped in foliage'; 'Remote from society, solitary.' The adjective can mean 'fierce, ferocious, cruel' but also 'Indomitable, intrepid, valiant.' We should not forget that the word derives etymologically from the Latin *sylvaticus*, meaning 'of the woods.' It is a verbal cousin of 'sylvan.' Woods, of course, could be dangerous places (in North America at least as much as elsewhere), and the implication of 'wild' – and so potentially dangerous – soon becomes associated with the term. (The word 'heathen' with its original meaning of 'heath-dweller' represents a similar case.) Nonetheless, it is possible that early writers who employ the term were using it in a more neutral sense than that now customary in the late twentieth century. It is interesting to note, indeed, that Ernest Thompson Seton's extremely popular *Two Little Savages* (1906), which introduced the game of 'playing Indian' as wholesome training for non-Indian children, should employ the word with decidedly positive implications. We shall do well to approach earlier accounts with this awareness in mind.

Historical developments in North America in the mid-eighteenth and early nineteenth centuries did nothing to challenge this basic dichotomy between the ferocious and the primitive. Bitter rivalry between Britain and France had inveigled local tribes into the active support of one side or the other, whether the matter involved was commercial struggle for the control of the fur trade or the more general fight for military domination. A little later, a similar split occurred during the American War of Independence, with the Indian tribes divided into those supporting the 'rebel colonies' and those loyal to the British crown. Moreover, if symbolic Indian figures were required for both extremes of the spectrum, they could readily be supplied. For British North Americans, Pontiac represented the antagonist, with the famous lacrosse match leading to the fall of Fort Michilimackinac in 1763 providing a classic example of treacherous cunning, while Tecumseh, with his crucial support in the War of 1812, became the very epitome of the noble and the loyal.

So far as literary presentation is concerned, another and less tangible factor was involved. The main thrust of white settlement in present-day Ontario coincided with the great period of European romanticism in which the claims of primitivism and the natural were revived to counter what was seen by many as an excessive emphasis on the artificial and the sophisticated. While philosophical thinkers might have to choose between the claims of Hobbes and Rousseau, others, not encumbered with any need for consistency, were free to form their own personal *mélange* of these opposed attitudes. For many, indeed, the primitive could be seen as combining the attractions of freedom and lack of constraints with a *frisson* of the exotic and even of the forbidden. One could register emotions of envy and revulsion, vicariously, at the same time. Thus for readers of the novel-romances of Sir Walter Scott, the untamed Highlanders represented a contradictory but nonetheless powerful balance of the primitively heroic and the politically threatening. In the United States, James Fenimore Cooper provided a North American equivalent in his 'Leatherstocking' novels, where the hostile raids of the Iroquois are balanced by the romantic loyalty of the Mohicans, rendered all the more poignant, of course, by virtue of the fact that they were 'the last of the Mohicans.' In Canadian literature, and contemporaneously with Cooper, John Richardson could exploit, and in a sense stabilize, both the extreme archetypes. In *Wacousta* (1832) Pontiac's capture of Michilimackinac is a crucial element in the sensationalist plot, while Tecumseh (also celebrated by Richardson in an ambitious and flamboyant poem) is a prominent character in its sequel, *The Canadian Brothers* (1840). (And it may be worth noting at this point that the pattern continues until surprisingly late in Ontarian literary history. In E.J. Pratt's heroic poem *Brébeuf and His Brethren*, published exactly a century later in 1940, the Indians play the role of torturing villains, yet at the same time Pratt subtly manages to convey a sense of heroism in the Indian antagonists as well as one of primitive determination in his Jesuit protagonists.)

A particularly dramatic instance of the combination of these extreme images of the Indian is to be found in Alexander Henry's *Travels and Adventures in Canada and the Indian Territories between the Years 1760 and 1776* (1809). Henry's exploits took him through the area that later became Upper Canada and Ontario, since he followed one of the main voyageurs' routes from Montréal up the Ottawa and the Mattawa rivers to Lake Nipissing and along the northern shore of Lake Huron to Fort Michilimackinac. The more adventurous details in his account read like fiction, though the main events must be at least roughly autobiographical. The shrewd and anything but credulous Anna Jameson accepted his testimony without question, recognizing in his plain, unaffected, and economical prose style 'the internal evidence of truth' (3.17), but the continual violent contrasts between dependency and triumph, the regular juxtaposition of security and seemingly overwhelming dangers, conform so faithfully to the conventions of popular adventure stories that it is difficult to accept them as unadorned fact. Be that as it may, not only was Henry disguised as a 'Canadian' because of Indian hostility to the English at that time, but he was actually present at the fall of Michilimackinac when the fateful lacrosse game was planned by the Indians as a ruse to penetrate the fort. He does not spare his readers any of the horrors that he claims to have witnessed on this occasion:

The dead were scalped and mangled; the dying were writhing and shrieking, under the unsatiated knife and tomahawk; and, from the bodies of some ripped open, their butchers were drinking their blood, scooped up in the hollow of joined hands, and quaffed amid shouts of rage and victory.   (80)

Yet Henry is able to observe all this because he has been smuggled into at least temporary safety within a garret, for no clear reason, by a Pawnee woman who appears to act out of a basic human compassion.

Henry is ultimately saved from the general massacre by a circumstance that sounds decidedly closer to romance than to prosaic fact. According to his account, not long after he had arrived at the fort he was approached by a 'Chipeway' named Wawatam who claimed that he had been instructed by the Great Spirit to adopt an Englishman 'as his son, brother and friend' (74) and now recognized in Henry the person he was bound to protect. After various adventures in which he escapes death by a hair's breadth, Henry is eventually ransomed by Wawatam and freed. This story of an Indian's loyalty and fidelity is, however, immediately followed by a scene of horror. The next day, a chief who had been absent when the main massacre occurred, demonstrated his approval of the uprising by butchering seven of the remaining prisoners. The fattest body is then cooked and the other Indians, including Wawatam, are invited to a cannibalistic feast:

Wawatam obeyed the summons, taking with him, as is usual, to the place of entertainment, his dish and spoon.

After an absence of half an hour, he returned, bringing in his dish a human hand, and a large piece of flesh.   (102–3)

Henry spends the best part of a year disguised as an Indian and living an Indian life. His account seems intent, however, on artfully juxtaposing merciful actions on the part of his Indian hosts with others of unprecedented barbarity.

Fort Michilimackinac itself was outside the boundaries of what became

Ontario, though its strategic position in British North American territories of the eighteenth century made its fortunes an integral part of the early history of Upper Canada (the area was ceded to the United States in 1796, captured by the British during the War of 1812, but returned to the Americans shortly thereafter). Henry's travels are of importance here, however, for his accounts of the journeys to and from Michilimackinac and, in the less sensational second part of the book, for his subsequent expeditions around the northern shore of Lake Superior. So far as his presentation of Indians is concerned, he concentrates on their religious beliefs (which he considered superstitions) and takes a rather conspicuous interest in stories involving cannibalism (199–201, 214–15). The overall impression he leaves with his readers is one of unpredictable actions whether of friendliness or of barbarity.

John Richardson, by his own admission, was deeply indebted to Cooper's early Leatherstocking novels, and the origin of the fatal feud in *Wacousta* originates in a Scotland that bears more than a casual debt to the writings of 'the author of *Waverley*.' At the same time, he had read Henry (whom he mentions in the introduction to the 1851 edition); Henry's influence is at its clearest when one of the novel's most sensational scenes – and Richardson carries sensationalism to the point of obsession – is devoted to the fall of Michilimackinac. Clara Beverley watches the massacre under circumstances that closely resemble Henry's purported experience, though Henry's description is stylistically a model of restraint in comparison with Richardson's. Here we are confronted with 'sounds that curdled [the] blood,' 'images of death in their most appalling shapes,' 'mangled corpses,' 'horrid butchery,' 'the unpitying steel of the blood-thirsty savages,' 'scalpless and disfigured forms' (309–10), and much of the same. Yet all this is self-consciously played out by Richardson against a backcloth of intense natural beauty: 'the sun shone in yellow lustre, and all Nature smiled and wore an air of calm' (310). Because Richardson is the reverse of a subtle artist, the basic archetypes in which he traffics are all the more prominent.

As in the case of Henry's *Travels*, the main locales in *Wacousta* lie just beyond the technical borders of Ontario, but the combination of terrain and political situation associates the novel inevitably with the culture of Upper Canada. However, Richardson's sequel, *The Canadian Brothers*, though partly set in the United States, not only offers a vivid presentation of parts of the southwestern extremities of the modern province but even includes accounts of the battles at Moraviantown and Queenston Heights during the War of 1812. (The presentation of the former has an additional claim to our attention, since Richardson himself fought in the battle at the age of seventeen and was taken prisoner.) Particularly noteworthy, however, is the fact that the violence and depravity previously laid at the door of the Indians is here for the most part transferred to American villains. The novel opens with a quite lyrical chapter in which the Indians at Amherstburg are described as 'these simple mannered people' (3). Characteristically, however, they are specifically commended, though with more than a trace of condescension, for having 'lost much of that fierceness which is so characteristic of the North American Indian in his ruder state' (8). An 'imposing fleet of canoes' appears at this point, and these are filled in the main by Indians as yet unaffected by white civilization. Richardson now embarks on Rousseauistic eulogy:

In these might have been studied the natural dignity of man. Firm of step – proud of mien – haughty yet penetrating of look, each leader offered in his own person a model to the sculptor, which he might vainly seek elsewhere. Free and unfettered in every limb, they moved in the majesty of nature ...   (9)

Here we find the Indians exploited as convenient embodiments of the picturesque. Among them, however, is Tecumseh, presented unequivocally as a paragon, since 'in nobleness of deportment, [he] even surpassed those we have last named' (9).

  The Canadian Brothers is also noteworthy on account of a remarkable scene in which the Indian braves are entertained to dinner at Amherstburg by Colonel D'Egville, Superintendent of Indian affairs, along with a captured American major and his niece and other members of the British garrison. I lay emphasis on this scene because the comparison and contrast of Indian primitive with fashionable European is a curious effect which recurs surprisingly often in Canadian literary texts. Richardson being Richardson, however, the precise degree of satire and grotesquerie intended is somewhat uncertain. He begins by observing that the social mix would 'inspire an English exclusive with irrepressible horror' (53). There follows a flippant description of three Indian warriors in which they are imagined as wanting to take the American's scalp. The dinner is not, as the narrator notes dryly, 'particularly gay' (58), and as soon as the ladies withdraw (along with Tecumseh), the group splits into two. The Indians settle down to drinking whiskey and smoking 'kinni-kinnick, a mixture of Virginia tobacco, and odoriferous herbs,' from their pipebowl tomahawks, while 'Colonel D'Egville and his more civilized guests quaff their claret' (59). The American remarks approvingly on the figure of Tecumseh ('What a truly noble looking being' [60]), and the white soldiers go on to discuss the whole political situation and the disposition of the Indians in the presence of the now-intoxicated braves. Individual readers are free to interpret the scene as artificially and impossibly contrived or as mordantly and disturbingly humorous.

Richardson's scene recalls a curious passage in Elizabeth Simcoe's diary. The date is 3 July 1792, and the place Kingston. She writes: 'There are Mississaga Indians here they are an unwarlike, idle, drunken, dirty tribe. I observe how extremes meet. These uncivilized People saunter up & down the Town all the day, with the apparent Nonchalance, want of occupation & indifference that seems to possess Bond street Beaux' (72). On the face of it, this would seem the least likely comparison to come to mind, but the inevitable contrast that the early settlers perceived between the elegant manners of the British garrison and the crude appearance of the Indians appears to demand, through a kind of psychological embarrassment, some kind of connection even if it is forced or even grotesque. Besides, similar references recur, as I have said, in other accounts. Richardson himself, earlier in *The Canadian Brothers*, has included such an allusion in one of his characteristically extreme confrontations: 'It would not a little have surprised a Bond street exquisite of that day to have witnessed the cordiality with which the dark hand of the savage [Tecumseh] was successively pressed in the fairer palms of the English officers' (12). And here is Anna Jameson in a passage that, although set in the American part of her 'rambles,' is especially germane to my subject: 'The dandyism of some of these Pottowottomie warriors is inexpressibly amusing and grotesque; I defy all Regent Street and Bond Street to go beyond them in the exhibition of self-decoration and self-complacency. One of these exquisites ... I distinguished as Beau Brummel' (3.43). (Brummel, still alive at the time of the book's publication, might have anticipated Queen Victoria in not being amused.)

It is Jameson, moreover, who provides perhaps the most revealing account of an initial meeting with Indians, and one which represents a non-fiction equivalent to Richardson's almost contemporaneous portrayal of the mixed dinner-party. Much of the special interest in Jameson's anecdote derives from the fact that, although she is at pains to present an accurate account, she is interested at least as much in analysing her own responses. In addition, she is well aware of her ignorance of her subject and of the contradictory nature of her preconceptions. 'Notwithstanding all I have heard and read,' she confesses, 'I have yet but a vague idea of the Indian character; and the very different aspect under which it has been represented by various travellers, as well as writers of fiction, adds to the difficulty of forming a correct estimate of the people' (1.26–7).

The meeting occurs under oddly artificial circumstances. Soon after her arrival in Toronto, Jameson had expressed her wish to meet 'some of the aborigines of the country,' and one morning the principal Indian agent 'had accordingly brought some Indians to visit us' (1.23–4). There follows a description of their dress, and she reports that they replied to questions 'with a grave and quiet dignity' (1.24). It is then revealed that they are Chippewas from Lake Huron who have come to report that their tribe was in dire extremity on account of a poor hunting season and an excessively harsh winter, that they have walked a hundred and eighty miles over the snow and have not eaten for two days. There is something disturbingly indecorous about the whole situation – one for which, of course, Jameson is not herself directly responsible – and she skilfully emphasizes the incongruity of the scene. She has already noted that, after the introductory courtesies, they had been seated on chairs although, the agent assures her, 'they would certainly have preferred the floor' (1.24). The account continues as follows:

A breakfast of cold meat, bread, and beer, was immediately ordered for them; and though they had certainly never beheld in their lives the arrangement of an European table, and were besides half famished, they sat down with un-embarrassed tranquillity, and helped themselves to what they wished, with the utmost propriety – only, after one or two trials, they used their own knives and fingers in preference to the table knife and fork.   (1.25–6).

What in Richardson is grotesque becomes in Jameson something comic and poignant at the same time.

She goes on, sensitively, to record that she was left with an impression of melancholy:

The sort of desperate resignation in their swarthy countenances, their squalid, dingy habiliments, and their forlorn story, filled me with pity and, I may add, disappointment; and all my previous impressions of the independent children of the forest are for the present disturbed.   (1.26)

For Jameson, then, both extremes of the literary image of the Indian have been rendered suspect. Despite a number of stock responses and verbal clichés ('swarthy countenances' and the like), Jameson's account is remarkably honest and effective through its presentation, in what seems close to a symbolic construct, of the uneasy commerce between sophisticated and primitive, a dominating administration and a subject race, a life of cultured elegance and one of basic desperation. Later in the book, Jameson is to encounter other Indian people on their own ground, so to speak, but she never forgets – and never lets her readers forget – that any white account of Indian ways is inevitably partial, incomplete, and therefore distorted.

Virtually all early travel writers register a combination of fascination and embarrassment when the subject of Indians is broached. John Howison, for example, writing in 1821, promises to introduce his readers gradually and gently to 'the barbarians of Upper Canada' by beginning his account in the civilized surroundings of Montréal: 'were I to plunge suddenly into the woods, and bring you among bears, Indians, and log-huts, your nerves might receive such a shock as would render you timid about continuing longer in my company' (2). 'Bears, Indians, and log-huts' well expresses one version of the widespread Canadian clichés, but Howison has not quite reached the border before he offers a suitably romantic scene containing all the exoticism that a goodly part of his readership might have anticipated:

Not a sound could be heard, but the dull paddling of a canoe which had just left the shore. The picturesque dresses of the Indians who sat in it, the glittering of their tomahawks, and the figure of the chief, as he stood erect, appearing almost gigantic from the state of the horizon, were all impressive in the highest degree.   (7–8)

By contrast, Basil Hall in his *Travels in North America* (1829) surprises his readers with the prosaically unexpected while recounting his visit to the area around Burlington Bay:

In the course of the next day, we made an acquaintance with the chief of an Indian tribe. But our friend, if he will permit us to call him so, was any thing but what the imagination paints to itself of such a character. In his speech, dress, manners, and conduct, as well as in his opinions, and also in his tastes and habits, he is quite an Englishman.   (1.255)

He turns out, indeed, to have travelled 'in England and other countries' and to be 'the owner of a landed property which he lives upon and cultivates.'

A similar instance is to be found in one of the letters of John Langton, who begins in a flippantly conventional manner but creates surprise with a contrastingly prosaic image. He too, like Jameson, is preparing for his first confrontation with an Indian:

And now that I am fairly amongst the savages you will perhaps expect some romantic description; the tomahawk and scalping knife, the chivalrous tuft of hair, the moccasins, the robe, the war paint and barbaric ornaments should all have been detailed to you; but imagine my disappointment at being introduced to a respectable-looking young man, dressed decently like a Christian in coat, waistcoat and trousers, wearing a checked shirt and neckcloth, and covering his thick black hair with a common straw hat. This person, who owned no long unpronounceable name, but answered to the familiar appellation of Stephen Elliot, agreed to become my conductor for $1 a day.   (7–8)

Clichés seem to be radically challenged; later, however, Stephen Elliot conforms to the dictates of popular myth by getting at Langton's whiskey bottle.

Many of the accounts of Indians in the early writers are statistical and impersonally informative in nature, some offering little more than a second-hand amalgamation of facts and figures as well as the occasional tall tale and evidence of entrenched prejudice. These I shall ignore here. Where personal impressions are involved, one finds expected reference to dirtiness, the wicked effects of drink, instances of quaint simple-mindedness, and intimations of cunning. Another quality listed in several accounts – and one that may have significant implications – is idleness. I have already quoted Elizabeth Simcoe on this subject; she is echoed by Anne Langton, somewhat ironically in view of the fact that her memoirs have been published under the title *A Gentlewoman in Upper Canada* and so suggesting that she was herself a representative of the idle rich. But the idle poor are another matter, and she responds with obvious disapproval to a group of Indians seen in a 'state of complete idleness' (36). A casual remark in George M. Grant's *Ocean to Ocean* (1872), the account of Sandford Fleming's expedition to establish a practical route for the Canadian Pacific Railway, may explain this emphasis. 'Poor creatures!' he exclaims, 'not much use have they ever made of the land' (33). The readiness to establish idleness as a basic Indian characteristic may well be connected with a bad conscience; the expunging of their rights to the land seems a little less culpable if they can be represented as unprepared to make proper use of it.

Other responses are either contradictory or teasingly ambiguous. A tendency to compare North American Indians to European gypsies is a case in point. Like the gypsies, the Indians are envied as free spirits who have evaded the constraints of modern life; at the same time, one suspects that the analogy conceals implications of dirtiness, untrustworthiness, and doubtful morals. Prejudices clearly arise when standards of beauty are involved. Elizabeth Simcoe, for instance, generalizes about the Ojibwa (she says 'Gibbeway') as 'extremely handsome' (103), while Susanna Moodie designates them as 'perhaps the least attractive of all these wild people, both with regard to their physical and mental endowments' (*Roughing It* 298). The last remark connects with Mary O'Brien's curt reference to a local chief as 'a stupid-looking man' (58) and George

Head's observation that 'their ideas are so limited, that they cannot be brought to reason upon the most trifling operation of the mind' (305). Such remarks clash with those of more open-minded commentators who pay due attention to special Indian skills and abilities (reading clues in the bush, for example) that the whites lack.

As might be expected, the two most valuable personal accounts of relations with the Indians of Ontario in the nineteenth century come from Catharine Parr Traill and Susanna Moodie. And, as usual, the differences in their temperaments give us a welcome variety of response. With her usual positive attitude, Traill makes much of Indian capacities. In the course of several sections devoted to Indian matters in *The Backwoods of Canada*, she remarks on their skills in duck-shooting, expertise in the use of bows, ingenuity in handwork, acquaintance with dyes, and offers details concerning the making of moccasins and birch-bark canoes. Where character is concerned, she notes their reliability when borrowing (very different from Moodie's comments on her fellow settlers!), describes them as 'gentle and amiable' (163), praises their tenderness as parents and their general good humour. She offers two detailed accounts of visits to Indian encampments, one in winter (211–17), one in summer (285–8). Other details include an acknowledgment of their shrewdness in bargaining, and (in contrast to many white reporters) she praises the 'sweet and soft' cadences of the Indian tongue (215). Her emphasis is firmly on a change from fierceness in the past to peaceful behaviour in the present. She bears witness to their 'considerable advancement in civilization and knowledge of agriculture,' though, like most commentators of the period, she adheres to the belief that the race 'is slowly passing away from the face of the earth' (220). This is stated, however, as a considered opinion without any trace of superior satisfaction.

Susanna Moodie's impressions, all concentrated in the chapter of *Roughing It in the Bush* entitled 'The Wilderness, and Our Indian Friends,' are very different. Indeed, her opening remarks (quoted two paragraphs back) seem to prepare us for a totally unsympathetic and prejudiced account. As it turns out, however, she provides a curious blend of pros and cons. Many of the details (skill in hunting, bargaining, music, and affection for children) echo Traill's, and in addition she praises their humorous propensities, 'strictest honour' and truthfulness (305), capacity for gratitude, generous impulses, and powers of imagination. She even, unexpectedly, praises their 'great taste' and 'elegance' in artistic matters (301). At the same time, there is generally an underlying qualification. When she acknowledges their skill in bargaining ('No Jew could make a better bargain' [303] is a typical Moodie attitude), this is also associated with cunning and avarice. She goes on to tell a vivid story of an Indian woman attacked by a bear which she bravely and dexterously kills. 'What iron nerves these people must possess,' she comments (304), but she also conveys a sense of savage wildness accompanying such courage. Moodie tends to take back in one phrase what she has just offered in another. Of one Indian she remarks: 'This man was handsome, but his expression was vile' (311), and one is left with a sense that her attitudes to the race as a whole are similarly paradoxical. This is Moodie's own characteristic version of the ambiguous Indian. On one page, she seems damning; on another she can insist: 'An Indian is Nature's gentleman – never familiar, coarse, or vulgar' (314-15). She is an infuriatingly protean witness, but one gets the uneasy feeling that, for all the attraction of Traill's clarity and directness, Moodie may have succeeded in communicating a more authentic complexity.

One of the controversial topics concerning Indians at this time was the influence of Christianity upon their attitudes and behaviour. Here again, opposed opinions are readily found. In the earlier period, however, the reports tend to be positive. Basil Hall comments on an experiment with the Mississaugas on the banks of the Credit river. A social program under the influence of a Methodist missionary claimed to have transformed the tribe from 'the most profligate, drunken, and it was supposed, irreclaimable of savages' to a society that was 'industrious, orderly, and, above all, sober' (1.257, 259). Now, according to Hall, the 'whole tribe profess Christianity, attend divine service regularly, and, what is still more to the purpose, their conduct is said to be in character with their profession' (1.259). Traill is particularly forceful in this matter, insisting that 'the introduction of the Christian religion is the first greatest step towards civilization and improvement' (*Backwoods* 63); her book emphasizes the 'simple piety' (164) of the Indians she describes, including several affecting accounts of hymn-singing and devout practices. Jameson, under the influence of Mrs Schoolcraft, wife of the well-known Indian agent and authority, herself an Indian and a convert, agrees. Susanna Moodie, typically, is not so sure. She finds their ideas of Christianity 'vague and unsatisfactory,' even claiming to have met an Indian who asked if she 'came from the land where Christ was born' and 'had ever seen Jesus' (*Roughing It* 319). The most forceful testimony on the negative side, however, comes from George M. Grant. He claims that the Methodist missionary on Manitoulin Island

confessed that there was little, if any, difference in morals between the Christianized Indians around him and the two or three hundred who remain pagan; that, in fact, the pagans considered themselves quite superior, and made the immorality of their Christian countrymen their great plea against changing from the old religion.   (18)

I have left to the end an image of the Indian that is to be found again and again in these writings. We have, indeed, encountered traces of it already, notably in Howison's description of the Indian canoe (p. 45 above). I refer to the presentation of Indian figures according to the aesthetic dictates of the Picturesque. This is familiar enough in early paintings of the Canadian wilderness that so often contain Indian groups within the picture performing much the same function as the habitual groups of *banditti* on a Salvator Rosa canvas. Verbal descriptions often follow the same formula. Here is an early instance from Elizabeth Simcoe:

An Indian Woman came today with Pitch which is made by the Indians from Fir Trees, to gum the Canoe if any part of it is worn off by bringing it hither. She held a piece of pitch in her hand & melted it by applying a piece of burning wood. Her figure was perfectly wild & witchlike & a little fire with her kettle on it by her side, in a stormy dark day the waves roaring on the beach near which she stood formed a scene very wildly picturesque.   (111)

A similar *chiaroscuro* effect is presented by Moodie. Here the scene is the inside of a wigwam on a clear night:

As [an elderly Indian woman] ceased speaking, the old blanket that formed the door of the tent was withdrawn, and the girl, bearing two pails of water, stood in the open space, in the white moonlight. The glow of the fire streamed upon her dark, floating locks, danced in the black, glistening eye, and gave a deeper blush to the olive cheek! She would have made a beautiful picture; Sir Joshua Reynolds would have rejoiced in such a model – so simply graceful and unaffected, the very *beau ideal* of savage life and unadorned nature.   (*Roughing It* 314)

Such scenes are often memorable and affecting. One cannot help feeling, however, that these Indian figures are being regarded as aesthetic objects, painterly elements within sublime landscapes. Perhaps the final image of the Indian in early Ontario was one that was romantic, aesthetically powerful, emotionally gripping, excitingly different – but, alas, not accepted as fully human.

4 *The Farming Life*

Why do I stick to the farm?

You might as well ask a woodchuck why he sticks to his hole.   (Peter McArthur 197)

Most people who come off farms never go back. They talk about it, cry about it – but they don't really go. They know better.   (Stephen Leacock, *Uncle* 20)

After the forests have been felled, the land cleared, the Indians rendered passive, what then? In virtually every civilization where there is a choice between rural and urban living, opinion is likely to be divided between the sentimentally loyal and the gruffly disillusioned. Ontario is no exception; however, if the more prominent writers on farm life are to be trusted, the farming life is most often portrayed negatively. Peter McArthur, who was born in Ekfrid Township, Middlesex County, in 1866 and subsequently came to be known half-humorously as 'the Sage of Ekfrid,' is one of the minority that upholds the positive view, and this may be because he is tied to his immediate locality through ancestral and childhood bonds. As he wrote in a newspaper article:

I have the good fortune to be living on the farm on which I was born – the farm which my father cleared ... The history of the clearing of the land, the first crops, the names and characters of the horses and cows on the place, are so interwoven with my youthful recollections that I seem to remember them all as if I had taken part in the battle with the wilderness myself, and had shared in all its triumphs and sorrows.   (6)

More nostalgically, he can write of the farm as 'a place of peace, a place of refuge and a home,' and argue that '[t]o be born on a farm is the greatest good that can befall a human being' (197). In the course of a life-time of rural journalism he could be humorous, lyrical, bitter, philoso-phic, sentimental, resigned, though even McArthur was prepared to admit: 'As a matter of fact, winter life in the country does get monotonous' (95).

On the other hand, Leacock, coming to Ontario as a small boy and as part of a decidedly unhappy family, looked back with very different reactions. For him the farm of his childhood, in a community with the symbolic and possibly sardonic name of Egypt, was simply 'the rotten place' (*Boy* 67). A deeply felt seriousness takes the place of his habitual humour when he writes of the monotony of his boyhood in 'My Remarkable Uncle':

We lived in an isolation unknown, in these days of radio, anywhere in the world. We were thirty-five miles from a railway. There were no newspapers. Nobody came and went. There was nowhere to come and go. In the solitude of the dark night the stillness was that of eternity.   (*Uncle* 14)

The same point is made by a narrator in one of Raymond Knister's short stories, a man who had grown up in a pioneer settlement in western Ontario: '"I don't need to waste your time telling you about isola-tion and the denseness of the bush, and that sort of thing"' (*First Day* 335). Similarly, Knister's novel *White Narcissus* is full of phrases like 'the impression of monotony' and the 'sense of futility and uncert-ainty' (23, 32).

As one can see from a writer like Susanna Moodie, the pioneer settlers could either be feckless and sloppy or responsible and disciplined to the point of oppressiveness. The feckless and sloppy either didn't survive or declined into a disreputable existence on the extreme fringes of local society. This state rarely found its reflection in literature, though one encounters such people occasionally in stories by Alice Munro (Joe Phippen living in a roofed-over cellar of a burnt-out house in 'Images' from *Dance of the Happy Shades*, Uncle Benny and his untidy shack in the opening pages of *Lives of Girls and Women*). More common within imaginative writing are stories and memoirs about families immersed in what Munro calls 'the hard-set traditions, proud poverty, and monotony of farm life' (*Lives* 7).

The representative background to this life is caught perfectly in a passage from an unlikely source, Ernest Thompson Seton's *Two Little Savages*. Seton is referring to an invented community of Sanger based on his own experience in the Lindsay area in the 1870s, but it provides a perfect introduction to the claustrophobic farm worlds of such writers as Knister and James Reaney:

In Sanger settlement the farmhouse parlour is not a room; it is an institution. It is kept closed all the week except when the minister calls, and the one at Raften's was the pure type. Its furniture consisted of six painted chairs (fifty cents each), two rockers ($1.49), one melodeon (thirty-two bushels of wheat – the agent asked forty), a sideboard made at home of the case the melodeon came in, one rag carpet woofed at home and warped and woven in exchange for wool, one center-table (!) ($9.00 each cash, $11.00 catalogue). On the center-table was one tintype album, a Bible, and some large books for company use. Though dusted once a week, they were never moved, and it was years later before they were found to have settled permanently into the varnish of the table. (111–12)

The image of the closed room is frequently used by Ontario writers to convey the sense of dour custom and propriety characteristic of this way of life. We find it, for example, in Patrick Slater's memoir-reconstruction of nineteenth-century Ontario, *The Yellow Briar*:

The new farm house brought a deal of comfort and a dash of pride to the members of the Marshall household. But we kept the family pride locked up behind the heavy, drawn curtains in the chilly parlour ... The sad truth is that for generations the best room in an Ontario farm house stood closed up as a place of gloom, awaiting a death or a marriage feast. (205)

The tenacity of the practice is indicated when a character in Robert Laidlaw's chronicle-novel *The McGregors* remarks: '"I hope you do not plan to make a room into a parlour and close it up into a musty-smelling place, fit only for a corpse"' (98).

A whole culture and way of life are skilfully captured in these passages: the set procedures, the canny bargaining, the thrift, the conventionality, the sombre pride, the unchanged routine – above all, the virtuous complacency. They provide the perfect setting for families which, in Knister's phrase, 'did not have much time for living' (*Poems, Stories* 92). An especially dramatic form of rural puritanism is portrayed by Alice Munro in 'The Stone in the Field,' a story that recounts a visit to the solitary family farm from which the narrator's father had escaped. The basic image here is that of an aunt's hands 'red as a skinned rabbit' caused by scrubbing floors and furniture with lye. The clash between work ethic and religious ethic is succinctly caught by the mother: '"They must have got a Presbyterian dispensation to let them scrub on Sundays."'

Here, in the apparent absence of a parlour, they are all ushered into the kitchen: 'The room was cleaner and barer than any I had ever been in. There was no sign of frivolity, no indication that the people who lived here ever sought entertainment. No radio; no newspapers or magazines; certainly no books' (*Moons* 26). Given the prevalence of such moral attitudes, we can appreciate the force of Knister's dead-pan comment from 'Peaches, Peaches': 'That was one of the chief demarcations of virtue and vice in the community; some sold peaches on Sunday' (*First Day* 30).

The oppressive monotony so frequently described was, of course, exacerbated by the distance between farmhouses and the resultant lack of even a limited society. Once again Munro catches the essence of such a life in the simple phrase 'houses set apart' (*Dance* 42). The over-whelming loneliness becomes a recurring preoccupation in the poetry of James Reaney, where a favourite subject is the bored farm boy surrounded by the deadening bric-à-brac of an inert past. 'The Canadian' begins by evoking a scene remarkably close to Seton's:

> this winter farmhouse parlour
> Coloured like the bindings of religious books ...
> And the stove as black as a bible ...
> this dowdy stuffy room
> Where I sit in the centre of the Christmas vacation
> Alone, with only the ticking clock
> For Company, and the fire and the wind outside.   (*Poems* 38)

Reaney's rural world takes the form of claustrophobic images from which there is no escape. The house is oppressive enough, but in another poem, more specifically entitled 'The Upper Canadian,' it is part of a

> dull township
> Where fashion, thought and wit
> Never penetrate,

and we are offered a frustrating image of

> this round pond
> Where the geese white as pillows float
> In continuous circles
> And never get out.   (*Poems* 56)

(The reference to geese connects with Reaney's whimsical Ontario pastoral, *A Suit of Nettles*, where the chief characters are geese rather than human beings, and where they are contained within the relentless pattern of the seasonal year in which December brings not human/divine birth but inevitable death as victims for Christmas festivities.)

But it was not only monotony and strait-laced prohibitions that made Ontario farm life unattractive for many members of the younger generation. There was, for example, the curse of ague, recorded throughout the nineteenth century. According to Catharine Parr Traill, the disease was a particular feature of newly cleared land, since 'it arises from the exhalations of the vegetable soil, when opened out to the action of the sun and air' (*Settler's Guide* 206). Be that as it may, Susanna Moodie gives a harrowing account of an occasion when the ailment struck their settlement. Her husband 'was confined to his bed on each alternate day, unable to raise hand or foot, and raving in the delirium of the fever,' while in her brother's and sister's families 'scarcely a healthy person remained to attend upon the sick' (*Roughing It* 343). The 'aig,' Laidlaw recalls in support of Traill, was 'a common complaint until more of the forest was cut down and the land drained' (59); its character is most vividly described by Seton in his autobiography:

we shook every day. Quotidian ague the doctor called it, or 'daily shakes' in folk tongue. It took us all in the same way; that is, each afternoon, about three, we began to shiver and shake. It was impossible, even with the fire and the blankets, to give us any semblance of warmth.

From two till seven, we had this deadly chill; then it would leave us. And from about seven till two next morning, we were in a raging fever. All we could do would be drink water, and grow weaker. At about two, the fever left us, and we lay feebly, snatching spells of sleep till sunrise.   (*Trail* 118)

Some of the stringent folk remedies for this condition are chronicled in Knister's 'Heart of Ironwood Tea,' the title cure being termed 'worse than the disease' (*First Day* 335).

Additional discouraging features included depressing environmental conditions and the sheer hardness of the rural life. Leacock, for instance, is one of the few writers to comment on an aspect of the traditional farm that can too easily be forgotten through the selective processes of memory – the smell of the place:

To me as a child the farm part just seemed one big stink. It does still: the phew! of the stable – not so bad as the rest, the unspeakable cowshed sunk in the dark below a barn, beyond all question of light or ventilation, like a mediaeval *oubliette*: the henhouse never cleaned and looking like a guano deposit island off the coast of Chile.   (*Boy* 44)

All in all, one can readily comprehend the unsentimental reaction of the narrative voice in Knister's 'Peaches, Peaches':

If a fellow could make a living without all this running his legs off, and packing peaches until midnight before market days, with no time off except to catch a little sleep or bolt enough feed to hold you up for another six hours, he would be silly not to try to do it.   (*First Day* 10)

The implications of this last remark expand when we realize that the life here being described is that of the fertile agricultural area of southwest Ontario. If conditions in these surroundings are considered too hard, how much more oppressive would be heavy labour on the poor soil of the Canadian Shield. (Part of the difference in attitude between McArthur and Leacock, incidentally, may be explained by the fact that the Leacock farm was situated on the edge of the Shield.) The most vivid and best-known evocation of farming life in the Shield region is contained within Al Purdy's poem 'The Country North of Belleville':

> this is the country of defeat
> where Sisyphus rolls a big stone
> year after year up the ancient hills
> picnicking glaciers have left strewn
> with centuries' rubble
> > backbreaking days
> > in the sun and rain
> when realization seeps slow in the mind
> without grandeur or self-deception in
> > noble struggle
> of being a fool.   (*Poems* 61)

Another poem focusing on the same landscape, 'My Grandfather's Country (Upper Hastings County),' conjures up a desolate scene

> where failed farms sink back into earth
> the clearings join and fences no longer divide.   (147)

These last lines introduce one of the most conspicuous and recurrent literary images of the Ontario countryside: the decaying farm and its doomed inhabitants. For many settlers, the hard work and low returns proved too depressing. In his third civil elegy, Dennis Lee catches the neurotic psychology of families overwhelmed by the unequal struggle with the Canadian Shield. Lee understands how

> men who worked their farms for a lifetime
> could snap in a month from simple cessation of will

and also how

> reaping stone
> from the bush their fathers cleared, the sons gave
> way, and they drank all year, or went strange, or they sat and
> stared outside
> as their cars settled back to slag.   (40)

The moral narrowness of one generation ironically gave way to failure or decadence in the next. In a similar spirit, Raymond Souster writes of 'these old farms waiting / for the weeds to cover them' (*Collected Poems* 3.113) or a more recent poet, Joan Finnigan, of 'the farm gone to pasture, / going to ruin, soon for the subdividers' (61). That the image is not confined to the Canadian Shield is proved by Souster's title, 'Old Farms, Bruce Peninsula'; besides, Alice Munro's work contains several variations on the same image from the same part of the province. In 'Walker Brothers Cowboy,' for instance, the narrator recalls '[o]ne yard after another ... the old cars, the pumps, dogs, views of grey barns and falling-down sheds and unturning windmills' (*Dance* 9) and has earlier observed: 'what could look more unwelcoming, more deserted than the tall unpainted farmhouse with grass growing right up to the front door, green blinds down and a door upstairs opening on nothing but air?' (7). (Max Braithwaite, incidentally, emphasizes *unpainted* barns as a distinguishing feature of the Ontario landscape [3].)

But the image of the decaying farm appears most frequently and relentlessly in the fiction of Matt Cohen. One of the most detailed of these descriptions occurs in the story 'Glass Eyes and Chickens,' a passage in which physical and psychological landscapes blend inextricably:

In the time of his father's sobriety, there had been a white frame farmhouse surrounded by four barns, two hundred acres of only mildly rocky land, and a huge maple bush that backed down to the lake. Successive waves of alcoholism and fire had swallowed the land and burned down the original house. The new house was only the pig barn in disguise; it was flanked by the two other remaining barns, which sat in front of it like twin warnings of disaster. Between them, leading from the house to the highway, was a hundred-yard driveway littered on either side with dead vehicles and spare parts, a true cornucopia of ancient and rusting cars and trucks. They filled the barnyard better than pigs or cows ever had.   (*Night Flights* 94)

It is an all-too-familiar picture, the pattern of loneliness, alcohol, neglect, and fire representing a recurring literary combination. The country of our defeat, indeed.

The most versatile writer on rural Ontario in the crucial period between the clearing of the forests and the triumph of industry and megalopolis is undoubtedly Raymond Knister (1899–1932). This is not merely because of his versatility – he wrote poetry, novels, short stories, and prose sketches – but because he himself experienced both the attractions and frustrations of farm life and so is by no means an unthinking champion of rural values. At the same time, 'farm country,' in Dorothy Livesay's words, 'was Knister's milieu, the central column of his thought' (xi). We know comparatively little about his early life, but his father farmed in Kent and Essex counties, and the future writer describes himself as 'a farm lad of little academic education or worldly acquirements' (*Poems, Stories* 161). He was clearly a sensitive child unsuited to the ceaseless and often demoralizing toil of farm work, yet the beauty and integrity of the agricultural landscape, and the labour and endurance of the people who worked within it, affected him deeply. He soon realized, moreover, that '[t]here was something about the life that I lived, and all the other farm people round me, something that had to be expressed, though I didn't know just how' (161–2). Although he goes on to assert that the attempt 'would have to be made in the form of short stories,' in fact he embraced many literary modes, and it will be convenient here to begin with a discussion of his poetry.

Knister's poems are almost invariably short, and for the most part descriptive – 'Spartan-plain celebrations of ploughing, or horses, or bees,' according to his own account (*Poems, Stories* 164). Generally avoiding the self-consciously poetic, he records as faithfully as possible the sights, sounds, smells, and tastes, all the varied texture of farm life. He possessed not only sharp eyes but a fine retentive memory for telling details, and had the capacity to recognize the significance of the minutiae of country scenes that most observers would either fail to notice or take for granted. Clearly influenced by the contemporary movement that became known as Imagism, he often presents a series of imagistic vignettes that are juxtaposed to form a complex though often elusive representative picture of a landscape or a way of life.

Here, for example, are some lines from 'Lake Harvest,' the poem that, following one of Knister's own listings, his editor places first in the most complete edition of his poems, *Windfalls for Cider*:

> Down on the flat of the lake
> Out on the slate and the green,
> Spotting the border of Erie's sleeping robe of silver-blue
>   changeable silk ...
> The men are sawing the frosted crystal.   (17)

What is remarkable here is the uncluttered directness of description, the unostentatious factual atmosphere. A Krieghoff subject is filtered through the sensibility of a modernist poet. Knister makes no attempt to invest the scene with a special symbolic importance; instead, the rural practice (all the more interesting to us now that it has passed into history) is described lovingly – and accurately *because* lovingly – as a human activity that deserves to be recorded and remembered. The poem is characteristic, since in writing it, while making no sallies in the direction of a conspicuous or flag-waving modernism, Knister resolutely avoids the metrically regular. Indeed, here as so often in his work, a clearly deliberate rhythmic hesitancy prevents the writing from becoming excessively 'poetic.' Knister, we might say, has the eyes and the attitudes of a Lampman, but without the nineteenth-century poet's sense of languid melancholy.

His ability to find suitable subjects for verse in the most mundane aspects of farm life is remarkable. For instance:

> I like to go to the stable after supper, –
> Remembering fried potatoes and tarts of snow-apple jam –
> And watch the men curry the horses,
> And feed the pig, and especially give the butting calves their milk.   (21)

The reference in the final line recalls the poem entitled 'Feed' about a young man giving swill to the young pigs. One can imagine few less 'poetic' subjects than that presented in the opening lines:

> For Danny whistling slowly
> 'Down in Tennessee'
> A fat white shoat by the trough
> Lifts his snout a moment to hear,
> Among the guzzling and slavering comrades,
> Squeezing and forcing ...   (20)

(It is interesting to note that James Reaney encountered this poem by

chance while he was an undergraduate; it taught him that he could find
suitable subjects for verse in his own rural background.) As these examples suggest, such poems are concerned not so much with rural
landscape itself as with the details of rural labour that take place within
it. The opening stanza of 'Stable-Talk' may be accepted as typical:

> We have sweat our share;
> The harrow is caught full of sod-pieces,
> The bright discs are misted yellow in the wet.
> Hear tardy hesitant drips from the eaves!
> Let the rain work now. (26)

Despite its calculated avoidance of verbal luxuriance, the multi-sensual
reference here recalls John Keats's 'To Autumn,' and it is no coincidence that Knister also wrote a novel, the posthumously published
My Star Predominant, based on the life of Keats.

I must not, however, give the impression that all Knister's verse is of
this kind. He can respond evocatively to the sights and sounds of the
natural world, but his characteristic spareness of expression remains,
and he invariably retains, in his own phrase 'the eye on the object'
(*Poems, Stories* 162). In 'The Hawk,' for example, he watches the bird's
shadow as it passes

> Across the bristled and sallow fields,
> The speckled stubble of cut clover.   (*Windfalls* 21)

'Reverie: The Orchard on the Slope' opens with a view of

> Thin ridges of land unploughed
> Along the tree-rows
> Covered with long cream grasses
> Wind-torn. (22)

On the rare occasions when he attempts a more conventionally poetic
effect, it generally takes on the elusive quality of Japanese *haiku*, as in
'Whip-Poor-Will in the Woods,' which ends:

> A wing
> Over lakes resting,
> And the ghost-trees
> Who do not forget
> Hot stormlight
> Muffling stars. (41)

The effect depends upon skilful interweaving of related impressions to create a unique atmosphere.

When he writes a more meditative poem, the character who emerges is identical, as we shall see, with the sensitive and frustrated young countrymen whom we find in his short stories and out of whom Richard Milne, protagonist of the novel *White Narcissus*, has clearly grown. One of his best-known poems, 'The Plowman,' is ostensibly an account of a young man intent on ploughing the perfect furrow yet always defeated:

> Sometimes even before the row is finished
> I must look backward;
> To find, when I come to the end
> That there I swerved.   (20)

One realizes, however, that the subject has become a correlative for the poet in quest of the perfect poem or any artist resolutely seeking an impossible goal. Here, as so often in Knister, the satisfaction and irritations of the rural life are held in balance while at the same time they are presented as typical of all human endeavour and ambition. Another poem, 'Plowman's Song,' makes a similar point in a rare outburst of resonant lyricism:

> Turn under, plow,
> My trouble;
> Turn under griefs
> And stubble.   (46)

The juxtaposition of abstract and particular internal emotion and external situation ('griefs / And stubble') embodies the essence of Knister's vision.

His shorter prose narratives often take the form of brief sketches almost entirely lacking in plot that, poised between fiction and the best kind of journalistic reporting, provide memorable accounts of normal village activities. These (which have not yet received the literary-critical attention that they deserve) will be considered in the next section. Whereas they tend to concentrate on social activities, his more traditional short stories focus on rural loneliness and isolation. Many of them, including 'Mist Green Oats,' 'The Loading,' and 'The First Day of Spring,' centre upon the relationship between a strong assertive father and his sensitive rebellious son, the one content with farm routines, the other dissatisfied and continually responsive to the lure of the city.

'Mist Green Oats' may not be Knister's finest achievement in short fiction, but it certainly qualifies as his most representative story of this kind. It begins with Len Brinder saying goodbye to his mother as she leaves for a holiday in 'the remote city' (*First Day* 58), after which he returns reluctantly to the farm and the company of his father and a hired man. The presentation of the relentless drudgery is brilliantly achieved here: 'he forgot everything about him except the wrenching heavy plow and the rhythmic swinging single-trees and the creaking harness' (61). A fine sense of rural atmosphere is conveyed a little later in the description of the all-male supper where physical closeness does not mitigate the fact of isolation:

Now, as they ate heartily, they said little, except to urge upon each other and accept or refuse more food. The room became warm and filled with the soft sounds of their eating and the steaming kettle on the stove. There was the humming of one or two flies about and between them recurrently.   (65)

The story builds up emotional power as the boy becomes increasingly dissatisfied with his lot: 'It seemed that he had never known anything else than the dolorous wrestle in the dust' (70). There seems little chance, however, of a way out, and it is interesting that Knister encountered difficulty in finding a satisfying conclusion. As it is, 'Mist Green Oats' exists in two versions. In one (reproduced in *The First Day of Spring*), Len leaves a packed suitcase in the kitchen as a sign to his father that he intends to leave. In the other (printed by Robert Weaver in *Canadian Short Stories*), the feelings of rebellion come to nothing and he concludes with the words: '"What's the use? What's the weary use?"' (Weaver 137).

More probing in their psychological insight are 'The First Day of Spring' and 'Elaine.' In the former, the son is told a depressing neighbourhood story of an unwanted pregnancy and the discovery of the child's dead body (possibly stillborn, more probably killed) in the pigs' swill-barrel. The father clearly tells him the story as a cautionary tale, but the boy is appalled because the girl involved was a class-mate in school to whom, it is suggested, he had once been attracted. Above all, the story is told on 'the first day of spring,' which had hitherto implied growth and promise but is now spoiled. What boy and reader alike learn is the grim sordidness, violence, and desperation that can underlie the dramatically beautiful rural background and what otherwise appears to be the idyllic serenity of rural life. The revelation in 'Elaine' is similar. A girl is returning with her mother to high school, and they chat with various acquaintances as they wait for a street-car. In terms of plot, nothing much seems to happen, but we gradually realize, with Elaine, that her return to school has been made possible by the financial rewards of her mother's adultery. As so often with Knister, the real action of the story takes place beneath the surface of the narrative. Since the story is not, like 'The First Day of Spring,' told from the first-person perspective of the main character, and the narrative voice remains at an emotional distance, we can only imagine what Elaine must feel as the fragmented clues gradually and inexorably come together. Once again, the surface of rural life is seen to conceal traumatic hidden depths.

When we turn to Knister's one published novel about an Ontarian farming community, *White Narcissus*, we find that the pros and cons of rural life are at the centre of the plot. Richard Milne, the protagonist, resembles so many of the leading characters in Knister's short stories in that he is too sensitive for the hardships of farm life. As a result, he leaves for the city where he lays the foundation for a career as a writer. When the novel opens, he is returning to his native village with decidedly ambivalent feelings. The monotony and frustrations are certainly still there; he remembers how 'the hamlet was so torpid' (19) and is acutely conscious of 'the rebellious period in which he nearly had hated the place and its inhabitants' (21). His mixed feelings – those, we might say, of McArthur and Leacock combined – are nicely caught: 'How beautiful all this has been, and as the years of his boyhood slipped past without more than a dream of wider freedom, how dreary!' (23). We begin to detect here signs of a subtle balancing. As he recognizes the old fields once again, they become 'more poignant at every yard he traversed' (21), yet part of the reason is that he is looking at the landscape with new eyes: 'he reflected that he was no longer much of a countryman, since he was allowing mere impressions of the place to take his mind, his eyes, from its utilitarian aspect' (20). The past is recalled as 'acrid' (43); at the same time, 'it seemed that the only real and personal part of his life had been lived here' (32). For all his reluctance, Milne cannot help but be moved by memories of 'those days mysterious and full of homely poetry, when he had been a boy in these fields' (37).

White Narcissus is one of those frustrating books that tend to annoy because they show the potential of being so much more profound and important than they actually are. The plot concerns itself with Milne's efforts to rescue Ada Lethen, the woman he loves, from an emotionally constrained life in the home of her estranged farmer-parents. This strand in the novel is weakened by some exaggerated Gothic overtones and forced symbolism, but the contrast between the man who has escaped from his origins and the woman who has not contains the makings of a fruitful tension. 'For so much of her life,' we are told, Ada 'had been bound to this place and to these slowly petrifying people' (43). Within the delicate description of simple and unidealized rural scenes (so different from the angular artificiality of his dialogue) Knister holds in a rather desperate but impressive suspension his rural sensibility and his urbane artistic skill; but the conflicting responses of attraction and repulsion are never finally resolved.

5 *When Work Is Done*

As we read about the lives of the earlier pioneer-settlers, and consider the deep sense of loneliness felt by inhabitants of solitary dwellings in sparsely populated parts of Ontario even in relatively recent times, it is easy to get the impression that life consisted of endless work and virtually no play. This would not, however, represent a complete picture. The very fact of isolation impressed on most families the necessity for occasional social contact and relaxation. Besides, pressure of work varied considerably from season to season. At certain times, bad weather or other adverse conditions rendered regular work impossible; in the natural cycle of the agricultural year, some periods – after the spring sowing, for instance – were less busy than others. Moreover, there were always the traditional festivals to be kept up.

Pleasures were simple, and often circumscribed, but the enjoyment was all the greater by contrast with the harsh conditions of everyday living. This is well brought out by a little-known description from Catharine Parr Traill's *Canadian Settler's Guide* of her family's 1837 Christmas festivities in the bush. Because her husband was on military duty as an aftermath of the Rebellion, Susanna Moodie was left alone with her children, and they were duly invited by the Traills to the feast. We hear of expeditions to bring home evergreen decorations from the woods, the preparation of a 'glorious goose' (229) and 'a large plum pudding' (230), and the delight of the small children as they 'glide and roll' on a snow drift with a newly made sledge. But the most impressive moment comes later when Traill accompanies her sister and family back home:

Just as we were issuing forth for our moonlight drive through the woods, our ears were saluted by a merry peal of sleigh bells, and a loud hurrah greeted our homely turn-out, as a party of boys and girls, crammed into a smart painted cutter, rushed past at full speed. They were returning from a Christmas merry-making at a neighbour's house, where they too had been enjoying a happy Christmas; and long the still woods echoed with the gay tones of their voices, and the clever jingle of their merry bells, as a bend in the river-road brought them back on the night breeze to our ears.   (230)

The scene seems close to the clichés of conventional old-fashioned Christmas cards, but Traill succeeds in conveying the vigorous conviviality of a special occasion.

The combination of basic social needs and occasional periods of enforced idleness required that various kinds of relaxation should develop, whatever the physical obstacles involved. As a young matron remarks in one of Raymond Knister's rural sketches, 'The Dance at Corncob Corners' (1926), '"even if we do live on a back road that's no sign we're going to give in and not go anywhere"' (*First Day* 312). Furthermore, because of the rarity of organized entertainment in the modern sense, small communities had to fall back upon their own resources; activities had to be chosen, organized, and provided by the participants themselves. The literature that comes down to us contains various intriguing hints concerning these occasions, that can most conveniently be divided into communal entertainments and private pastimes.

In the early years, communal entertainments tended to arise as a by-product either of work or of social and religious obligation. This explains why, to the surprise of some modern readers, there are remarkably few references to sport. Various settlers, notably Samuel Strickland, who mentions his interest in the sporting activities of the English country gentleman, primarily riding and shooting, tried to continue their pastimes in the backwoods, but most were compelled to give their time to more pressing matters or at least to confine their shooting to the practical needs of the cooking pot. The most detailed account of any sporting activity in the literature of early Ontario seems to occur in Ralph Connor's *Glengarry School Days*, where the final chapters are centred upon the rivalry between two schools that takes the form of a shinny match, shinny being a primitive form of hockey. The game ('fight' might be a more appropriate word) is eventually won by the Glengarry team that has been trained by a schoolteacher noted for his prowess at lacrosse. The sequence appears to be offered as heroic adventure; many contemporary readers will find it childishly immature. Other sporting references are sparse and minor. The attention of most early writers focuses on matters more directly related to basic survival.

The most widely described and discussed communal activities were the festivities that brought to a close those collaborative work-gatherings known as 'bees.' We find an enlightening account of this tradition, taking the significant form of an old-timer reminiscing about past days (itself an instance of another type of rural entertainment, as we shall see) in Knister's short story 'Laying a Ghost':

'People were more neighbourly them days, and they used to have bees to get most of the jobs done. If a man wanted to get his corn husked he held a bee, and the neighbours came, and the womenfolk got a lot of cooking ready, and a good time was had by all. Or if a man got sick and couldn't get his haying done properly, the neighbours would turn [to] and make hay for him. Used to have bees for pretty near everything – buzzing for stove-wood, butchering, and all that sort of thing, not to mention clover hulling, bean-pulling, and all kinds of threshing.'   (*First Day* 329)

Traill bears out this testimony in her mid-nineteenth-century account of 'those friendly meetings of neighbours who assemble at your summons to raise the walls of your house, shanty, barn, or any other building.' With her unfailing sense of practicality, she goes on to describe the practice as 'highly useful, and almost indispensable to new settlers in the remote townships, where the price of labour is proportionately high, and workmen difficult to be procured' (*Backwoods* 121).

Her sister, almost predictably, has very different views. Moodie would certainly have challenged the assertion of Knister's veteran that 'a good time was had by all.' Though she acknowledges rather reluctantly that, '[i]n raising a house or barn, a bee may be looked upon as a necessary evil' (*Roughing It* 334), for her it presents 'the most disgusting picture of a bush life' (333). She disapproves on moral grounds, of course, but also questions the usefulness of bees in most instances:

They are noisy, riotous, drunken meetings, often terminating in violent quarrels, sometimes even in bloodshed. Accidents of the most serious nature often occur, and very little work is done when we consider the number of hands employed, and the great consumption of food and liquor.

I am certain, in our case [a logging-bee is in question], had we hired with the money expended in providing for the bee, two or three industrious, hard-working men, we should have got through twice as much work, and have had it done well, and have been the gainers in the end.   (333–4)

It is clear, however, that Moodie's main objection lies in the 'unhallowed revelry, profane songs and blasphemous swearing' that accompany these 'odious gatherings' (342), Her husband (who incidentally, she reports as having been 'twice seriously hurt' while attending other people's bees

[342]) even contributes – at Susanna's vigorous urging, one suspects – a doggerel poem in the course of which 'The Devil sat on a log heap ... / A-grinning at the bee' (333).

The evidence, then, is contradictory. Since Traill's logging-bee passed off without incident (though she was 'a little nervous' at one point about the danger of fire [*Backwoods* 192]), and since I see no reason to doubt either the accuracy or sincerity of either writer, it is only reasonable to conclude that such gatherings were sometimes wholly beneficial but that they sometimes degenerated into excessive horseplay, violence, and misrule. Moodie's decidedly refined tastes may tip the balance here – I shall return to those 'profane songs' a little later – though it is only fair to point out that her sporting brother Samuel Strickland comes down on her side. Such practices all too often lead, he asserts darkly, to 'a continual round of dissipation – if not of something worse' (1.37). What emerges clearly from all these accounts, however, is the way in which mutual help provided an occasion for entertainment and revelry that seems to have been much needed, however 'unhallowed' the festivities might become as the hours passed.

The convivial aspect of bees is emphasized in Ralph Connor's fictional account of a logging-bee in *The Man from Glengarry*:

now the day's work was over, and the hour for the day's event had come, for supper was the great event to which all things moved at bees. The long tables stood under the maple trees, spread with the richest, rarest, deadliest dainties known to the housewives and maidens of the countryside. About the tables stood in groups the white-aproned girls, tucked and frilled, curled and ribbon-ed into all degrees of bewitching loveliness. The men hurried away with their teams and then gave themselves to the serious duty of getting ready for supper. (123–4)

Connor's account also suggests that customary practice varied drasti-cally from place to place. Whereas Moodie lays emphasis on the hard work and expense involved in providing for the assembled workers, Connor remarks that 'little baking was required, for the teams that brought the men with their axes and logging-chains for the day's work at the *brûlé* brought also their sisters and mothers with baskets of provi-sions.' He acknowledges, indeed, that a bee 'without the sisters and mothers with their baskets would hardly be an unmixed blessing' (115). Even more noteworthy, perhaps, is the fact that, in a novel packed with physical violence, this logging-bee, though the occasion for smouldering rivalry, passes off, like Traill's, without incident. It ends not with a fight but with the minister's speech and prayer. Given Connor's predilection for both rough-house and piety, one would have expected his logging-bee to contain both.

Connor also furnishes us with a vivid account of another combination of work and entertainment, the 'sugaring-off.' He gives only the sparsest details of the sugar-making itself – perhaps this was too hackneyed a 'Canadian' subject even for Connor, or perhaps it seemed so familiar that any lengthy·description would be superfluous. Instead, he emphasizes the festive occasion that forms its climax (and includes an exciting and potentially disastrous accident for good measure). 'The sugar time,' he insists, 'is, in many ways, the best of all the year' (58), and the festivities that accompany it are clearly presented as some sort of seasonal rite. When Don, the master of ceremonies, begins to organize the proceedings, he announces: '"the programme for this evening is as follows: games, tea, and taffy, in the order mentioned"' (59). One suspects, indeed, that the celebratory climax of the sugaring was considered (albeit unofficially) as important as the utilitarian motive of producing maple-sugar.

Church functions also provided convenient excuses for communal get-togethers, though some of these, like bees, could get out of hand. Even the wake, Connor tells us, which began 'for the guarding of the dead,' gradually turned into an occasion 'for the comfort of the living' and ultimately might degenerate 'into a frolic, if not a debauch' (97). Since we live in an age when church-going, or some equivalent form of supposedly religious gathering, seems oriented more towards social cohesion than theological instruction or the performing of a sacred rite, we are likely to understand better than the early settlers why attendance at divine service was regarded as so desirable a part of a well-balanced life. There is little reason to doubt, for example, that many (perhaps unconsciously) repaired to church not for the doctrine but the music there; others may have been dimly aware of the inevitability – even the psychological necessity – of social release. Anne Langton offers a characteristically perceptive and witty comment when she reports in her journal (October 1838): 'We had an excellent sermon on evil-speaking, and by way of showing how much we had profited by it, we began talking over the weak points of our several neighbours immediately afterwards' (80). This is not, I think, merely a sharp irony; she recognizes the need for communal gossip alongside the need for communal worship.

In early times, to be sure, moral and social norms ostensibly supporting religious teachings could lead to more dubious forms of communal activity. A notorious instance is the 'charivari' or 'shivaree,' in which individuals involved in, among other things, marriages considered unsuitable or improper were subjected to rough horseplay and sometimes serious violence. Although both Moodie (*Roughing It* 221) and Mary O'Brien (26) claim that this practice was imported from Lower Canada, it is clearly related to the skimmington-ride well known in English rural districts until the beginning of the present century and portrayed unforgettably by Thomas Hardy in *The Mayor of Casterbridge*. Moodie devotes a whole chapter to the custom, during which one of her acquaintances is made to recount local instances with disapproval but also with an apparent relish. These include the more typical examples of old men marrying young wives or the marriage of 'two old people, who ought to be thinking of their graves' (221). On such occasions, the protests usually ended in nothing more objectionable than some noisy threats accompanying extortion for drinking money. Moodie's source claims, indeed, that a charivari 'would seldom be attended with bad consequences if people would take it as a joke, and join in the spree' (225). But one story culminates in the death of a runaway black slave who had married an Irishwoman, and shows how ugly such traditional customs could become. Alice Munro chronicles a related scene of violence in the fatal horse-whipping of an unpopular resident in *Who Do You Think You Are?* (7–9) – and, furthermore, has asserted that the scene was based on an old newspaper story and 'really did happen in a town I know' ('What Is Real?' 225). A related scene in Robertson Davies's *What's Bred in the Bone*, in which a dwarf is goaded into suicide (120–1), has a similar local-historical foundation.

A little later, when communities developed and the network of roads improved, more varied (and less rough) activities became possible. One of these, for an account of which we may turn to Knister at the beginning of this century, was the harvest-home supper. In his documentary sketch 'Harvest Home Chicken Supper at Birdseye Centre,' he records – and with his characteristic artistry the information comes at the end of the action rather than at the beginning – how a 'thrill' spread through the church when the minister announced the event (*First Day* 305). Clearly, a social gathering attains respectability, becomes something close to a pleasurable obligation, when recommended during divine service. Knister describes the supper in all its organized gaiety: the carrying of baskets down to the church basement; the setting out of cake booth, meat booth, pie booth; the children interrupting their game of tag to wonder at 'the variety of food at every hand' (303); the general good cheer of the feast itself. But there is a sense in which what comes *after* the feast is even more significant; this was called 'the program,' an entertainment including visiting 'people from the town' (304). We hear of 'songs, recitations, readings, quartets, instrumentals, more songs, recitations' (305). We may be tempted to sympathize with the new schoolteacher's comment, "'Oh, isn't it awful?,' yet 'the good of getting together' is clearly exempt from the gently gathering irony.

One related function was the box-social in which successful bids by young men for lunch-boxes included the company of the young women who made them. Alice Munro's story 'Visitors' contains a comic anecdote about switched wrappings and an agonizing choice between a poor lunch with a pretty girl and a lavish feast with a plain one (*Moons* 207–8). By contrast, in a grisly story entitled 'The Box Social' that gained notoriety on its first publication in 1947, James Reaney presents a girl avenging herself on her seducer by filling the box with 'the crabbed corpse of a still-born child wreathed in bloody newspaper' (151). Most box-socials, one hopes, passed off less melodramatically.

Other excuses for communal entertainment, which may well overlap with excruciating duty, include school functions, glimpses of which we are continually receiving from Munro's fiction. In 'An Ounce of Cure,' for instance, the retrospective narrator recalls a Christmas production of *Pride and Prejudice* during which, as a girl, she had predictably fallen in love with the boy who played Darcy (*Dance* 76). In *Lives of Girls and Women* we watch the habitual school routines annually interrupted for the 'ceremony' of an operetta. (Robertson Davies offers a similar Torontonian example in *The Manticore*.) In 'Accident' (from *The Moons of Jupiter*) we are invited to hear strains from a rehearsal for the Christmas concert: 'He Shall Feed His Flock,' 'The Huron Carol,' 'Hearts of Oak,' 'The Desert Song,' 'The Holy City.' The time setting for this last example is 1943 – which accounts for the (British) patriotism of 'Hearts of Oak' – but an equivalent potpourri of musical favourites could represent numerous decades stretching before and after.

Elsewhere, Munro touches on adult amateur dramatics (*Something* 12) and the picture-show that once went by the quaint appellation of 'lantern slides' (*Who* 196–7). In 'The Time of Death,' Patricia Parry is a youthful member of a local concert-party group regularly introduced as 'the Little Sweetheart of Maitland Valley, the Baby Blonde, the Pint-Size Kiddie with the Great Big Voice' (*Dance* 89). In addition, Munro, writing in a less pious age, is a shrewd if somewhat sceptical commentator on the non-spiritual rewards for church attendance; it is not accidental that Del Jordan, the protagonist of *Lives of Girls and Women*, finds her first serious sexual partner at a revivalist meeting and in a chapter entitled 'Baptizing.'

Gradually, a pattern of formal celebrations became established, a regular succession of fairs and parades. In Sara Jeannette Duncan's *The Imperialist* (1904), Victoria Day has become 'a real holiday, that woke you with bells and cannon' (13). Duncan is mildly ironical about the event itself and some of its features (on one occasion, the cannon 'blew out all the windows in the Methodist Church' [13]), but she has no doubts about its importance as a social festivity – 'a day with an essence in it, dawning more gloriously than other days and ending more regretfully' (12). It was a day when countryfolk came into the town in holiday mood dressed 'in their honest best' (13), when the chief local industry, the Milburn Boiler Company, took its employees by train 'to the lakeside or "the Falls" at half a dollar a head' (14), when a local lacrosse match generated keen support for the home team, a day that 'ended up splendidly with rockets and fire-balloons and drunken Indians vociferous on their way to the lock-up' (13). (Some commentators, in our over-sensitive age, have sniffed racist prejudice here, but Duncan, who had begun her career as a brilliant and responsible journalist, was, of course, being honestly realistic.) From morning till night, a spirit of carnival reigned.

In *Sunshine Sketches* a decade later, Stephen Leacock half-parodied, half-celebrated the succession of seasonal festivities when, in a small community, everyone takes part in everyone else's anniversary. On St Patrick's Day 'everybody wears a green ribbon' (37); on St Andrew's Day a thistle; on St George's Day everyone feels 'glad that he's an English-man' (38); on the Fourth of July, Mariposa is bedecked with stars and stripes. And at about the same time, probably on Dominion Day (when, in the small town George Elliott presents in *The Kissing Man*, there are 'harness horse races' [41]), the Knights of Pythias organize their annual 'marine excursion.' More ambitious and more popular, however, was the annual county fair or fall fair, referred to in *The Kissing Man* (which seems to be based on Strathroy) as 'the carnival,' with its tents and prizes, the barkers, 'the merry-go-round and Ferris wheel' (20), the 'fun house' with its 'labyrinth of mirrors' and its 'winding tunnel of terror' (21).

For the young people of an earlier age, this was a world of wonders indeed, a phrase that reminds us how Robertson Davies has recorded this aspect of village and small-town life in the greatest detail. Deptford, we learn, 'had a proud local reputation for its fair. School children were admitted free ... the Fair Board liked to run up the biggest possible annual figure' (*World* 23). We are invited to see it through the impressionistic eyes of the young Paul Dempster who approaches the fair in 1918

like a gourmet savouring a feast. Begin at the bottom, with what was least amusing. That would be the Women's Institute display of bottled pickles, embalmed fruit, doilies, home-cooking, and 'fancy-work.' Then the animals, the huge draught-horses, the cows with enormous udders, the prize bull (... some of my schoolmates were lingering there ... gaping at his enormous testicles), the pigs so unwontedly clean, and the foolish poultry.   (25)

The display from the nearby Indian Reservation ('slim walking-canes,' 'fancy boxes made of sweetgrass' [26]) is a little more exotic, but the small boy is more intrigued by the non-local booth selling 'gaudy celluloid, kewpie dolls.' But the main attraction, of course, to which he succumbs fatefully, is the visiting circus, Wanless's World of Wonders, with its Fat Woman and Strong Man, its fire-eater and knife-thrower, snake-charmer, fortune-teller, midget juggler, armless foot-painter, hermaphrodite, and 'Missing Link' – and, of course, its magician. Paul Dempster becomes part of this world, in fact a world of sleaziness rather than of wonder, and so comes to play an important part in the chief aim of the company – deceiving 'the Rubes.' Magic and deception go hand in hand. Davies well conveys the mixture of cynicism and companionship, of kindness and cruelty. Wanless's World of Wonders is offered as a curiously ambiguous microcosm.

In *The Manticore*, which, though published earlier, describes a later version of the fair in the mid-1930s, the eight-year-old David Staunton is cast as the bridegroom in a Tom Thumb wedding organized by the United Church. The general standard of the fair remains much the same. Whereas Paul Dempster had noted the 'endless jokes about minorities' in the circus (*World* 100), here a representative carnival game is revealingly called 'Hit the Nigger in the Eye' (95). But the Ladies' Aid hoped to offer 'a refined alternative to the coarse pleasures of the carnival shows' and revived an entertainment that was 'already old-fashioned.' In the supposedly innocent fun, during which the bridegroom kissed the bride so frequently and enthusiastically that the comic parson had to part them, a sentimental cuteness combined with 'just that spice of sanctified lewdness that the Ladies' Aid loved' (97). The scene is a minor episode, and holds its place in the psychological pattern of the novel (young David acts up and provokes comparisons with his 'swordsman' father), but it speaks volumes for the 'representative' attitudes of the small-town Deptfords of that time.

But the great public celebrations in old-time Ontario must surely have been the parades. Here, as so often, though one finds tantalizing references in Duncan and Leacock and elsewhere, it is Alice Munro who evokes their spirit most memorably in imaginative literature. The frequency and variety of their origins are alike memorable:

There used to be plenty of parades in Hanratty. The Orange Walk, on the Twelfth of July; the High School Cadet Parade, in May; the schoolchildren's Empire Day Parade, the Legion's Church Parade, the Santa Claus Parade, the Lions Club Old-Timers' Parade.   (*Who* 191)

The Orange Walk is given pride of place here because it was

the most splendid ... King Billy at the head of it rode a horse as near pure white as could be found, and the Black Knights at the rear, the noblest rank of Orangemen – usually thin, and poor, and proud and fanatical old farmers – rode dark horses and wore the ancient father-to-son top hats and swallow-tail coats. The banners were all gorgeous silks and embroideries, blue and gold, orange and white, scenes of Protestant triumph, lilies and open Bibles, mottoes of godliness and honor and flaming bigotry. (191–2)

These parades were, of course, important because they were participatory. One doesn't have to go to the lengths of Leacock and see everyone wearing each other's national emblems to realize that most members of the community could be involved on one occasion or another. Friends and relatives could readily be watched at one parade, and duly become watchers at the next. The sense of spectacle – and especially of locally produced spectacle – was paramount. Above all, though this may not have been immediately obvious to the participants, local rivalries – most notably those of national origin and religious affiliation – could be triumphantly acknowledged in the interests of a more permanent social cohesion.

Otherwise, as in most societies, the chief social activity was dancing. Susanna Moodie, rather surprisingly in a book called *Roughing It in the Bush*, lists 'music and dancing' as the 'chief accomplishments' of Canadian women of her time, and continues: 'The waltz is their favourite dance, in which old and young join with the greatest avidity; it is not unusual to see parents and their grown-up children dancing in the same set in a public ball-room' (218). But times change, and dance fashions change along with them. At Knister's Corncob Corners, country dancing has taken the place of the more elegant waltz, 'those old-time dances without which no truly rural assemblage for this sort of jollification is complete' (*First Day* 310). But Knister catches the rural dance at a crucial moment of transition. He observes that the younger people may 'devote their attention to two-steps, turkey-trots, waltzes, or even the Charleston' – more than half a century later we might find ourselves rephrasing that to read 'even waltzes' – but they are prepared, Knister notes, 'to take part in the square dances which their elders enjoy so much' (310). Yet such intergenerational relaxation was soon to be challenged. Alice Munro's George in 'Thanks for the Ride' has a different reaction when told that the only dance that evening in the small town he is passing through was at a local school:

'That old-time? No, no, I don't go for that old-time. *All-a-man left* and that, used to have that down in the basement of the church. Yeah, *ever' body swing* – I don't go for that.'   (*Dance* 45)

The older traditions are in the process of giving way to newer, non-local tastes. The widely disseminated communications media altered the old ways, and led to an inevitable decline not only in the dances performed but in the parades. The reason, we note with interest, is not a decline in bigotry. Once again Munro clinches the point. The aging Flo comments: '"Parades have fallen off a lot. All the Orangemen are dying out and you wouldn't get the turnout, anyway, people'd rather stay home and watch their T.V."' (*Who* 201).

Public entertainment, then, was a regular but still occasional phenomenon in early Ontario. It provided events to be anticipated with excitement and later remembered with pleasure. But what of the periods in between? What of the long winter evenings in isolated farmhouses without any of the entertainment-at-the-touch-of-a-button that the later twentieth century tends to take for granted? Even in the early days of the automobile, ambitious excursions to local centres might prove unpractical, but local visits to neighbours within walking distance were still feasible. In his sketches set in what we consider the rather condescendingly named Corncob Corners, Knister skilfully conveys the warmth and sense of expectancy and excitement involved in such modest excursions. The need for such companionship is clearly articulated in the opening paragraphs of 'Corncob Corners Folks':

The long winter evenings when the weather makes people disinclined to venture out, if that involves getting a recalcitrant car ready and taking the risk of getting stuck in the snow of country roads – the long winter evenings are the time for neighbours to renew acquaintanceships.

They trudge from their farms through the snow carrying a lantern to light their steps, their stamps resound upon the veranda, and you are ready to welcome them before you hear the knock. Evenings would be tedious without such visits, when the men have done all the chores and are inclined to fall asleep over the farm paper, while the women-folk gossip or mend or read, or gather a quorum for a game of cards.   (*Poems, Stories* 116)

Ironically, the emphasis on visiting, gossiping, and general getting together draws attention to the oppressive sense of rural loneliness that is being so deliberately avoided.

Clearly, whether neighbours come to visit or not, families had no recourse but to provide their own pastimes. For those with musical abilities, the playing of instruments would obviously be a major source of self-entertainment. We hear of a piano being imported by the Stewarts from Ireland in 1826–7, since Frances Stewart 'was an accomplished performer' (103); on the other hand, Patrick Shirreff met a Miss Somerville in the backwoods and reports: 'her piano had remained untouched in the corner of the room since her arrival in the country, the churn being now her favourite instrument' (120). Otherwise, pastimes would generally have taken the form of story-telling, song-singing, reminiscences of the past told by the elderly to the younger generation, and in at least some homes family readings out of books and magazines. Once again we can catch glimpses of these activities in literature, though detailed evidence for such fleeting oral occurrences is inevitably scant. Nonetheless, it is still intriguing to ask ourselves: what kind of stories would they have told, and what forms did such stories take?

We can gather some clues from writers' own reminiscences as well as from incidents embedded within imaginative literature itself. The former, however, do not always produce a clear and consistent picture. Catharine Parr Traill, for example, doubted whether the traditional tales from her own culture would survive the passage across the Atlantic: 'The Canadian settlers' children will probably never listen to any of the wild tales of ghosts and witches and robbers and fairies and seer [sic] – that formed at once the blight and terror of their parents' childhood' (qtd in Gerson 42). One wonders, however, what stories she herself told to her own children in the backwoods, and one wonders also if other settlers would be so squeamishly critical of their own childhood experience. It seems likely that such stories were transmitted in Ontario as they were elsewhere. We know, moreover, that immigrants brought with them a wealth of ballads and songs from their native countries, and that these were passed down through their families and so spread from one community to another. Edith Fowke, the most prominent collector of the ballads, songs, and folklore of Ontario, has found Ontarian specimens of many of the traditional English and Scottish ballads originally collected and published by Francis James Child and others. Moreover, she has uncovered an unusually impressive store from Irish sources, her researches persuading her that 'our richest folk-song heritage' has come from the nineteenth-century Irish settlers in the province (*Traditional* 2). Other material that gradually filtered down into Ontario homes included broadside street-ballads, ancient rebel songs, murder ballads, bawdy ballads, drinking and vaudeville songs.

Many of the last-mentioned would doubtless have shocked Traill's genteel tastes, and especially those of her sister Susanna Moodie (we recall that earlier reference to 'profane songs' at the logging-bee). Neither sister could or would imagine a small child like the young Al Purdy hearkening to the stories of his disreputable grandfather; still less would either of them acknowledge that such hearkening could furnish a legitimate entrance into an authentic past. Purdy recalls the occasion in one of the poems that make up *In Search of Owen Roblin*, where the grandfather is graphically described as

> all-night boozer and shanty wrestler
> prime example of a misspent youth
> among ladies of the church-sewing circle
> poker player and teller of tall tales
> to a boy – Listen he'd say Listen   (n pag)

Purdy did listen, and if we want to gain anything approaching a complete picture of the popular culture of the province, we must be prepared to listen too.

Even in more 'respectable' situations, however, a wide range of story would doubtless be standard fare. In his appropriately titled poem 'Winter's Tales,' James Reaney presents a more traditional picture of story-telling in isolated farmhouse families. Here

> the farmer and his children sit
> About their stove whose flamey wit
> Giggles in red and yellow laughter

and watch through the window

> The cold wind herd a river of snow
> Beneath the moon.

This conspicuous metaphorical style reflects the imaginative mood of the group, and in due course leads into the subject of story-telling:

> Then the farmer told them stories
> That his father had told him
> Of the massacre at Lucan ...   (*Poems* 36)

The group-killing of the Donnellys at Lucan in 1880 is, of course, a story that Reaney himself was later to tell in more ambitious form in his trilogy of plays, *The Donnellys*, in the 1970s. It is a more sensational story than most. I mention it here because it contains two elements that are essential to my subject: first, it is an Ontario story, comparable in its starkness and savagery to many of the imported tales but significantly a local product; second, in alluding to the story in an early poem and retelling it dramatically a generation later, Reaney is demonstrating the power of such stories and how they are handed down, retold, and imaginatively recreated.

The farmer in Reaney's poem was indeed telling a local story, since the setting is close to Reaney's Stratford and the Donnelly murders took place in a nearby township. But the story has now become part of Ontario's history; indeed, since we now know that it originated in a religious blood-feud in Ireland, it is itself part of a larger historical subject. This reminds us that historical reminiscences can themselves stimulate the writing of historical fiction. The novelist John Richardson, author of *Wacousta* (1832), is on record as acknowledging a literary debt to the historical reminiscences of his grandmother who 'used to enchain my young interest by detailing various facts connected with the siege [at Michilimackinac] she so well remembered, and infused into me a longing to grow up to manhood that I might write a book about it' (585). Richardson was later to draw upon his own appointment with history at Moraviantown in the War of 1812 when he came to write his sequel to *Wacousta* entitled *The Canadian Brothers*. Other historic events produced a crop of ballads and rhymes that would undoubtedly have become part of the local store of song. Many of these deal with the 1837 rebellion, and John S. Moir has made a collection, in *Rhymes of Rebellion*, of both loyal and rebel contributions. One of the best-known is 'The Battle of the Windmill,' which gives a rousing version of the defeat inflicted on a group of American invaders near Prescott in 1838. A similar incident in the Niagara peninsula in 1886, when rebel forces enjoyed a brief initial success, is celebrated from a different viewpoint in 'A Fenian Story.' Both these examples are conveniently accessible in Fowke's *Penguin Book of Canadian Folk Songs*. They offer dramatic instances of how historic event can be transformed, through the imperative of story-telling, into popular myth.

Many of the local stories would be cautionary, like the tales of children lost in the woods that so obsessed Catharine Parr Traill. Others would be less serious and more fanciful. These include the hoard of tall tales, mainly emanating from northern Ontario, that imaginatively exaggerate such matters as the extent of the cold or the size and viciousness of mosquitoes. This humour of desperation is common in pioneering communities. Settlers in or near the Ottawa valley would exchange stories of Joe Mufferaw, a legendary Paul Bunyan character known for his giant physique and his enormous feats of strength. Key figures in the dissemination of this orally transmitted popular culture were the shantymen from the northern logging camps. Their songs and stories had a wide currency because, as Fowke has reminded us, '[u]ntil recently it was the custom for farmers to work their fields in the summer, and spend the winter in the [northern] woods, coming back each spring with their winter's wages and a fresh batch of songs' (*Traditional* 3). While this material included such widespread favourites as 'Barbara Allen,' 'The Croppy Boy,' and 'The Foggy Dew,' which were handed down in something close to their original form, other songs were adapted to local conditions, including a jail song naturalized in Ontario as 'The Soo St Mary's Jail.' Others again were specially composed to celebrate events, generally either tragic or sentimental, that took place within the province. Two songs, 'Jimmy Whalen' and 'Lost Jimmy Whalen,' commemorate a raftsman killed in a logging-jam accident in eastern Ontario in the 1870s; another, 'John R. Burchell,' following a sanctioned tradition of street-ballads that publicized executions, records the last hours of an Englishman hanged for murder in Woodstock in 1890. Shipwrecks on the Great Lakes were another fruitful source for local story.

Other musical influences came from church and school. The appeal of hymns must have been a welcome alternative in strongly religious families to some of the more secular songs and stories already considered. The tradition goes back a long way. On two occasions in *The Backwoods of Canada* Traill refers to the satisfaction of listening to Indians singing their hymns on Sundays (164, 215), and although this may in part be explained by her partiality for exotic incident and her desire to make pious allusions to missionary efforts, it also conveys a hint of traditional practices. Certainly, the popularity of hymn singing in Ontario can be attested from a variety of sources, and literature adds its mite to the store. Munro's fiction, for instance, is studded with allusions to and quotations from popular hymns, not only sung in choirs but remembered in private. She is also fond of reproducing scraps of children's rhymes learned in the schoolyard – some of them traditional, others travestied in profane versions. Naturally, these last rarely graced the printed page until the post-1960s age of permissiveness, but they undoubtedly existed earlier (as did the obscene versions of hymns that anyone with army experience will know). These need not be over-emphasized – and they would not, of course, have been openly acknowledged within the domestic context – but they make a not insignificant contribution to the tangled skein of oral culture.

Poetry recitation, then as now, is likely to have been a much less popular form of literary expression, but the amount of local verse published in small-town newspapers testifies, as Pauline Greenhill has shown, to the continuing life of the genre, whatever reservations we may have about its quality. In *Twelve Letters to a Small Town*, Reaney records one amusing incident possibly fabricated but more probably encountered while going through the local archives:

When the Crimean War comes someone writes a poem that starts Hail Britannia, Hail Terrific Gal. Next Week we are informed that he didn't mean Gal, he meant Hail Terrific Gaul.   (*Poems* 218)

But some of Ontario's local bards were comic without the excuse of typographical error. In *The Four Jameses* (1927), William Arthur Deacon immortalized three Ontarian instances, including James Gay of Guelph, self-styled 'Poetic Laureate of Canada, and Master of the Poets,' and James McIntyre of Ingersoll, remembered for his 'Ode on the Mammoth Cheese' ('We have seen thee, queen of cheese, / Lying quietly at your ease' [64]). Nowadays, such verse-making is for the most part deliberately light in tone, and serves on public occasions as the equivalent of a comic speech.

Although there are comparatively few records of ghost stories as a popular tradition preserved in high-quality fiction, it is reasonable to assume that they must have constituted an appreciable part of the winter entertainment. In early times, it was common to assume that real-life ghosts had been left behind in 'the old country' (the traditional folk belief, immortalized in Robert Burns's 'Tam o'Shanter,' that ghosts were unable to cross water, may have contributed to this confidence). Thus Traill claimed that 'ghosts or spirits ... appear totally banished from Canada,' since it is 'too matter-of-fact [a] country for such supernaturals to visit' (*Backwoods* 153); and her brother Samuel Strickland makes the same point: 'Canada is no place for ghosts. The country is too new for such gentry' (2.184). But the reality of the case is very different. Indeed, only a few years before, presumably unbeknownst to Traill or Strickland, a dramatic case of poltergeist activity had taken place at Baldoon in southwest Ontario. In 1976 Reaney, along with C.H. Gervais, produced a play about the incident (entitled simply *Baldoon*), and we can be sure that the events were widely discussed at the time. Such stories recur. Munro has one of her characters relate a local poltergeist story in the opening chapter of *Lives of Girls and Women* (8), and 'A Queer Streak' (in *The Progress of Love*), like Knister's 'Laying a Ghost,' centres upon fake poltergeist phenomena that are ultimately exposed. Knister even contradicts Traill and Strickland by observing that 'in those days no community was complete without a haunted house' (*First Day* 329).

As John Robert Colombo has pointed out in *Mysterious Canada* (127–9), we now know that even the respectable Susanna Moodie showed a great interest in the supernatural, and insisted on meeting Kate Fox, one of the founders of modern spiritualism, who had been born near Belleville, when the latter revisited her native area in the 1850s. The Moodies themselves then began dabbling in spiritualism, and Susanna even goes so far as to describe the seemingly down-to-earth Catharine Parr Traill as 'a very powerful Medium' (129). It may be reasonably assumed that stories of ghosts and poltergeists, as well as other strange happenings, were common in early Ontario, especially in the rural areas. Indeed, R.S. Lambert, who gives a readable if journalistic account of the Baldoon mystery and other hauntings in *Exploring the Supernatural: The Weird in Canadian Folklore*, remarks that, while there is 'a dearth of ruined castles, moated granges, decayed country houses and dilapidated rectories, such as provide good cover for the ghosts of the Old World' (10), lonely farms are a favourite site for supernatural phenomena in the country and in the province. Between them, Lambert and Colombo compile an impressive list of strange stories, the most common in Ontario being ghost stories, tales of buried treasure, sightings of lake monsters, and puzzling accounts surrounding shipwrecks in the Great Lakes. These, we may be sure, provided ample excuse for eerie story-telling around farmhouse kitchens.

In the work of Alice Munro, we encounter various hints concerning the oral transmission of traditional lore, including ghost stories. In the name-story of *Something I've Been Meaning to Tell You*, Blaikie Noble tells a story on his lakeshore bus-tour about a reputedly haunted house where a woman is supposed to have killed her husband. He assures his women tourists that 'the ghost walked up and down in the garden between two rows of blue spruce. It was not the murdered man who walked, but the wife, regretting.' Significantly, this was '[t]he first Et [the leading character] had ever heard of it, living ten miles away all her life' (2), and the strong supposition is lodged in our minds that Blaikie has invented the whole tale. In any case, it is yet another instance of the development of local story. Munro also emphasizes the taste for mysterious gossip and rumour. In the 'Age of Faith' section of *Lives of Girls and Women* Del Jordan lists the anti-Catholic stories promulgated by her relatives who lived across from the Catholic church: 'they knew, they could tell you, all there was beyond jokes, babies' skeletons, and strangled nuns under the convent floors, yes, fat priests and fancy women and the black old popes. It was all true. They had books about it' (78).

Another glimpse into the heart of Protestant Ontario.

'[F]or a collector of curiosities about his fellowman,' Knister tells us, 'village gossip is a treasure-vault' (*Poems, Stories* 39), and Munro would agree. For her, gossip is one of the chief origins of story; indeed, the fact of gossip frequently becomes part of the story itself. In the opening section of *Lives of Girls and Women*, 'The Flats Road,' she shows how the gossip that circulates about Uncle Benny's newspaper-advertisement bride gradually turns into the stuff of local story. 'Stories of Madeleine were being passed up and down the road ... After a while [Benny] started telling stories himself' (15). Similarly, the ailing mother in 'The Peace of Utrecht' became 'one of the town's possessions and oddities, its brief legends' (*Dance* 194). Other legends preserved in this way include the inevitable tale of wolves overrunning a sleigh and eating a baby (*Something* 116), of the woman who lost her way in a snow blizzard and was found frozen to death (*Something* 164), of a man who is supposed to have disappeared in a local swamp but is still occasionally seen (*Moons* 213). In addition, of course, there are the comic anecdotes and the dark rumours concerning sexual scandals and improprieties. These are circulated, debated, refined, and the more sensational of them inscribed in local memory. Munro lays considerable emphasis on this corporate story-telling function and the way it ultimately graduates to the status of oral history – hence her unflagging interest in 'the whole business of how life is made into a story by the people who live it, and then the whole town sort of makes its own story' (Struthers, 'Alice Munro' 103–4).

Munro, then, is the most fruitful source for an imaginative understanding of how the process of local story-telling grows and develops. Her own stories, however, though they may contain intriguing examples of such story-telling, extend towards other fictional concerns. Only rarely do such stories get translated faithfully into written literature, but a particularly choice example is preserved in the prose of Peter McArthur. This, one suspects, is how local tales were actually passed down in earlier times:

And that reminds me of a story. One spring many years ago two young men were paying court to the same girl. Both had to cross the creek that wound before her home, and one of them had a bright idea. As soon as it was dark he hurried to the creek, carrying a pail of soft soap. Straddling the log, he worked his way backwards across and spread the slippery soap lavishly on the little bridge over which his rival was to follow. He then washed his hands and went to the house to press his suit. About an hour later he was quietly gratified to hear a loud splash in the swollen stream. This put so much courage in him that he pleaded his cause with complete success. Some time about midnight he tore himself away from his future bride and was so exultingly happy that he forgot all about the soaped log. There is no need telling you what happened.   (14)

Whether such stories belong to fact or fiction (or perhaps to a disputed area between the two) is, for our purposes, not especially important. More significant is the undoubted fact that characters like Munro's Del Jordan are prepared to accept the traditional, albeit far-fetched stories as 'all true.' Most of the stories I have so far mentioned – even Blaikie Noble's probably spurious haunting – are offered as authentic local tales. The taste for 'story' frequently exists alongside an almost passionate concern for 'fact.' As one of the characters remarks in 'Visitors': "'It's not a story. It's something that happened''' (*Moons* 215). Moreover, many family stories, presented as being handed down from one generation to another, sound convincingly authentic. Munro is unparalleled in her ability to introduce such anecdotes into her stories. One thinks of the practical jokes played by Aunt Elspeth and Auntie Grace on their brother and the hired man in *Lives of Girls and Women* (28–9), the story of the lemonade and the sewn-up fly-buttons in 'The Ottawa Valley' (*Something* 187–8), the epic story of driving through a blizzard to win a darts tournament (*Moons* 206). Even a casual anecdote, like Flo's assumption that 'Spinoza' must be a new kind of vegetable (*Who* 3), sounds more likely to have happened than to have been invented. Part of Munro's artistry lies in her capacity to leave us tantalizingly unsure; another part is to convince us that, in the final analysis, the distinction is unimportant.

Such reminiscences are clearly made up in large part of the domestic talk of days gone by. Peter McArthur, himself in reminiscent mood, thinks back to the ancient fireplaces of the past and the tales told around the blaze. As often as not, they qualified as 'something that happened' rather than mere 'story':

I had heard pioneer stories told around that old fireplace by veritable pioneers ... I remembered the tenor of these stories. They dealt with home-building and the struggles through which men and women passed in getting a foothold in the new land.   (12)

Many of these accounts never got written down and were eventually forgotten. But some have been given a new lease of life in books of retrospective memoirs – some of them imaginative and even artful in construction – that preserve in print some of the oral experiences of the province. Such books, as it were, gather, sift, and systematize the records of the folk memory.

One of these is *The Yellow Briar* (1933), ostensibly by 'Patrick Slater,' though the author's name was in fact John Mitchell. Mitchell was born on a farm in the Caledon Hills in 1880, and his best-known book preserves a record of his grandparents' generation by inventing as narrator 'old Paddy Slater,' who claims to have been referred to in the neighbourhood as 'an historical landmark' (14, 15). As he observes, 'the only theme I have in this simple narrative is the homely and commonplace in the lives of pioneer Irish folk in the Ontario countryside ... They are all dead and forgotten; but such simple, natural, wholesome lives make the history of the country where their bodies lie' (182). As the tone of this passage suggests, *The Yellow Briar* is a somewhat sentimental re-creation of a vanished world, but it is important as a witness to the Irish contribution to Ontario's population and life. For some reason, the Scots contribution has been much more prominently portrayed in literature, and Mitchell's book helps to restore the balance. As Paddy Slater notes both ruefully and gallantly, '[t]he Scottish Presbyterians may have been the salt of the earth in Upper Canada; but the Irish women gave it sweetness and light' (21).

A similar historical record is to be found in Robert Laidlaw's *The McGregors* (1979), a tribute to that Scottish 'salt of the earth.' Though subtitled 'A Novel of an Ontario Pioneer Family,' it might better be described as a representative chronicle, the typical story of an immigrant, Jim McGregor, who came to Canada as a child in the mid-nineteenth century (at approximately the same time as Leacock), spent the rest of his life in Ontario, watching his immediate area turn from a rugged wilderness 'into a land of plenty, tamed and obedient' (5). In an introductory preface the village is identified by the author as 'a combination of Lucknow and of Blyth where I grew up,' and the book categorized as 'a partial history of this part of South Bruce and North Huron counties.' As with Mitchell's book, 'the early pages are largely based on memories of conversations with parents and grandparents' (vii).

Although it is somewhat over-descriptive, and occasionally verges on the ponderous, *The McGregors* is a warm evocation of the early stage of Ontario settlement. The effect is a kind of literary equivalent to visiting a reconstructed pioneer village. We appreciate the rigorous hardness of a life with few amenities, where even the building of an outside privy was considered 'uppity' (5, 44), where a supper meal consisted of 'pieces of yellow cheese cut in squares,' 'two small plates of butter,' '[a] cup of milk ... at each plate,' 'a loaf of bread,' and 'a large dish of preserved fruit' (51–2). Here, as elsewhere, the rough log cabins of the earlier generation were replaced by houses of brick and frame or even stone, to be downgraded themselves into pigpens or chicken houses (55–6). It was clearly a hard life, though Laidlaw's anecdotes of co-operation between settlers appear much more mutually satisfying than those described by Susanna Moodie. He presents the standard pioneering events – a brush with timber wolves (chapter 12), a quilting bee (chapter 13) – but presents them convincingly with a matter-of-fact directness that is impressive. Laidlaw offers an accurate if somewhat standard accumulation of traditional attitudes and manners. (So far as Ontarian literature is concerned, however, his main contribution is not so much this chronicle novel as the fact that he was the father of Alice Munro.)

These stories are doubtless 'all true,' at least in a representative sense, but the way of life they record has for the most part disappeared into the mists of history. The events they chronicle were 'something that happened' but they have now become 'story.' The last word may be given to McArthur, who recalls how most of his childhood dreams 'were dreamed while gazing at the dancing flames or the dying coals' of the old farm fireplaces:

But when I got back to the country, the fireplaces were gone, and the wood mostly gone, and the big, strong men who used to chop wood for a dollar a day were all gone. Instead of the romantic open fireplace I found the prosaic kitchen stove, which has all the appetite of the fireplace without its charm.   (87)

We inhabit a different world, but one that forgets the ways of the past at its peril.

6 *In Search of History*

In 1925, in an address to the Canadian Historical Association, Stephen Leacock remarked: 'When I was a boy, history meant to me the story of Greece or Rome, of Achilles in his tall helmet, or at best of Nelson sending up the string of coloured signal flags on the bright autumn day of Trafalgar. I never realized that there was history, too, close at hand beside my very own home' (qtd in Legate 13). Characteristically, Leacock remembers pictorial images appealing to a child's imagination, and complains that local equivalents were not forthcoming. After his time, this complaint became increasingly common until the impetus of Centennial Year and Expo '67 persuaded many Canadians – and Ontarians – not only that their country possessed a history which ought to be known to its citizens and taught prominently and imaginatively in its schools, but also that it offered splendid material for artistic presentation. Before Leacock's time, the most common response was a virtually unchallenged assumption that Canada lacked a substantial history – at least any history that could be mentioned in the same breath with that of Europe. There were, of course, exceptions. A few historians persisted, though their findings rarely caught the popular imagination. Some poets were also attracted to this material; one thinks of Charles Mair with his poetic closet-drama *Tecumseh* in the nineteenth century, and E.J. Pratt with his long narrative poem *Brébeuf and His Brethren* in the twentieth. A number of historical novelists also explored – and exploited – local material, including John Richardson's fictions based on Indian skirmishes and the War of 1812. However, the most fruitful period for the historical novelist in the early chronicles of eastern Canada proved to be the years immediately prior to the fall of New France, which resulted in such romantic and swashbuckling novels as William Kirby's *The Golden Dog* and Gilbert Parker's *The Seats of the Mighty*. But these, unfortunately, were set outside the boundaries of Ontario; inside, the early settlers' assumption that they inhabited a land without a history tended to prevail.

An early instance of this assumption is to be found in Edward Allen Talbot's *Five Years' Residence in the Canadas* (1824):

No monuments of ancient glory or of ancient magnificence display their venerable heads, directing the imagination to a retrospect of days that have passed. – No 'ruined palaces,' the once splendid domiciles of monarchs who have mouldered into dust, – no antique towers, the castellated guardians of feudal independence, – no 'cloud-capt' pyramids, the sacred resting-place of sleeping majesty, – present their ponderous remains, to please the antiquarian curiosity of age, or to foster the rising patriotism of youth. A few glittering steeples, whose resplendent spires never saw the sun of centuries pass over their youthful vanes, or an aged oak whose trunk has become weary of conveying annual nutriment in its decaying boughs, are the only objects in America calculated to awaken a sentiment of sadly-pleasing recollection concerning times that are gone for ever, or heroes that have measured out their span.   (1.146–7)

The arguments and images presented here recur again and again. For a classic formulation by a much more skilled writer than Talbot, we may turn (as so often) to a passage in Catharine Parr Traill's *Backwoods of Canada*:

Here there are no historical associations, no legendary tales of those that came before us. Fancy would starve for lack of marvellous food to keep her alive in the backwoods ...

... I heard a friend exclaim, when speaking of the want of interest this country possessed, 'It is the most unpoetical of all lands; there is no scope for imagination; here all is new – the very soil seems newly formed; there is no hoary ancient grandeur in these woods; no recollections of former deeds connected with the country ...'   (153–4)

It is easy to be condescendingly superior in our response to such sentiments, easy to point out, for example, that Traill was writing in the area of Peterborough which was later found to contain the dramatic Serpent-mound and some of the most spectacular petroglyphs on the continent. Secure in our belief that Indians 'first appeared in southern Ontario about 9,000 BC' (White 32), we may find it difficult to understand why it never seemed to occur to the early immigrants that the Indians in whom they often took such a romantic interest might have a history to be explored. In Traill's case, however, two personal factors need to be remembered: first, *The Backwoods of Canada* was structured as a series of letters to her family at home, including her elder sister Agnes Strickland, who was soon to distinguish herself as the author of *The Lives of the Queens of England from the Norman Conquest*; second, both Traill and her other sister Susanna Moodie came to Canada in 1832, the year of Sir Walter Scott's death, when the romance of historical association which had been fanned by his Waverley novels was at its height. Upper Canada could hardly compete with a literary landscape strewn with memories of Bonnie Prince Charlie, the Covenanters, and Rob Roy.

But a further point needs to be made. In *The Backwoods of Canada* Traill had turned to the study of natural history, especially botany, as a substitute for the lack of historical stimulation. By the time she came to publish *Canadian Crusoes* in 1852, however, she was in a position to write a story set in her local area that laid conspicuous stress upon the difference between the present situation and that of the historical past. In the intervening sixteen years, Traill had discovered local history, lived through its making, and even invented it in so far as she transforms it in terms of fictional conventions. Indeed, the modern reader's interest in *Canadian Crusoes* is likely to focus not on its rather rickety adventure plot but on its intriguingly early presentation of historical change. She writes, she tells us, of a time when 'the neat and flourishing town of Cobourg ... was but a village in embryo,' when 'the wild and picturesque ground upon which the fast increasing village of Port Hope is situated, had not yielded one forest tree to the axe of the settler' (1–2). Often (like Scott) in extensive factual notes, but also within the narrative itself, Traill deliberately presents her story as an example of events that have actually happened in a specifically identified place. A story of an Indian feud, Mohawk versus Ojibwa, is offered as 'a matter of history' (134n), and the narrator frequently breaks into the story in the role of historical guide:

On that spot where our Indian camp then stood, are now pleasant open meadows, with an avenue of fine palms and balsams ...   (184)

What changes a few years make in places! That spot over which the Indians roved, free of all control, is now a large and wide-spreading town.   (209)

where Louis saw the landing of the Indians – now a rising village – Gore's Landing.   (224)

A palpable historical perspective is maintained throughout.

This chronicling of local change continues in the area of non-fiction memoir, but its potential as a basis for imaginative exploration of a poet's or novelist's native place failed to develop in the nineteenth century. The two classic texts that embody a human interchange between past and present did not appear until the 1970s. One is a long poem, Al Purdy's *In Search of Owen Roblin* (1974), the other a novel, Hugh Hood's *A New Athens* (1977). Both will repay detailed attention at this point.

In Search of Owen Roblin takes the form of a composite of shorter poems on a common subject that Purdy had written over the years; these are held in place by some rather prosaic bridge-passages that give an unfortunate impression of slackness. Purdy has since dismantled the structure and reprinted the discrete, shorter pieces, but (despite the publishers' irritating failure to provide pagination, which explains the absence of page references in the discussion to follow) I refer to the extended version here. The combination of poetry with some evocative photography makes *In Search of Owen Roblin* an imaginative production that unites various arts while it takes the art of researching and recreating the past as its dominating subject. At the same time, it is a poetic record of how Purdy and his wife built a house near Ameliasburg in the 1950s and were, by that decision, almost inevitably drawn into rediscovering the past of the area in which they had settled – an area in which the poet found traces of his own ancestors.

Purdy is characteristically offhand about the initial stages in the historical process –

> I got interested in the place
> I mean what the hell else could I do?

– but the quest is in fact both serious and intense. He wonders why the small village nearby was once called Roblin's Mills, and becomes fascinated by the late-nineteenth-century houses in the immediate countryside which seemed to represent 'a silent kind of triumph or survival.' Typically, Purdy does not turn to local histories but feels the need to investigate the situation himself. At last he finds

> the old ruined grist mill
> built by Owen Roblin in 1842
> four storeys high with a wrecked mill wheel.

Purdy imagines Roblin as a dour Victorian materialist

> dreaming not of houris and other men's wives
> but his potash works

and decides that 'his wife whelped every nine months.' But the attempted flippancy cannot conceal the seriousness of this almost Proustian quest for past time. He writes of

> the privilege of finding a small opening
> on the past

and begins to realize that he is himself a part of a greater continuity:

> First my grandfather, then Owen Roblin
> me hanging on their coattails
> gaining strength from them
> Then I went still farther back
> trying to enter the minds and bodies
> of the first settlers and pioneers here
> – how did they feel and what were their thoughts?
> I tried to feel as they felt and thought as they did.

Ultimately,

> In search of Owen Roblin
> I discovered a whole era
> that was really a backward extension of myself
> built lines of communication across two centuries
> recovered my own past my own people.

Purdy learned, we might say, to read the countryside in which he found himself. This is an important gift. For an early instance, we may turn once again to Leacock. In his unfinished autobiography, *The Boy I Left behind Me*, he writes, with an initial flippant deprecation that anticipates Purdy: 'Anyone of my experience could drive you through the present farm country [he is thinking particularly of the area around Lake Simcoe] and show you (except that it would bore you to sleep) the mark of the successive waves [of depression and prosperity] like geological strata.' Again anticipating Purdy, he alludes to 'the remains of what was the original log-house of a settler' abandoned during the prosperity of the Crimean War period when 'the farmer, suddenly enriched, ... built a brick house,' or a similar process when 'reflecting the boom years of the closing 90's and the opening century are the tall hip-roofed barns with stone and cement basements below for cattle and silos at the side' (46).

'... like geological strata.' Hugh Hood enlarges upon this simile in *A New Athens*, a novel specifically devoted to the unearthing of the Ontario past. In its opening pages Matt Goderich, Hood's protagonist in his ambitious twelve-volume novel series entitled *The New Age/Le nouveau siècle* (of which *A New Athens* constitutes the second volume), is walking along Highway 29 in eastern Ontario. Matt, who had been a student in the course of study that used to be known in the University of Toronto as 'Art 'n Ark' (Art and Archaeology), is also well versed in local history and is preparing a master's thesis – rather daringly at that time – on a Canadian historical subject, an architectural study called 'Stone Houses in Loyalist Country.' He is sufficiently a historian to be aware of the fact that Highway 29 was originally known as the Victoria Macadamized Road, since it was begun in 1837, the year of Queen Victoria's accession, and used the system of broken-stone tar-bound paving invented by J.L. McAdam, who had died the previous year (the same year, as it happens, in which Traill's *Backwoods of Canada* was first published). Matt, like his creator, has a remarkable breadth of interests, and he begins to look more closely at the road surface.

Everywhere the provincial engineers have been at work, straightening a curve here, introducing a fatal approach from a sideroad there, on the whole improving and embellishing the old road with an excellent surface and safe sight-lines. Sometimes you can see an earlier roadbed cutting a sharp curve around a knoll a hundred feet off, while new paving lies above it on the wider, more direct course.
     This provides a kind of instant archaeology ... (5–6)

What has all this got to do with literary images of Ontario? In my view, a good deal. Consider that last phrase, 'instant archaeology' (akin, I suppose, to the recently fashionable phrase, 'industrial archaeology'). We have here a quite profound poetic image, the successive surfaces and realignments of the road offering visible strata (we may even recall the famous levels of Troy) that take us back, gradually but inexorably, from 1977, the date of publication, to 1966, the novel's present, eventually to the 1830s, the historical origins of the road. A little later, Matt notices 'a long, receding, overgrown mound or embankment which led away from the highway deep into fields, in a line so straight as to preclude the suggestion of purely geophysical origin; the hand of historical man had been at work' (8). This turns out to be the abandoned track of a railway that had led a brief life between 1888 and 1952. Hood turns this recognition into a Proustian moment of *temps perdu*, important in Matt's personal history as well as significant in local record. Matt first saw the young woman who was to become his wife at the events commemorating the railway at the time of its closure; and the railway itself ran from

Hood's Stoverville – in actuality, Brockville – through a small Ontario community once called Farmersville but which, because it was so proud of its educational facilities, changed its name in 1890, with a curious blending of the sublime and the ridiculous, to Athens. (This, I must make clear, is authentic history.) Hence Hood's title, taking up a quotation from Alexander Pope, 'A new Athens rising near the Pole,' a line quoted by Frances Brooke in *The History of Emily Montague*, the first Canadian (and perhaps even the first North American) novel, published as far back as 1769. We are enmeshed in history indeed.

Hood's thought here provides a perfect complement to Traill's. The 'earthwork' resembles a prehistoric 'barrow or burial mound' (8), and this leads Matt to a remembrance of age-old footpaths traversed while on holiday in England, to thoughts of Thomas Hardy and the ancient region of Wessex about which he wrote, and at last, more generally, to ghosts haunting their landscapes in both the old and the new worlds. He never mentions Traill, but the following sentences are almost a point-by-point answer to the passage I have quoted from *The Backwoods of Canada*:

Other personages lurk near these [i.e., Hardy's] barrows, ghosts of rare pre-Celts already in the day of the Caesars vestigial, almost forgotten, haunting outland downs and sea-caves on the Channel coast, emerging occasionally from concealment on unwarlike purpose, food-finding, shelter-seeking, little black men from a removed myth.

Such folk are neither found nor feared in southern Ontario in Anno Domini 1966, I thought. There are no elvish scurrying westerners retreating toward our Cornwall; we haven't the culture-memory of the people who live in Anglaland, layer on layer on less discernible layer on faint mark on mere suspected prehistoric spume of cross-hatched human purposes, or have we, or have we? Who tarred over those scratches on the roadway? How much past is past? (10–11)

Layers, levels of reality, the signs of history available beneath our feet. *A New Athens* is a book about the discovery of history and so of identity, personal or communal. A foreshortened history, perhaps, by Hardy's standards, but history nonetheless. 'How much past is past?'

I labour this point because it illustrates so dramatically how, in the last quarter of a century, Canadians – and Ontarians – have woken up to the fact not only that they possess a history (that is a fairly obvious, even banal realization) but that they possess an intricate texture of pasts which can be drawn upon for imaginative purposes. It is no coincidence that Hood begins his novel in 1966; by the end of that year the local centennial celebrations of 1967 were in the planning stage. Hood therefore pivots his novel – even, as he has recently suggested, his whole series – on the extraordinary combination of national and local pride, of growing awareness and self-consciousness, that characterized, in ways that had both positive and negative consequences, the heady years of the late 1960s. From then on, Traill's remarks about the absence of history, implicitly accepted as accurate within the popular consciousness for so long, were at last recognized as no longer valid. We had a past, and it was therefore reasonable to suppose that we had a future. In literary terms, this was the recipe for an exciting present.

The sense of history that we find emerging here makes it possible for us to recognize Ontario as a distinct regional entity that has developed over the passage of time. This is underlined later in *A New Athens* in a magical scene where Matt and his girl-friend, at what becomes the moment of their engagement, see beneath the waters of the St Lawrence the outlines of a submerged ship which is later brought to the surface (the past literally recovered) and identified as 'one of a flotilla of gunboats built for escort duties along the river, to protect the sailing ships that plied between Kingston and Prescott from raids by American pirates' (194) in the uneasy years after 1812. Which fits in yet one more piece to the historical jigsaw. Later, Matt is employed as historical consultant by the 'South Nation Village' project, clearly based on Upper Canada Village and described in the text as a 'colonial Williamsburg' (165). It is compromised by plans for a phoney parking garage for a period hotel/motel, which Matt wants built at a distance but which has to be 'on-site' at the insistence of the 'American-owned chain of franchises' (165). In these instances, the interrelation of Ontario and the States, in both the nineteenth and twentieth centuries (including the two-nation co-operation on the building of the St Lawrence Seaway, also mentioned in the text), is clearly indicated as a vital socio-historical background to the individual (but representative) lives that are central to the novel.

Purdy and Hood both bear witness to the importance of a combination of historical interest and imaginative perception. The historical facts, they imply, are inert unless revivified by a more creative response to their meaning and significance. Another, briefer text from the 1970s, earlier than either Purdy's or Hood's, provides us with a dramatic illustration of the same point. This is a section of 'Heirs of the Living Body,' one of the chapters in Munro's *Lives of Girls and Women* (1971). Here the narrator, Del Jordan, reminisces about her Uncle Craig, who had ambitions in the area of local history. He 'gave out information,' we are told, but 'was not moved to curiosity' (25). He had devoted much of his spare time to a history of the local county as well as 'a family tree, going back to 1670, in Ireland' (26). The young Del, herself determined to become an imaginative writer, cannot raise any enthusiasm for mere lists of dead people, especially since '[n]obody in our family had done anything remarkable' (26). Similarly, the history of the county is a chronicle of ordinary events and what she calls 'only modest disasters' (27). Later, after his sudden death, Del is presented with the unfinished manuscript by his surviving sisters, who assume, since she has literary inclinations or what they call 'the knack for writing compositions' (52), that she will be both willing and eager to complete it. '"You'll be interested,"' they assure her. '"Didn't you always get good marks in history?"' (51). Munro provides a specimen of Uncle Craig's uninspired and lumbering prose, and we cannot help agreeing with Del when she remarks: 'It seemed so dead to me, so heavy and dull and useless' (52). She stashes it away in the cellar of her home where, ironically, it is ruined by a spring flood, an instance of the 'regular flooding of the Wawanash river' (27) which was one of those 'modest disasters' that the manuscript had so scrupulously recorded.

But this is not the final judgment on Uncle Craig and his attempts at historical scholarship. Even as a child, Del gains a dim perception of a larger dimension to his work, palpable though never achieved, which the older narrator sums up as follows: 'It was not the individual names [in the family tree] that were important, but the whole solid, intricate structure of lives supporting us from the past' (26). That last phrase is essentially in tune with Purdy's 'lines of communication across the centuries' and Hood's 'spume of cross-hatched human purposes.' It is therefore appropriate that, years later, Uncle Craig's example has an effect on Del's own practice. She has tried her hand at a novel about Jubilee, her native place, but has cast it, falsely, in a Gothic mode where the characters are anything but ordinary and the disasters anything but modest. Recognizing her error after the poignancy of everyday reality has broken in upon her consciousness, she comes to understand that her sensationalist approach is as much a distorting extreme as Uncle Craig's plodding servitude to unadorned fact.

The point is made in an eloquent passage from the 'Epilogue' to the book that deserves quotation at length:

It did not occur to me then that one day I would be so greedy for Jubilee. Voracious and misguided as Uncle Craig out at Jenkin's Bend, writing his history, I would want to write things down.

I would try to make lists. A list of all the stores and businesses going up and down the main street and who owned them, a list of family names, names on the tombstones in the cemetery and any inscriptions underneath. A list of the titles of movies that played at the Lyceum Theatre from 1938 to 1950, roughly speaking. Names on the cenotaph (more for the First World War than for the Second). Names of the streets and the patterns they lay in.

The hope of accuracy we bring to such tasks is crazy, heart-breaking.

And no list could hold what I wanted, for what I wanted was every last thing, every layer of speech and thought, stroke of light on bark or walls, every smell, pothole, pain, crack, delusion, held still and held together – radiant, everlasting. (210)

Lives of Girls and Women is itself an attempt to express this radiance, to achieve this everlastingness. Munro's book is neither a local history in the Uncle Craig tradition nor a work of pure imaginative fiction like the young Del's projected novel. It is, rather, a re-creation, a transfiguration of daily experience in a small town in southwestern Ontario at a particular moment in historical time. Del's unique yet representative life stands for the unchronicled lives of the whole community. The fortunes of ordinary men and women – those in Uncle Craig's family tree that she had once dismissed as of no interest – are found to possess a new attraction and depth: 'People's lives, in Jubilee as elsewhere, were dull, simple, amazing and unfathomable – deep caves paved with kitchen linoleum' (210). Some of these lives – typical, often humble, but potentially fascinating – and the places in which such lives are lived, reproduced meticulously but also lovingly and imaginatively, provide the literary images of Ontario that are being examined in this book.

Part Two:
Region and Community

7 Landscapes and Localities

The adjectives attached by writers to the word 'Ontario' over the years have varied drastically in both meaning and tone. I have already quoted John George Bourinot's 'prosaic Ontario' (24), dating from 1893. Others that appeal to me include Sara Jeannette Duncan's 'long-settled Ontario' (193) as early as 1904, and more recent examples like Hugh MacLennan's unexpected 'gentle Ontario' (102) – applied to the nature of the terrain rather than to the inhabitants – and especially 'lovely Ontario,' a phrase Hugh Hood puts into the mouth of Matt Goderich (*Tony's Book* 253). Eager as we may be to accept this last, flattering designation, it nevertheless raises a question: in what does this loveliness consist? The answer is by no means easy to formulate. With the exception of a brief period of spectacular fall colour and the splendour (however commercially vulgarized) of Niagara Falls, there is little in southern Ontario to evoke any firm image of identifiable beauty in the picture-postcard sense – no Rocky Mountains, no Gaspé or Cabot Trail, nothing quite like Peggy's Cove.

Alice Munro's Del Jordan feels her way tentatively but thoughtfully towards an articulation of the paradox. She is fascinated by

country we did not know we loved – not rolling or flat, but broken, no recognizable rhythms to it; low hills, hollows full of brush, swamp and bush and fields. (*Lives* 57)

Similarly, Raymond Souster, taking time off from his love/hate relationship with Toronto, paints a comparable impressionistic portrait in verse:

> this land, these fields,
> the red barns, standing cattle, lazy villages
> north of Toronto stretching to Georgian Bay and the sterner land
> of a thousand lakes, short birch and mossed boulder ....
>
> (*Collected Poems* 1.89)

Such passages evoke a decidedly generalized sense of difference, which may well be characteristic.

It is tempting to remain content with a general picture, to accept a representative, quintessential 'Southern Ontario.' The problem becomes pressing if an urgent motive is to distinguish *this* terrain from a different one elsewhere: is there such a thing as a typically Ontarian landscape? Here, however, an interesting historical development begins to emerge. As we have seen, the first immigrants from the Old World tended to emphasize those aspects that reminded them of home. Yet in the course of time, when the new land itself became recognized and accepted as home, a conflicting impulse arose: to articulate the particular qualities that made the new land different from 'the old country.' Such a tendency increases when the real or imagined readership resides abroad. Throughout the nineteenth century, the trend is to establish Ontario landscape as a recognizable entity. Later (and this is facilitated, of course, by the changes that took place as forests were cleared and the areas around the settlements were increasingly affected by human labour) the extent to which localities *within* the province differ from each other becomes a matter of general – and literary – interest. This did not happen, however, until well into the twentieth century. Both these processes will be explored in the course of this chapter.

The urge to record and praise the aesthetic beauties of the Upper Canadian natural scene did not pass unchallenged. Thus, although Daniel (later Sir Daniel) Wilson, a professor of history and English at the University of Toronto, was himself an immigrant, he was quick to come to terms with what he called 'the rugged realism of this vigorously practical Canada' (132), and remained suspicious of attempts to interpret the local landscape in words. In 1858 he wrote a review article which raised some important issues concerning contemporary attitudes to the natural world. There was something in the Canadian make-up, he claimed, which shied away from the emotionally appreciative:

We cannot yet respond, amid these charred stumps and straggling snake-fences of our rough clearings, to Hiawatha's appeal to those:

> Who love the haunts of nature,
> Love the sunshine of the meadow,
> Love the shadow of the forest,
> Love the wind among the branches,
> And the rain-shower and the snow-storm,
> And the rushings of great rivers,
> Through their palisades of pine-trees.

We want our pine-trees for lumber, and so long as they spare us a surplus of kindling wood, we ask no kindling inspiration from them. The rushing of our rivers we estimate rejoicingly – for their water privileges.   (132)

Wilson is being somewhat comically facetious in a decidedly Victorian way, but his point is a serious one. The time is inauspicious, he argues, for the poetry of nature popularized in England by Wordsworth and the Romantics: 'it is not greatly to be wondered at that such poetry as we produce is less redolent of "the odors of the forest" than of the essences of the drawing room'   (133).

Wilson's arguments fall rather oddly on modern ears. He claims, for example, that love for 'the shadow of the forest' belongs to what he calls 'our squatter age of infancy,' which has been overtaken by the energetic concern for clearing that rejoices in 'the crash of falling pines' (132). I have already suggested that these distinctions are less those of historic periods than of class and education on the one hand or the differing attitudes of temporary visitors and permanent settlers on the other. Furthermore, Wilson does not seem to have considered the possibility that an aesthetic interest in landscape would evolve and flourish once the process of clearing was over. It is well known that landscape cannot easily be appreciated aesthetically while it is still oppressive, untamed, and potentially dangerous. Furthermore, perhaps because as historian and antiquarian he saw the study of the past as a formal academic discipline (he coined the word 'prehistory'), Wilson apparently disapproved of any poetry that seemed to him backward-looking. The nineteenth century, he felt strongly, was one of action and achievement, not of brooding and meditation. He was looking for a Canadian Tennyson open to the contemporary march of mind rather than a Wordsworth searching (as he saw it) for reactionary impulses from vernal woods.

Unfortunately, he was reviewing *The St. Lawrence and the Saguenay* (1856), a volume of poetry by Charles Sangster, who was frequently compared to Wordsworth (improperly, I think) in his own time. Wilson can hardly be called a sympathetic reader, yet his critique is decidedly perceptive. He recognizes Sangster's book, justly if a trifle harshly, as essentially Old-World poetry that is reproducing imported traditions and attitudes rather than evolving more suitable new ones. Nonetheless, we must acknowledge that Sangster is here caught in a classic bind. The reviewer casts doubt on the possibility of a Canadian poet's persuading his Canadian readers of the beauty of nature for its own sake. Rejoicing at 'the crash of falling pines' is a more appropriate response for Wilson than love for 'the shadow of the forest.' As he remarks with more of his heavy Victorian irony, 'we wonder what would be the estimate of the emigrant settler who should apostrophise the giants of the Canadian

back-woods, as they bowed beneath his steady stroke, after the fashion
of the Ayrshire bard to the "wee, modest, crimson-tipped flower" over
which he so reluctantly drove his plough-share' (132). (The reference is
to Robert Burns's poem 'To a Mountain Daisy.') For Wilson's taste,
Sangster is an old-fashioned Romantic unable to adapt to new conditions
in a new country. At the same time, however, he also faults Sangster for
seeing the St Lawrence, for all its beauty, only as 'the great navigable
highway from Ontario to the Sea, with its daily steamers, its wooding
stations, its locks and canals' (133). A true nineteenth-century poet, he
argues, must write of a modern industrial world with the kind of passion
and vigour that the Romantics gave to a now outmoded 'Nature.'

Sangster was, however, a pioneer in Canadian poetry, with the same
combination of endearing stolidity, lone perseverance, and palpable but
generally unspectacular results that characterizes pioneers in the more
conventional sense. An interesting but uneasy forcing of New-World
materials into Old-World forms and tropes is especially noticeable in
'The St Lawrence and the Saguenay,' the long poem that gives its name
to his first and most impressive volume. Here he undertakes a symbolic
journey from Kingston (where the poet was born in 1822) down the St
Lawrence past Montréal and Québec, and up the Saguenay River to that
real but archetypal goal of any allegorical quest, Cape Eternity. Sangster
is therefore moving in the opposite direction from the incoming settlers,
his eyes generally facing east rather than west. Similarly, his overall
form (a descriptive travel narrative interspersed with lyrics), his metric
(mainly Spenserian stanzas), and his language are all backward-looking
in imitation of Lord Byron and *Childe Harold's Pilgrimage*. These are
fused to a philosophical attitude strongly suggestive of Shelley's ethereal
idealism.

He begins with an enthusiastic poetic portrait of the Thousand Islands:

> Many an isle is there,
> Clad with soft verdure; many a stately tree
> Uplifts its leafy branches through the air;
> The amorous current bathes the islets fair,
> As we skip, youth-like, o'er the limpid waves.   (10)

The vocabulary is generalized and unoriginal. Sangster is aware of the
lack of Old-World associations, but for him these are mitigated by the
conventional beauties of Nature:

> No Nymphic trains appear,
> To charm the pale Ideal Worshipper

Of Beauty; nor Neriads from the deeps below;
Nor hideous Gnomes, to fill the breast with fear:
But crystal streams through endless landscapes flow,
And o'er the clustering Isles the softest breezes blow.   (11)

Sangster provides a number of natural details – 'a proud young eagle,'
'stately evergreens,' 'two majestic deer,' and a 'strong-antlered stag'
(11) – but for the most part the 'lovely Archipelago' (14) is presented in
disappointingly general terms. At one point we find Sangster desperately
trying to insert romantic excitement into both the landscape and his
poem by fabricating an unlikely story of a 'stately Maiden' and 'the
Brigand Chief, / Her father' (13), which recalls much too obviously
Byron's Haidée and Lombroso in *Don Juan*. It is all rather flat-footed –
and decidedly earnest.

Ultimately, however, Sangster is able to suggest a sense of both the
historical and the uniquely Canadian by means of a genre-picture commemorating the *coureurs de bois*:

Long years ago the early Voyageurs
Gladdened these wilds with some romantic air;
The moonlight, dancing on their dripping oars,
Showed the slow batteaux passing by with care,
Impelled by rustic crews, as debonnair [*sic*]
As ever struck pale Sorrow dumb with Song:
Many a drooping spirit longed to share
Their pleasant melodies, that swept along
The echo-haunted woods, in accents clear and strong.   (15)

Just as Sangster leaves the boundaries of present-day Ontario for what
in his day was Canada East, he introduces the Indians as a combination
of the historical and the picturesque:

Many a tale of legendary lore
Is told of these romantic Isles. The feet
Of the Red Man have pressed each wave-zoned shore,
And many an eye of beauty oft did greet
The painted warriors and their birchen fleet,
As they returned with trophies of the slain.   (24)

Wilson may well be right in complaining that Sangster provides few
fresh insights into a contemporary Canada and only a stereotypical picture
of the past, but he set a worthy example upon which later poets could build.

A.J.M. Smith, disagreeing with Wilson, has described Sangster as the 'first person who arose with a sufficient command of language and feeling to treat what were felt to be the particularly "Canadian" aspects of scenery with the enthusiasm of a genuine romantic poet,' though he admits that 'Romantic enthusiasm and literary polish kept his work vague and general,' and that he represented 'the common heritage of European romanticism' (*Towards a View* 36–7). Sangster's river-poem conveys, however, something of the crude and stiff effectiveness of primitive painting. The rest of his work tends to be conventional, but a series of 'Sonnets Written in the Orillia Woods,' in *Hesperus and Other Poems* (1860), is worth noting in view of the more meditative strain that characterizes him in less violently Romantic landscapes. Sangster's concern to combine love of nature with duty to God is expressed in the third sonnet, where he writes:

> I sit within the quiet woods, and hear
> The village church-bell's soft insisting sound.   (164)

More significant, however, is his explanation of the relation between inner and outer landscapes:

> Blest Spirit of Calm that dwellest in these woods!
> Thou art a part of that serene repose
> That ofttimes lingers in the solitudes
> Of my lone heart ...   (166)

Later, in more critical mood, he sees leaves as 'sere / As my own blasted hopes' (170), and he can wish that his 'heart / Were calm and peaceful as these dreaming groves' (175). The woods are seen specifically as an emblem ('Our life is like a forest' [168]). And once again the Indian is seen as providing historical associations: 'My footsteps press where, centuries ago, / The Red Man fought and conquered' (177). He is only too well aware, however, that ' No record lives of their ensanguined deeds.' Instead, all that remains is 'A few stray skulls; a heap of human bones' (178). Sangster's mood, however, is less that of Gothic sensation than of stoic *memento mori*.

Wilfred Campbell (1860–1918), though born a generation later than Sangster, spent his teenage years in a much more primitive community, since Wiarton, on the Bruce Peninsula and therefore close to Georgian Bay and Lake Huron, had barely established itself as a settlement when the Campbells arrived in 1872. Although Campbell went on to become a writer of tiresome rhetorical verse advocating the Empire and general moral uplift, he began as Ontario's first genuinely local poet. His phrase 'the lake region' is itself symptomatic. As might be expected, his dominant images, reflecting the general experience of early Ontario, are those of wood and water:

> Miles and miles of lake and forest,
>   Miles and miles of sky and mist,
> Marsh and shoreland where the rushes
>   Rustle, wind and water kissed;
> Where the lake's great face is driving,
>   Driving, drifting into mist.   (23)

This is typical of the dreamy but vigorous and individual rhythms of his best verse.

Perhaps because the Wiarton district is very close to qualifying as 'northern Ontario,' Campbell is especially remarkable for his wintry landscapes. Many of his titles reflect this: 'A Winter's Night,' 'The Winter Lakes,' 'How One Winter Came in the Lake Region,' 'In the Winter Woods,' 'December.' Indeed, the reader often senses in Campbell that aesthetic fascination for northern Thule over southern Tempe that Thomas Hardy discusses in the well-known opening chapter of *The Return of the Native*. There are times when Campbell seems to revel in the stark coldness of his 'iron-bound land' (30):

> Out in a world of death far to the northward lying,
>   Under the sun and the moon, under the dark and the day;
> Under the glimmer of stars and the purple of sunsets dying,
>   Wan and waste and white, stretch the great lakes away.
> ...
> Lands that loom like spectres, white regions of winter,
>   Wastes of desolate woods, deserts of water and shore,
> A world of winter and death, within these regions who enter,
>   Lost to summer and life, go to return no more.   (26)

These last lines are, however, more negative than Campbell's norm. As often as not we find an attractive landscape of wintry dream –

> Here I have wandered all a frosted day
> In faery dream of sheeted ice and snow.   (35)

Alternatively, the emphasis is on a bracing sharpness: 'the tingling silence' (36); 'the still, rich frosted days' when 'airs are keen and stars grow sharp and clear' (24). This last mood is finely caught in the final stanza of 'How One Winter Came in the Lake Region':

> That night I felt the winter in my veins,
>   A joyous tremor of the icy glow;
> And woke to hear the north's wild vibrant strains.   (35)

Campbell is also concerned to establish whatever historical and legendary associations the region can claim. As he notes in a grotesquely over-alliterating, pseudo-Swinburnian poem,

> I lie and listen, O lake, to the legends and songs you throw me,
> Out of the murmurous moods of your multitudinous mind.   (30)

Occasionally, he is not above creating a dubious legendary association, as in 'A Storm Picture' where the 'night-haunted' landscape is decked out with imported bogey-men. After the 'lake's far booming' is likened to the 'hammer of Titan that thunders at doors of the night,' Campbell abruptly switches mythologies:

> And the settlers' children quake in their beds and whisper, 'the
>   Norsemen!'
> They've come again from the north, as they came long ages ago ...   (39)

Elsewhere, however, the hint of Indian tradition enters the poetry – and naturally so, since, as Carl F. Klinck has documented, there were several reserves in the vicinity, and Campbell was well aware of Indian associations, especially in the youthful '"Nama-Way-Qua-Donk" – the Bay of Sturgeons,' with its invocation 'O ancient Indian shore and town' and its sadly romantic meditation over 'A wild and passionate broken race' (19). Campbell's talent was a minor one, and he soon abandoned his humble but effective early gifts for the temptations of high moral and political assertions, but in these rhythmic lyrics of the Ontario lake district he sounded an original note that has never been quite equalled.

I have already discussed Isabella Valancy Crawford's 'Malcolm's Katie' on account of its accomplished and informative presentation of the realities of the lumbering life. But that represents only one side of the poem. Elsewhere – and this is for many readers the poem's chief claim to attention – Crawford provides vigorous passages of seasonal description that preserve the mythic resonance of the Indian culture that intensive logging and increased industrialization have now displaced. (This is all the more remarkable, since Crawford, unlike Sangster and Campbell, was an immigrant, having been brought to Canada while still a child.) Daniel Wilson might still have lamented the backward look, but in Crawford's most lyrical passages he would have found an endemic Canadian – even Ontarian – style that makes few concessions to European tradition.

Although the only non-white character in the poem is Max's assistant, 'a half-breed lad / With tough, lithe sinews, and deep Indian eyes' (203), the spirit of the Indian past permeates the imaginative dimensions of the poem. There is perhaps nothing so remarkable and, within the literary tradition, so unexpected in nineteenth-century Canadian poetry as the following well-known passage describing the decline of summer and the coming of the wintry cold:

> The South Wind laid his moccasins aside,
> Broke his gay calumet of flowers, and cast
> His useless wampum, beaded with cool dews,
> Far from him northward; his long ruddy spear
> Flung sunward, whence it came, and his soft locks
> Of warm, fine haze grew silvery as the birch.
> His wigwam of green leaves began to shake;
> The crackling rice-beds scolded harsh like squaws ...
> ...
> In this shrill moon the scouts of Winter ran
> From the ice-belted north, and whistling shafts
> Struck maple and struck sumach, and a blaze
> Ran swift from leaf to leaf, from bough to bough,
> Till round the forest flashed a belt of flame ...   (198, 199)

The contrast with the viewpoint of the early immigrants is astonishing: no recollections of Capability Brown clumps here, no comforting comparisons with a known English landscape. Crawford grew up close to the area first settled by the Traills and Moodies but her literary sensibility is far removed from theirs. This is a Canadian forest seen from within its own culture, and the luxuriant audacity of colour and strong line surely looks forward to the violently beautiful paintings of this kind of landscape produced a generation later by the Group of Seven.

Like the rest of Crawford's work, 'Malcolm's Katie' is frustratingly uneven. The first three-and-a-half parts (from which all the above quotations derive) are original and impressive, but the last half of the poem degenerates into a contrived melodrama that can hardly be taken seriously. Most of Crawford's other poems are conventional and uninspired, but a handful derive a remarkable imaginative strength from the same source that produced the colourful descriptive passages in 'Malcolm's Katie.' In 'The Camp of Souls,' for example, the speaker is a dead Indian returning in his 'white canoe' to revisit the landscapes of forest and lake that he knew in life. It is a bold conception balanced perilously between the mysterious and the grotesque:

> Two hundred times have the wintry moons
>   Wrapped the dead earth in a blanket white;
> Two hundred times have the wild shy loons
>   Shrieked in the flush of the golden light
> Of the first sweet dawn, when the summer weaves
> Her dusky wigwam of perfect leaves.   (53)

Nothing very much happens in the poem, and the situation is a little stark in its Gothic oddity, but 'The Camp of Souls' succeeds in conveying the sense of an alien viewpoint that is surprisingly compelling. Similarly, 'Said the Canoe,' as its title suggests, describes an Indian scene idiosyncratically from the viewpoint of a canoe:

> My masters twain made me a bed
> Of pine-boughs resinous, and cedar;
> Of moss, a soft and gentle breeder
> Of dreams of rest; and me they spread
> With furry skins and, laughing, said:
> 'Now she will lay her polished sides
> As queens do rest, or dainty brides,
> Our slender lady of the tides!'   (67)

The last two lines suggest a pre-Raphaelite, intellectualized sensuousness that clashes with the sharply focused Indian details, but this is typical of Crawford's fitful genius. Where she derived her Indian inspiration is not known – one is tempted, indeed, to posit a deep psychological need to create a world totally distinct from her dull life of spinsterish genteel poverty – but even the awkwardnesses and inadequacies within her work convey a sense of the disunified texture of Ontario life at this period.

While Crawford may have produced the most original and startlingly imaginative effects, the poet who caught most accurately and exquisitely the spirit of the late nineteenth-century landscape of rural Ontario was undoubtedly Archibald Lampman. Lampman worked for most of his short life as a post-office clerk in Ottawa, and most of his poems are the product of walks and wilderness excursions in areas within or adjacent to the Ottawa Valley. This means that it isn't always possible, unless particular places are mentioned, to decide whether a given poem refers to the Ontario or Québec side of the provincial border. In most cases, however, the descriptions are broadly representative, less specifically topographical than uniformly mournful and elegiac. Lampman was a quiet, introspective man, with a strong vein of melancholy in his temperament. Most of his poems take the form of meditations in rural places to which he has withdrawn as if to a pastoral retreat in order to avoid the restlessness of city life. He needed the peace of the countryside in which to think; he needed to get away from what he calls, in 'The Railway Station,' 'The flare of lights, the rush, and cry, and strain' (*Poems* 116).

Lampman, who was born in 1861, belonged to the generation that had grown up after the main clearing of the forests had been completed. He therefore represents a later stage than that highlighted by Daniel Wilson; he could afford to appreciate the beauties of woodland scenery. The sonnet 'Solitude' records the kind of response to the surviving forest that would have been congenial to Catharine Parr Traill and Anna Jameson but not to Alexander McLachlan or Crawford's settlers. It also displays a technical expertise, an artistic control, that sets it well above the poetic standard of Sangster's similar verse-meditations:

> How still it is here in the woods. The trees
> > Stand motionless, as if they did not dare
> > To stir, lest it should break the spell. The air
> Hangs quiet as spaces in a marble frieze.
> Even this little brook, that runs at ease,
> > Whispering and gurgling in its knotted bed,
> > Seems but to deepen, with its curling thread
> Of sound, the shadowy sun-pierced silences.
> Sometimes a hawk screams or a woodpecker
> > Startles the stillness from its fixèd mood
> With his loud careless tap. Sometimes I hear
> > > The dreamy white-throat from some far off tree
> > Pipe slowly in the listening solitude,
> > > His five pure notes succeeding pensively.   (120)

This is more than *mere* description. Lampman subtly plays with the irony that the woods are full of sounds – the whispering and gurgling of the brook, the scream of the hawk, the tap of the woodpecker, the piping of the white-throat – yet these enhance rather than detract from the 'still,' 'quiet' peace of the woodland 'Solitude.' Lampman is not merely engaged in accurate delineation of a woodland scene; he is reproducing a personal, human experience.

He is, nonetheless, adept at focusing on a detail that, as in the Impressionist painters, contains the essence of a larger, more complex scene. In 'Across the Pea-Fields,' for instance, he evokes a whole countryside by concentrating on

> great elms and poplar trees
> That guard the noon-stilled farm-yards, groves of pine,
> And long dark fences muffled thick with vine.   (262)

Those 'dark fences' may well be the very snake-fences that annoyed the alien eyes of Howison and Traill. Also, as we might expect from a poet in a northern city, his landscapes are not confined to summer idylls. Indeed, Louis Dudek has argued that 'Autumn is Lampman's preferred season, because its theme is that of mortality.' Even in spring and summer, nature is 'only celebrated in order to introduce the elegiac note – that autumn comes, and then the snows!' (68). Certainly the details of Ontario in winter are regularly and skilfully invoked. These can vary from images of vigorous specificity – 'Tonight the very horses springing by / Toss gold from whitened nostrils' in 'Winter Evening' (243) – to the magnificently simple single line in the sonnet 'In November' that sums up winter and acute loneliness at the same time:

> Fast drives the snow, and no man comes this way.   (117)

Lampman's poetry, though narrow in mood, is wide-ranging in the kind of rural experience it describes. Emphasis may fall on particular species of wild life – 'The Frogs,' 'Snowbirds,' 'To the Warbling Vireo' – or a broad panorama – 'April in the Hills,' 'Comfort of the Fields,' 'An Autumn Landscape.' Often, he is content with an accurate presentation of what is observed, the poet as camera faithfully recording details of the local scene. Sometimes, as in the well-known 'Heat,' an experience is subtly recreated in words – not, of course, the experience of summer heat itself but an approximation to the languid effect that it produces. Nonetheless, he avoids extremes. While he enjoyed travelling into remote wilderness, and on such occasions, as I shall show in the chapter on northern Ontario, could produce a poetry that evokes and celebrates the satisfactions of vigorous physical action, he is temperamentally more skilled at preserving moments of stillness and rest. His most characteristic landscape, then, is one that is relatively tamed, wilder perhaps than the immediate environs of Wordsworth's Grasmere yet no longer hostile and threatening, like Huxley's tropics. His Ontario is therefore poised between the ruggedness of the early nineteenth-century landscape and the industrialized countryside of modern times. Within this middle range, he has few rivals. Though he lacks Keats's intellectual passion and poetic force, he can match him in richness of imagistic texture. A descriptive sonnet like 'Evening' may be said to represent both Lampman and the landscape of which he writes at their best:

> From upland slopes I see the cows file by,
> Lowing, great-chested, down the homeward trail,
> By dusking fields and meadows shining pale
> With moon-tipped dandelions. Flickering high,
> A peevish night-hawk in the western sky
> Beats up into the lucent solitudes,
> Or drops with griding wing. The stilly woods
> Grow dark and deep and gloom mysteriously.
> Cool night winds creep, and whisper in mine ear.
> The homely cricket gossips at my feet.
> From far-off pools and wastes of reed I hear,
> Clear and soft-piped, the chanting frogs break sweet
> In full Pandean chorus. One by one
> Shine out the stars, and the great night comes on.   (198-9)

The history of landscape description in Ontario during the nineteenth century may now be seen as forming a curious pattern. In the early years, the favoured medium was discursive prose, whether verbal portraits by travellers of the main characteristics of an unfamiliar land or personal accounts by settlers of life in the backwoods. Many of these contained passages of considerable imaginative force, and I have drawn generously upon these writings in earlier chapters. By mid-century, however, descriptive poetry came into its own. This can be partly explained as a delayed reaction to English Romanticism, as a not unprecedented example of Canadian cultural lag. In addition, Daniel Wilson may well have been right in detecting a tendency to look back nostalgically to a simpler age when the bustle of activity was losing some of its original impetus though he erred in failing to recognize Sangster's meditative verse as part of the wave of the immediate future. By the time of the death of Lampman in 1899, however, this period of achievement was itself drawing to a close. Raymond Knister continued the tradition, to some extent, in his verse, but it is significant that in his prose, especially his fictional prose, we begin to discern a preoccupation with the minutiae of his own local area within the province. There are, of course, occasional poetic renditions of a regional nature (Purdy's 'The Country North of Belleville' being the best known, and deservedly so); by and large, however, their local specifications are explored within the meticulously documented settings of modern novels and short stories.

The increased interest in the distinctiveness of local areas arose, as I have already suggested, with a realization of the ways in which human communities had set their individual stamp on the landscape. It was also encouraged by improvements in communications which allowed easier movement between place and place, and thereby stimulated a broader awareness of local differences. Thus the mother in Munro's short story 'Chaddeleys and Flemings' had grown up in the Ottawa Valley before moving to a community close to Lake Huron and eagerly stresses the contrasts between the two, generally to the detriment of the latter. This may be merely the result of prejudice ('the better quality of things for sale and the better class of people' [*Moons* 6]), but reference to the predominance of stone buildings rather than brick suggests a more basic regional distinction. The process is carried further in 'Friend of My Youth,' where another mother, whose origins were also in the Ottawa Valley, emphasizes 'things about it that distinguished it from any other place on earth' (*Friend* 4). It would be impossible in a book of this scope to attempt to cover all these different subregions, but a sampling of those that have stimulated some of our most provincially conscious writers will at least provide an indication of the rich variety of terrain existing within Ontario's boundaries. Our chief guides will be Knister, Munro, and Hugh Hood.

Knister, as already indicated, writes primarily about his native place in the extreme southwest corner of the province, the area bordering on Lake Erie. (This includes the area developed by Colonel Thomas Talbot in the early nineteenth century and celebrated – in decidedly non-specific terms, however – by Adam Hood Burwell in *Talbot Road: A Poem* [1818].) Knister's comparatively rare descriptive passages seem designed to communicate as much a pervasive atmosphere as a sense of particularized detail. For example:

The land was perfectly flat. From the slight elevation of the road he could see long bleached after-harvest grainfields, varied with dull tracts of beets, and rows of soiled-appearing corn-shocks, stretching sombrely, wire-fenced to the backs of the farms, where stood thin forests, which did not shut out streaks of gray sky. (*First Day* 152)

This is a country devoted to the production of fruit, grains, and vegetables, and from it emanates an aura suggestive at one and the same time of a languid Keatsian richness and the melancholy of Thomas Hardy's *The Woodlanders*. Knister conjures up a rural world dominated by unending hard work, stultifying heat, and a generally oppressive lethargy. The mood-piece 'Peaches, Peaches' catches the appropriate tone perfectly: 'The Burkins were eating, drinking, dreaming peaches, riding to town with baskets in the back seat, finding rotten peaches loose in the car on the way to church, thinking of peaches while the minister prayed, cursing peaches when, overwearied, they tried to sleep at night. Peaches!' (*First Day* 9).

A collection of brief quotations will best illustrate Knister's capacity to evoke a unique sense of locality – what he calls 'this oppressive atmosphere, this time and place' (*White* 81):

In the orchard the sunlight seemed to pack the heat down below the boughs and above the earth. The boughs seemed to hold it there, and to make room in some way for more heat.   (*First Day* 61)

The trees stood dozing, or whispering a little softly so as not to rouse the others.   (*First Day* 77)

the hamlet was so torpid ...   (*White* 19)

Meanwhile the crops were being smothered with weeds, the grain was beaten to the ground, in some cases left until overripe and then lodged and shelled by storm.   (*White* 104)

The oats field and the gloomy light were curiously lethargic in their tranquillity, even the forests seemed to toss with a heavy, slow resignation ...   (*White* 115)

The 'enervating odour' of the white narcissus that gives the title to Knister's novel (41) connects not only with the psychological oppressiveness of the homestead that contains it but also with the region that the protagonist regards with such mixed feelings. Knister here catches the pulse of a distinctive Ontarian landscape.

In Munro's 'Images,' the narrator reproduces a child's view from the top of a modest hill in the Wawanash area that Munro has explored in so much of her fiction:

The whole basin of country drained by the Wawanash River lay in front of us – greenish brown smudge of bush with the leaves not out yet and evergreens, dark, shabby after winter, showing through, straw-brown fields and the others, darker from last year's plowing, with scales of snow faintly striping them ... and the tiny fences and colonies of grey barns, and houses set apart, looking squat and small.   (*Dance* 42)

Like Knister – and, indeed, like most major writers – she is more concerned with atmosphere than with accurate topographical description. As she told Graeme Gibson in an interview, '[t]he part of the country I come from is absolutely Gothic' (Gibson 248), and she is clearly more interested in psychological interconnections between place and character.

Nonetheless, some distinctive features emerge, and one of these is her strong awareness of her local area as what might be called 'snow-belt country.' The point is made most explicitly in the short story entitled 'Fits':

Not much more than a hundred miles from Toronto, it is a different country. The snow-belt. Coming up here to live was not unlike heading into the wilderness, after all. Blizzards still isolate the towns and villages. Winter comes down hard on the country, settles down just the way the two-mile-high ice did thousands of years ago. People live within the winter in a way outsiders do not understand.   (*Progress* 110)

It is a season that affects the whole population. Children soon learn to recognize 'the time of year when snowdrifts curled around our house like sleeping whales and the wind harassed us all night, coming up from the buried fields, the frozen swamp' (*Dance* 112). In 'Wigtime,' Anita and Margot regularly set off for school 'struggling head down against the snow that blew off Lake Huron, or walking as fast as they could through a predawn world of white fields, icy swamps, pink sky, and fading stars and murderous cold' (*Friend* 246). The schoolgirl narrator of 'Winter Wind' (in *Something I've Been Meaning to Tell You*), who lives in the country, knows that, two or three times every winter, she will have to stay overnight with her grandmother when bad storms begin during the day. In the same story, an adult dies as a result of the storm. But Munro also chronicles the exhilarating release of spring in this area:

Spring in that part of Ontario comes in a rush. The ice breaks up into grinding, jostling chunks on the rivers and along the lake-shore; it slides underwater in the pond and turns the water green. The snow melts and the creeks flood, and in no time comes a day when you open your coat and stuff your scarf and mittens in your pockets. There is still snow in the woods when the blackflies are out and the spring wheat showing.   (*Friend* 257)

After all, Munro's country is not far from Wilfred Campbell's beloved 'lake region.'

While Knister and Munro are primarily concerned with evoking the essence of their own regions, Hugh Hood explores the difference between regions – between, for example, 'the small river towns' dotted along Highway 2 and the St Lawrence, and the way the towns 'shrink in size' and the farms are 'scrubbier and smaller and hillier' as the rocks 'begin to stick up through the thin topsoil and you are into the Canadian Shield' (*Flying* 102). A similar effect is achieved in 'New Country,' where the protagonists, driving along Highway 401, decide on impulse to make a diversion in to the area described on a tourist board as 'Highlands of Hastings.' It proves to be a temporal as well as a spatial change. They come upon

a terrain which was utterly novel to them, perfectly unlike the open countryside around Toronto or the limestone ridges, the granite shelves and narrow beds of good soil north of Stoverville [i.e., Brockville]. This was a central Ontario landscape seen by fewer and fewer people. They felt transported to the nineteen-thirties.   (*None Genuine* 73)

In 'Getting to Williamstown,' the narrator is driving in the opposite direction, from Montréal, but a similar regional change is noticed. At first it consists of 'pretty country down by the locks and the islands,' but 'soon, northwest of Cornwall, the geography changes; you can't see the river and the land is swamp. Scrub timber, marsh, cattails, and the occasional concession road running north into the scrub' (*Fruit Man* 16–17).

This pattern is most dramatically illustrated by the Bronson family's excursion in 'Bees, Flies and Chickens.' They set out from Toronto, and Hood begins with a detailed report of urban sprawl in the environs of Brampton:

Realtors' signs, my God! So many realtors' signs. He had not thought God had unleased so many. Pre-set traffic lights allowing the cars to move in sudden startling unpredictable directions. 'Advanced green when flashing!' Shopping plazas of grotesque proportions; little twinned movie theatres, devoted to *Star Wars* and soft-core porn. Here and there the dessicated [*sic*] remains of a farm.   (*August* 138–9)

They are on their way to a farm retreat north of Orangeville and are amazed, having escaped from this commercial-metropolitan landscape, to enter the unexpected moraine country near Shelburne. The narrator intrudes to present his own personal response to the terrain:

The country was void; on the right a vast falloff, the downwards slant of a
moraine ...
   ... get yourself out in a depopulated part of the province on a hot afternoon,
with the land dropping away on your right hand like the trough of an enormous
enveloping wave, with the next nearest swell plainly visible three miles away to
the east and you almost feel seasick. Turn off Highway 24 down a sideroad ..
and ... the sheer amplitude of the roll of moraine moraine moraine all the way to
the sky will unnerve you.   (139)

The forests have been felled, the countryside tamed, but the larger
determinants of geology and geography still exert their influence.

The Bronsons' journey then introduces us to a characteristic Ontarian
subregion, the product of industrial working patterns and the invention
of the automobile: 'cottage-country.' For many urban residents, especially
the inhabitants of Toronto, escape to 'the summer cottage' has been a
dream of the well-to-do for a century, and because Ontario is a land of
lakes the lakeside cottage has always been a particular favourite. Since
the end of the Second World War, thanks to increased economic prosperity, this luxury has been extended to a larger percentage of the
population. And writers, of course, have experienced the process and
duly written about it.
   Two poets who were fortunate enough to enjoy this pattern of life as
early as the 1920s were W.W.E. Ross and Douglas LePan. In 'One of
the Regiment,' LePan's soldier narrator looks back to his earlier life and
appropriately catches the balanced quality of this settled existence in the
line

   Skating at Scarborough, summers at the Island.   (118)

The capitalized, singular Island presumably indicates Toronto Island in
this case, but the LePan cottage was on Georgian Bay, and the poet
elsewhere sums up the essence of such summers as 'an escape for a city
boy into the splendour of wind blowing' (18). In the sonnet 'Islands of
Summer' he presents his own characteristically ornate but precisely
evocative sense of this leisurely world:

   A few acres of pines and cedars where he knew
   almost every tree. Abrupt granite rising from the clearest
   water in all the world. Crowned with a tangled diadem

of blue green foliage, with proud cedar-waxwings nesting there.
A secluded thicket where you could lie all afternoon, listening
to the warblers. And always beneath birdsong the sound of water.   (19)

This is, of course, the older poet's retrospective view of an idyllic, perhaps idealized past. By contrast, W.W.E. Ross wrote as an adult during the same period about the area around their cottage on Lake Scugog, and his style, when juxtaposed with LePan's, is so austere and understated as to seem almost minimalist. He offers not a description of his mood and emotions but a clearly etched account of what his eye sees:

A summer night,
a tall pine
black against
the cold starlight;
its branches outlined
sharply against
the studded sky
with brilliant stars.   (67)

But Ross is not confined to visual images. He is sensitive to the sounds of cottage country,

where the whippoorwill
repeats its call
through the revolving
hours of night,   (123)

and records how

the rocks around will soon
echo over the water below
the wild calling of the loon.   (110)

Moreover, he responds to texture as he memorably conveys the graini-ness of

rocks,
lichen-covered,
eternal, almost,
as the sun.   (45)

For a literary account of the history of this cottage-country phenom-enon, however, and for the most evocative description of its rewards and frustrations, we must return to Hugh Hood. In *A New Athens*, Matt Goderich records how, when he and his wife decided to build a summer cottage on an inland lake,

we were recapitulating – perhaps without being fully aware of it – the constitu-tive, essential story of life in the colony which became Ontario. Life along the river [St Lawrence] was enchantingly beautiful and easy, but dangerous, ex-pensive, likely to deliver us from one moment to the next into the hands of unwanted masters. Back in the difficult hinterland on the rocks near thick woods, where two trails met in 1785, people like us built the new Athens, and we built our summer home in the same place.   (185)

What he calls elsewhere 'the age of cottaging' (*August* 102) clearly has a long history, and one which altered rapidly with the improvements in roads and communications.

This history is developed further in the short story entitled 'Evolving Bud' and collected in *August Nights*. Set in the same district, the lake country centred upon the Rideau canal system, Hood quickly etches in the life-patterns of the 'aborigines who had built up the cottaging tradition early in the century,' families whose names 'were visible on hand-lettered signs tacked to trees, arrows pointing up shore roads or across limestone ridges on which no city-dwelling weekender dared risk his muffler' (81). But it is these same city-dwelling weekenders upon whom the economic variability of such an area now depends, and Hood per-ceptively identifies the subtle class gradations in this new summer soci-ety by describing the three stores with their respective docks that serve different segments of the population. The time is the mid-1970s:

The smallest dock, Minto's Marina, handled Fina products, fishing equipment, groceries, Coleman stoves and lanterns for the old-timers, folks with island cottages who only came in once a week to buy supplies; they came from really remote parts of the lake where there were no Hydro lines and a summer place might look exactly as it did in 1875 ...

The middle store, Hanlon's Groceries and Variety, was where the comfort-able middle-aged cottagers went for the papers, gas and oil mixed in the correct proportions for their big engines, paperbacks and memberships in the Cottagers' Protective Association.

The largest store at the public dock was the trading-post for the summer children and their local rivals in love. The summer children seemed to be mostly girls like Billie, fourteen, fifteen, with a talent for water-skiing and huge insatiable engines you don't see anymore.   (77–8)

This may at first sight seem like non-fiction, historical reportage; in fact, Hood builds up a richly textured scene through a highly skilful and selective literary impressionism.

Cottage country can, of course, include Muskoka and Haliburton as well as the Rideau lakes and several other less clearly defined areas. Each has its own local distinctions, but they are united in a common human pattern. Hood's accounts are especially valuable because they draw attention to overlapping time spans, even, as in this passage from *The Motor Boys in Ottawa*, within easy striking distance of Toronto:

you find yourself surrounded, as you draw away from the urban sprawl ... by the signs and artifacts of an earlier civilization, the old Ontario of the last century ... You are entering the first ring of cottage country ... As you approach, the odours and the atmospheric effects of the nineteen-twenties and early nineteen-thirties becomes almost overpowering, the tiny rickety cottages crowded together in little groves, the worn grass, the absurd lake, a stone's throw across, and then the dance hall where, in your tender youth, you came from the city in a carful of kids hugging their first cases of beer, mickey of rye, girls ...   (70)

Naturally, the ways of life within such country can vary enormously. In various stories in *August Nights* we encounter illustrations – in 'The Small Birds,' where the discomfort of a June of blackflies and mosquitoes on an appropriately named Beelzebub Lake develops into a fulfilling July and August when the family watches the successful hatching and growth of a brood of swallows under their porch; in 'Weight Watchers,' where dinner in 'a huge old summer hotel' is followed by a yuppie-style party on a 'sizeable unhandy inboard cruiser' (196, 197); in 'We Outnumber the Dead,' where the solitary Bronson spends his time bird-watching and generally pottering around in 'the back country where those abandoned nineteenth-century farmsteads lay open to the sky, walls fallen in, lilac overgrown above hidden foundations' (112). The whole phenomenon of 'cottage country,' then, enables writers to portray in illuminating fashion the complex interchange between geographical regions and the human needs and desires that develop and change them.

And the final emphasis must be on change. If the phenomenon of 'cottage country' has brought new life to struggling communities, it has led to adaptations and alterations which sometimes threaten to overwhelm the rural differences that once constituted the attraction of a home away from home. The process of 'winterization,' enabling cottage country to be more than just a summer resort area, has carried the tendency still further. Once again, Munro presents the pattern most forcibly. 'How I Met My Husband' is set 'just when the trend was starting of town people buying up old farms, not to work them but to live on them'

(*Something* 37). The more general features of rural change are caught in 'The Stone in the Field.' Dalgleish 'was no longer an out-of-the-way place. The back roads had been straightened; there was a new, strong, two-lane concrete bridge; half of Mount Hebron had been cut away for gravel' (*Moons* 33). But the most powerful accounts of the process occur in *Friend of My Youth*. Logan, in 'Oh, What Avails,' has now

greatly changed. Not many houses have been pulled down, but most have been improved. Aluminum siding, sandblasted brick, bright roofs, wide double-glazed windows, verandas demolished or enclosed as porches. And the wide, wild yards have disappeared ... and the extra lots have been sold and built on. New houses crowd in between the old houses. These are all surburban in style ...   (196)

Similarly, in 'Oranges and Apples,' '[e]verybody alive seemed to be yearning toward parking lots and shopping centers and suburban lawns as smooth as paint' (133). As time passes, one subregion becomes more and more like another – until southern suburbia gives way to the northern wilds.

8 *Northern Boundaries*

> ... north, to muskeg and
> stunted hackmatack, and then the whine of icy tundra north to the pole –
> despotic land, inhuman yet
> our *own* ... (Lee 40)

So Dennis Lee in the second of his *Civil Elegies*. A characteristic Canadian – and Ontarian – sentiment, yet, in our less rhetorical moments, we
realize that it isn't ours. The North recognizes no human boundaries. It
can be mapped and named, a small part of the whole terrain can be
classified under 'Ontario,' but it remains 'The North,' undifferentiated,
unassimilated. A well-known railway line is officially identified as
'Ontario Northland,' but its popular name is the 'Polar Bear Express,'
and if the third word records a sardonic joke, the first, however inaccurate
and unacceptable to geographers, makes its non-provincial, even anti-
provincial point. This is a rugged land that stifles human language as
easily as it obliterates human distinctions. In Duncan Campbell Scott's
short story 'Vengeance Is Mine,' reference is made to 'the mere essential
earth without the form of hill or valley' (*Witching* 47). For Scott, echoing Genesis, it is as if this land had only just emerged out of the water,
as yet unmoulded by the hand of God. The image of an uninhabitable
outer-space panorama is sometimes evoked. In 'The Winter Skies'
Archibald Lampman observes how

> The northern ridges glimmer faintly bright,
> Like hills on some dead planet hard and gray, (*Poems* 295)

while Scott himself, when a train stops unexpectedly in the northern
wilds, looks out and remarks: 'It seems a tiny landscape in the moon'
(*Green* 42). A similar impression strikes Abe Ross, Rudy Wiebe's pro-

tagonist in *First and Vital Candle*, as he flies up to a remote trading-station specifically located in northern Ontario: 'There was nothing below them but the land, indistinguishable from all that they had traversed for what under the unwavering drone of the motor seemed an endlessness. Look as he would, the land had no face' (105).

Poets may be fascinated by the harsh, sublime landscapes of the north, but they are also likely to respond with appalled shock to its apparent cultural emptiness. Earle Birney's impressive poem entitled 'North of Superior' (1.20–2) approaches the terrain in a way that recalls Catharine Parr Traill and some of the early settlers in the southern parts of the province. For him, the most memorable and disturbing aspect is the absence of any 'human story,' by which he means historical or literary associations. Characteristically, he employs a variant of ancient accentual verse to convey the primitive quality that he finds in the north; it is as if he views the landscape with the attitudes and sensibility of the lonely stoic narrators in Old English poems like 'The Wanderer' and 'The Seafarer.' Birney's poem begins:

> Not here the ballad or the human story
> the Scylding boaster or the water-troll
> not here the mind

and goes on to describe birch trees

> that never led
> to witches by an Ayrshire kirk nor wist
> of Wirral and a Green Knight's trysting.

The references are, respectively, to the Old English poem *Beowulf*, Robert Burns's 'Tam o' Shanter,' and the medieval *Sir Gawain and the Green Knight*, examples of heroic, popular, and romance poems that form part of the linguistic continuity of English-speaking peoples. This is Birney's somewhat desperate response to an alien silence. Reference is made to '*soundless* fugues / of stone and leaf and lake' (my emphasis), aspects of landscape here 'without a meaning' because the land knows no language that can contain or humanize it; if a 'pibroch' is to be heard, it will be 'inhuman.' Birney's poem is an awesome yet poetically memorable portrait of desolation, ending with a deadeningly alliterative elegy for a land

> that weeps unwept into an icy main
> where but the waters wap and the waves wane.

If to poets like Birney the north is, in Douglas LePan's well-known phrase, 'a country without a mythology' (75), others feel the necessity to fill the vacuum by creating an appropriate myth. Imaginatively, this landscape has been given its most vivid rendering by E.J. Pratt in a famous passage from his latter-day epic poem *Towards the Last Spike*. Once again the setting is north of Superior, though Pratt's creation extends ultimately far beyond the boundaries of the province:

> On the North Shore a reptile lay asleep –
> A hybrid that the myths might have conceived,
> But not delivered, as progenitor
> Of crawling, gliding things upon the earth.
> She lay snug in the folds of a huge boa
> Whose tail had covered Labrador and swished
> Atlantic tides, whose body coiled itself
> Around the Hudson Bay, then curled up north
> Through Manitoba and Saskatchewan
> To Great Slave Lake. In continental reach
> The neck went past the Great Bear Lake until
> Its head was hidden in the Arctic Seas.
> This folded reptile was asleep or dead:
> So motionless, she seemed stone dead – just seemed:
> She was too old for death, too old for life ...   (2.227–8)

Seldom has geological material been so magisterially transformed. What Pratt has done, of course, is to adapt and make new the medieval image of the dragon. The Canadian (or Laurentian) Shield must be conquered by the combined efforts of Sir John A. Macdonald, William Cornelius Van Horne, and the rest, if Canada is to become a dominion stretching from sea to sea. The traditional heroic struggle of knight against monster is transformed into a conflict between industrial technology and a recalcitrant natural world. At the same time, Pratt's reptile has all the attributes of a prehistoric monster (recalling his Tyrannosaurus Rex in 'The Great Feud'). Like no other poet, with the possible exception of Christopher Dewdney, Pratt can evoke the vast stretches of geological and biological evolution, fusing them into a single image.

Dewdney, as we have seen, confines his attention in the main to southwestern Ontario. In *Radiant Inventory*, however, he includes a poem entitled 'Halcyon July in Algoma.' Here, reversing the conventional trope by which a level prairie is compared to a sea, he envisages the motionless stretch of lake as a plain that nonetheless retains the attributes of water:

The clusters of offshore islands
interrupted this plain
like a frozen pod of granite dolphins,
their pink backs aligned
by a frozen glacier.
    Cetaceans forever bound
    for the heart
    of the Wisconsin ice age. (24)

There is an imaginative sweep expressed here, manifest in concept rather than in language, that captures a sense of primordial vastness, both temporal and spatial.

At noon, Dewdney reports, 'a haunted stillness / enclosed our island' (24); this introduces another northern characteristic. Doubtless because of the sparseness of any human associations, writers have tended to concentrate on the few legends and mysteries that have attached themselves to these shores. Such stories go back to the accounts of the first explorers. As early as 1766, for instance, when Jonathan Carver made his initial journey within North America and travelled around the northern shore of Lake Superior, he became fascinated by the legend of the golden sand:

One of the Chipéway chiefs told me, that some of these people being once driven on the island of Mauropas, which lies towards the north-east part of the lake, found on it large quantities of a heavy shiny yellow sand, that from their description must have been gold dust. Being struck with the beautiful appearance of it, in the morning, when they re-entered their canoe, they attempted to bring some away; but a spirit of amazing size, according to their account sixty feet in height, strode into the water after them, and commanded them to deliver back what they had taken away. Terrified at his gigantic stature, and seeing that he had nearly overtaken them, they were glad to restore their shining treasure; on which they were suffered to depart without further molestation. Since this incident, no Indian that has ever heard of it, will venture near the same haunted coast. Besides this, they recounted to me many other stories of these islands, equally fabulous. (135–6)

The 'island of Mauropas' was later given the name of Michipicoten Island. Alexander Henry, who quotes the above passage in a note to his *Travels and Adventures in Canada and the Indian Territories* (1809), independently heard similar stories three years later. The Indians had informed him that the island contained 'shining rocks, and stones of rare description,' but he could discover 'nothing remarkable' (217). However, his curiosity was roused by their accounts of another island to the south: 'This they described as covered with a heavy yellow sand, which I was credulous enough to fancy must be gold' (218). A legend similar to that recorded by Carver is recounted, though in this version the 'spirit of amazing size' is replaced by 'enormous snakes ... which are the guardians of the yellow sand' (218). Bad weather and other duties frustrated his immediate attempt to investigate, but two years later, in 1771, another opportunity occurred. Henry is a good raconteur, with an admirable control of tone. As soon as he lands on this new island, the stylistic mood of his story changes from the evocation of mystery to an endearing whimsical humour. He tells how he was himself the first to land, carrying a loaded gun and resolving 'to meet with courage the guardians of the gold.' However, since his comrades had not run their barge up the yellow sands, he dryly observes that 'no immediate attack was to be feared' (221), and continues:

A stay of three days did not enable us to find gold, nor even the yellow sands. At the same time, no serpents appeared, to terrify us; not even the smallest and most harmless snake. But, to support the romance, it might be inferred, that the same agency which hid the one had changed the other; and why should not the magic of the place display itself in a thousand varied exhibitions?   (222)

Henry soon became more interested in the caribou that inhabited the place, and it appears to be as a result of his report that the island is now known as Caribou Island.

Henry is clearly fascinated by legend. He explains the name of Manitoulin Island as meaning 'the residence of ... genii' (36), and recounts the traditional Indian stories associated with 'Nanibojou' that were widespread in the area. But he is also effective in his presentation of strange and disturbing incidents that take place in the northern wilderness. One example is the unprecedented appearance of a rattlesnake near one of his camping-places. Henry himself had wanted to kill it, but his Indian companions, fearing that he had offended the guardian spirit of the place, go to great lengths to placate it, by addressing it as 'grandfather' and blowing smoke from their pipes towards it. Henry duly reports: 'after remaining coiled, and receiving incense, for the space of half an hour, it stretched itself along the ground, in visible good humour' (167). A more troubling incident occurs when supplies are low, and he finds himself having to oppose two of his Canadian companions who are advocating cannibalism, a young Indian woman being the proposed victim (214). Henry's penchant, then, is for the startling and unusual. He is notably less successful in presenting a compelling description of the physical features of the land through which he passes. Thus on his first voyage along the north shore of Georgian Bay he describes the islands as 'either wholly bare, or very scantily covered with scrub pine-trees,' and goes on to claim that '[a]ll the land to the northward is of the same description' (33).

For an elegantly written refutation of this assumption we have to wait for well over half a century, until the publication of George M. Grant's *Ocean to Ocean* in 1873. Grant, it may be remembered, was acting as secretary to a surveying party that had been appointed to determine the best route for the Canadian Pacific Railway. Its descriptions are therefore an important part of the whole venture, and Grant reveals a keen eye for geographical and geological differences. As soon as they enter northern Ontario he remarks on '[t]he contrast between the soft and rounded outlines of the Lower Silurian of Manitoulin and the rugged Laurentian hills, with their contorted sides and scarred foreheads, on the mainland opposite' (17). He waxes lyrical about the north shore of Lake Superior: 'The scenery of Nepigon Bay is of the grandest description; there is nothing like it in Ontario ... Bluffs, from three hundred to one thousand feet high, rise up from the waters, some of them bare from lake to summit, others clad with graceful balsams' (24). And he is especially informative about the stretch between Thunder Bay and Shebandowan Lake:

Everything about this part of [the] country, so far, has astonished us. Our former ideas concerning it had been that it was a barren desert; that there was only a horse trail, and not always that, to travel by; that the mosquitoes were as big as grasshoppers, and bit through everything. Whereas, it is a fair and fertile land ... The road through it is good enough for a king's highway, and the mosquitoes are not more vicious than in the woods and by the streams of the Lower Province.   (30–1)

Gradually, legend and tall tale are giving way to information that is factual but no less inspiriting for that.

Meanwhile, however, Alexander Henry remained a trusted guide to travel in the area. Anna Jameson, for instance, considered his book an indispensable guide to these northern waters, though it may be significant that she associates him with story and romance rather than with accurate survey: 'He is the Ulysses of these parts, and to cruise among the shores, rocks, and islands of Lake Huron without Henry's travels, were like coasting Calabria and Sicily without the Odyssey in your head or hand' (3.18). Jameson herself, the product of a decidedly more sophisticated class and culture than Henry, specializes in lively observation and emotionally charged atmosphere. On Manitoulin Island she was a witness to the second annual distribution of governmental presents to the Indians of the district, and gives a detailed and historically valuable account of the scene. She is also vividly immediate in her presentation of the prosaic discomforts of travel – sleeping on hard rock, the ceaseless attacks of mosquitoes, etc.

But she is at her best in sensitively etched genre-pictures like the following, where her companion is Mrs Schoolcraft, the Indian wife of the well-known American agent at Mackinaw Island. They are journeying in 'a little Canadian bateau' (3.153) from Mackinaw to Sault Ste Marie, and are close to St Joseph's Island:

I cannot, I dare not, attempt to describe to you the strange sensation one has, thus thrown for a time beyond the bounds of civilised humanity, or indeed any humanity; nor the wild yet solemn reveries which come over one in the midst of this wilderness of woods and waters. All was so solitary, so grand in its solitude, as if nature unviolated sufficed to herself. Two days and nights the solitude was unbroken; not a trace of social life, not a human being, not a canoe, not even a deserted wigwam, met our view. Our little boat held on its way over the placid lake and among green tufted islands; and we its inmates, two women, differing in clime, nation, complexion, strangers to each other but a few days ago, might have fancied ourselves alone in a new-born world.   (3.163)

Jameson shows, of course, a notably self-conscious response here, but her evocation of human companionship and solidarity in a deserted terrain, all the more refreshing since the protagonists are uncharacteristically female rather than male, is an equally faithful and significant instance of what we too easily designate the spirit of the north.

Jameson's sense of strangeness and displacement is typical. Most writers on the north are inevitably outsiders without any intimate knowledge of the landscape they are describing. They bring fresh but uninformed eyes to the terrain; their reactions are spontaneous but limited. A notable exception is Fred Bodsworth, naturalist and fiction-writer, whose testimony is of special value because, in order that his readers may understand the full implications of what he writes, he feels the need not only to describe the area accurately and meticulously, but also to differentiate the various geographical and geological areas that constitute the north. He does this most clearly and succinctly in the opening pages of *The Sparrow's Fall* (1967). He explains how the land north of Lake Superior is divided into three basic regions. The first, extending for a hundred and fifty miles, is 'a rugged terrain ... of worn-down mountains carved by rivers,' containing 'a sporadic network of roads and railways, a spattering of lumbering and mining towns' (7). This is the area most often visited and described by travellers from the south. But further north there are stretches of 'forest and bogland broken only by a sprinkling of Indian settlements that cluster around the fur-trading outposts of the white man' (7). This is the landscape of Wiebe's *First and Vital Candle*, where there are no roads, communication is confined to aircraft and canoes, and the deciduous forests to the south are replaced for the most part by conifers. The southerly section of the area forms part of the Canadian Shield, but in the remaining two hundred miles up to Hudson Bay this is replaced by a bed of limestone resulting in 'a network of open ponds or lakes, or vast stretches of soggy, treeless sphagnum bog' (28), the terrain popularly known as 'muskeg.' In Bodsworth, imagination and science, poetic fancy and geographic fact, are skilfully united.

The north may be gruelling, but it is also a constant stimulus to the imagination. In *Brébeuf and His Brethen*, Pratt relates how the French Jesuits responded to

>   stories of those northern boundaries
> Where in the winter the white pines could brush
> The Pleiades, and at the equinoxes
> Under the gold and green of the auroras
> Wild geese drove wedges through the zodiac.   (2.48–9)

Throughout Canadian and Ontarian human experience, this awareness of 'northern boundaries,' of a cold and desolate periphery, has always been felt – and not merely in winter. It is a factor even in Leacock's 'little Town in the Sunshine.' The farms of Mariposa, we are told, 'end sooner or later in bush and swamp and the rock of the north country. And beyond that again, as the background of it all, though it's far away, you are somehow aware of the great pine woods of the lumber country reaching endlessly into the north' (*Sunshine Sketches* 4). Norman Levine, in the centre of Ottawa, could feel 'the pressure of those vast frozen spaces to the north' (*Canada* 56). Similarly, W.W.E. Ross in 'Island with Trees,' a poem about the cottage country of Lake Scugog, subtly catches the hint of northern influence in a passage of superficially innocent description:

> The trees are bent
> away from the north
> on this island

in the lake
wind-swept
in all the seasons

– windswept because 'the northern / wind is master' (51). And the general awareness of a strange northern frontier is later elaborated by Douglas LePan in 'Canoe-Trip':

And then up to the foot of the blue pole star
A wilderness,
The pinelands whose limits seem distant as Thule,
The millions of lakes once cached and forgotten,
The clearings enamelled with blueberries, rank silence about them.   (77)

'Rank silence about them.' Silence, mystery, emptiness, endlessness, solitude: these are the northern images – evocatively summed up by Duncan Campbell Scott's phrase, 'a country where essential solitude abides' (*Circle* 119) – images that the poets recognize and pass on.

The two principal Ontarian representatives of the so-called 'Poets of Confederation,' Lampman and Scott, both felt the call of the north as they searched for the same sense of wildness that was becoming harder and harder to find in the increasingly populated southerly parts of the province. As close friends they would often go on wilderness trips together, though these generally took them into the Gatineau area of Québec. It is clear, however, from what we know of Lampman's last and best documented trip into northern Ontario, to the area of Lake Temagami in the summer of 1896, an excursion that did not include Scott, that the two poets found very different subjects for their verse in the northern environment.

Lampman, though so often introspective and meditative in gentler southern landscapes, and although he is said on this particular trip to have been 'lost in reverie and enjoyment' (C. Connor 181), was generally content to record the dominant sights and sounds of the northern scene. He is especially skilled at evoking the quintessential images of this area within a single line or even a single phrase. In the sonnet 'On Lake Temiscamingue,' for example, we find 'The sombre forest and the wan-lit lake,' followed a little later by 'Bold brows of pine-topped granite' and 'A race of tumbled rocks, a roar of foam' (*Poems* 293). More specifically, he celebrates the harshness and strength in the north that he so much desired but knew was so lacking in himself. Thus the vigorous energy of 'In the Wilds' is relatively unusual in his work:

> The rain we take, we take the beating sun;
> The stars are cold above our heads at night;
> On the rough earth we lie when day is done,
> And slumber even in the storm's despite.   (294)

In 'Night in the Wilderness' he gives us a vivid picture of the shared companionship of the group, with deft vignettes of the camp-fire sending off 'its front of sailing sparks that light / The ruddy pine-stems,' the preparation of 'bouillon,' the exchange of 'forest lore.' But ultimately it is the images of the northland itself that bring forth his greatest eloquence. The following lines, for example, constitute a night scene caught on a poet's page rather than on a painter's canvas:

> On every side,
> A grim mysterious presence, vast and old,
> The forest stretches leagues on leagues away,
> With lonely rivers running dark and cold,
> And many a gloomy lake and haunted bay.
> The stars above the pines are sharp and still.
> The wind scarce moves. An owl hoots from the hill.   (294)

He yearns for the spirit of wildness, and the word 'wild' itself echoes through the sonnet entitled, simply, 'Temagami':

> Far in the grim Northwest beyond the lines
> That turn the rivers eastward to the sea,
> Set with a thousand islands, crowned with pines,
> Lies the deep water, wild Temagami:
> Wild for the hunter's roving, and the use
> Of trappers in its dark and trackless vales, .
> Wild with the trampling of the giant moose,
> And the weird magic of old Indian tales.

Yet, although he enthusiastically records 'the thunder-travelled sky / Purpled with storm,' it is the silence that ultimately prevails as he watches

> at eve the broken sunset die
> In crimson on the silent wilderness.   (292-3)

In 'The Lake in the Forest,' he even locates the soul of the Indian

Manitou within the all-pervading silence, a silence rendered all the more conspicuous by the sounds that occasionally break it –

> The silence of the midnight made more deep
> By the deer's footsteps and the loon's halloo,
> The lashing wings and laughter of the wild.   (316)

Scott's northern verse is very different. Often it was official duty rather than private pleasure that took him into this terrain. As a commissioner with the Department of Indian Affairs, he made several trips into the James Bay area in the first decade of this century to help negotiate Indian treaties, and he responded fully to the atmosphere of the northern landscape. But with Scott the emphasis is more intellectual than pictorial or sensual. Only too conspicuously, while escaping from the south, he brings the southerner's brooding thoughts with him into the wilderness. Description is incidental, preparatory to a meditation on the differences between north and south or between Indian natives and white visitor-intruders. This is most clearly evident in 'The Height of Land' (*Poems* 46–51), which might well be regarded as a paradigmatic poem of northern Ontario. It is, first, focused on the one genuine northern boundary, determined by geological factors rather than human decree: the geographical watershed at which streams flow either south into Lake Superior or north to Hudson Bay. The narrator, a projection of Scott himself, is a solitary white man dependent upon Indian guides and uncomfortably aware that this is their environment rather than his, that the accustomed noises of the region blend with their speech but are alien to him:

> The wind sounds in the wood, wearier
> Than the long Ojibwa cadence
> In which Potàn the Wise
> Declares the ills of life
> And Chees-qua-ne-ne makes a mournful sound
> Of acquiescence.

Like Lampman, Scott can paint a skilful impressionistic portrait of his surroundings. He notices the flakes of ash in the camp-fire

> that play
> At being moths, and flutter away
> To fall in the dark and die as ashes,

and can marvel at the clear beauty of the stars 'like marigolds in a water-meadow.' He can even evoke, in an image that combines associations of age-old chivalry and stark terror,

> the enormous targe of Hudson Bay,
> Glimmering all night
> In the cold arctic light.

Characteristically, however, these pictorial details are only the background for a sustained meditation. The cerebral takes precedence over the actual and immediate. Scott is ultimately more interested in the impact of this landscape on the human mind. His Indian guides soon fall asleep, and the narrator is left in the double loneliness of night and wilderness to brood upon a world of beauty that suggests at the same time a world of emptiness and desolation.

The poem becomes a debate – a wilderness version of Tennyson's 'The Two Voices' – between an exalted and exultant idealism on the one hand and a glimpse of the northern equivalent of the heart of darkness on the other.

> Here there is peace in the lofty air,
> And Something comes by flashes
> Deeper than peace.

In that kind of mood, 'where the air is clear,' it is possible to contemplate (perhaps to invent) a world of purpose and moral meaning. But the northern spirit that Scott calls '[t]he ancient disturber of solitude' can stir another potion, and he remembers

> The last weird lakelet foul with weedy growths
> And slimy viscid things the spirit loathes,
> Skin of vile water over viler mud
> Where the paddle stirred unutterable stenches,
> And the canoes seemed heavy with fear.

There can perhaps be no adequate resolution of Scott's dilemma – and therefore no satisfying ending to the poem. He is enough of a Victorian to attempt a positive, even uplifting conclusion, but the final verse-paragraph consists of a string of questions expressing a much-needed optimism but ultimately lacking in assurance. The 'ideal of hope and promise / In the blush sunrise' remains in the sphere of 'dream.' More memorable, at least for modern readers, is the ambiguous image drawn from the northern nightscape just before dawn:

> How strange the stars have grown;
> The presage of extinction glows on their crests
> And they are beautied with impermanence.

It is a chastening vigil, suggesting that inner mood and outer environment are alike in their capacity for enigma.

In 'Spring on Mattagami' (*Poems* 41–5), Scott invokes the same situation of a solitary white man awake while his Indian guides sleep, but in this case – and much less effectively – the dichotomy is converted to one between loneliness and lost love, between the harsh present of Mattagami and a remembered past of sensual yearning in Venice. The narrator tries to develop the contrast by seeing his New-World setting as a 'land of quintessential passion' opposed to the European 'land of fraud and fame and fashion,' but the effect seems forced. Nonetheless, the uneasy relation of white and Indian, of conflicting aims, life-style, and religious values, recurs in Scott's poetry. Sometimes it takes the form of sheer violence, as in 'On the Way to the Mission,' where an Indian is murdered for what his white killers believe to be valuable furs when he is in fact bringing the body of his dead wife for a Christian burial; sometimes it involves cultural contrast, as in his well-known poem 'The Forsaken,' where the white reader is presumably shocked by the action of the Indian tribe in abandoning the old woman to die in the snow, but is forced to acknowledge the tragic dignity of her death and the complex moral imperatives dictated by the need for tribal survival in a harsh climate.

But Scott's most compelling northern poem, after 'The Height of Land,' is 'Night Hymns on Lake Nipigon' (*Poems* 23–4), where the white/Indian split is expressed in a momentary blend of religious cultures that contains extraordinary power. A remarkable tension is set up between the threatening midnight storm scene and the brief coming-together of Christian faith and Indian spiritual vision. Scott catches an important symbolic moment in the history of the modern northland:

> Sing we the sacred ancient hymns of the churches,
> Chanted first in old-world nooks of the desert,
> While in the wild, pellucid Nipigon reaches
>   Hunted the savage.

> Now have the ages met in the Northern midnight,
> And on the lonely, loon-haunted Nipigon reaches
> Rises the hymn of triumph and courage and comfort,
>   Adeste Fideles.

> Tones that were fashioned when the faith brooded in darkness,
> Joined with sonorous vowels of the noble Latin,
> Now are married with the long-drawn Ojibwa,
>   Uncouth and mournful.

Scott refrains from a moralizing meditation here. The poem's meaning exists within the rendered scene: the regular strokes of the canoe maintain the rhythm of the imported hymn. This moment of shared worship is placed within a context of earlier Indian savagery and the history of Christian persecution. Moreover, the night hymns either lapse into the inexorable northern silence or are drowned out by the 'booming thunder' of the storm. What at first sight reads like a poem of conversion, of achieved white dominance through the influence of an imported religion, is later recognized as a joining of white songs with Indian language and voices in a concerted gesture against the unceasing, indomitable threat of natural forces.

But Scott's evocation of the north is not confined to verse. In his essay 'The Last of the Indian Treaties' he presents an account of travelling down the Albany River which seems to me unparalleled (at least since Anna Jameson) in conveying a sense of the loneliness of the region:

Occasionally, the sound of a conjurer's drum far away pervaded the day like an aerial pulse; sometimes we heard the clash of iron-shod poles against the stones where a crew was struggling up-stream with a York boat laden with supplies. For days we would travel without seeing a living thing, then a mile away a huge black bear would swim the river, slip into the underbrush through a glowing patch of fire-weed, then a lemming would spring across the portage path into the thick growth of Labrador tea; no birds were to be seen, but a white-throat sparrow seemed to have been stationed at intervals of a hundred miles or so to give us cheer with his bright voice.   (*Circle* 119)

Like Lampman accentuating the silence by listing interrupting sounds, Scott here introduces York boat, black bear, lemming, and white-throat sparrow to make the loneliness of river and underbrush seem all the more poignant.

For the Canadian modernists, poets who came into prominence between the mid-1920s and the mid-1950s, the north provided a variety of responses, especially as improvements in communications made parts of the northern wilderness not only more readily accessible but more familiar. I know of no evidence to suggest that A.J.M. Smith had ever travelled in the area; he seems to have been satisfied with a cottage at Lake Memphremagog on the Vermont/Québec border. Nonetheless, 'The Lonely Land' is a splendid transposition of northern scenery into verse, though it may be significant that, on its first publication in the *McGill Fortnightly Review* in 1926, the poem was subtitled 'Group of Seven.' The artists in question, for whom northern Ontario was a favourite choice for painting expeditions, were in the process of making the Canadian public aware of northern images, and Smith does the same in his poem. Poetry, however, is not confined to the visual, and Smith alternates effects drawn from sight and sound. The opening stanza evokes Group of Seven images of northern conifers uplifting 'sharp barbs / against the gray / and cloud-piled sky,' but the second stanza introduces other elements:

> A wild duck cries
> to her mate,
> and the ragged
> and passionate tones
> stagger and fall,
> and recover,
> and stagger and fall,
> on these stones –
> are lost
> in the lapping of water
> on smooth, flat stones.   (*Classic Shade* 38)

In poetic terms, this is very different from Lampman, and even from Scott, though Smith (who wrote two fine essays on Scott's poetry) may well have been influenced by Scott's effectively tentative, sometimes deliberately stumbling rhythms. What he emphasizes, in some frequently quoted lines from later in the poem, is the 'beauty of dissonance' that he comes to recognize (employing a phrase that telescopes sight and sound) in 'this resonance / of stony strand' (39).

The uncertainties of geographical boundary lines continue when we turn to the poetry of F.R. Scott (no relation to D.C.). From the poem itself, we cannot be sure which parts of this extended terrain he had in mind in his 'Laurentian Shield' (58), but Sandra Djwa informs us in her biography of Scott (225) that the poem was inspired by a train journey across northern Ontario. Central for Scott is the capacity of this landscape to stimulate the human – and, more specifically, the political – imagination:

> Hidden in wonder and snow, or sudden with summer,
> This land stares at the sun in a huge silence
> Endlessly repeating something we cannot hear.

Once again we get the sense of mysteriousness associated with both endlessness and silence. For Scott, this is a land '[n]ot written on by history, empty as paper,' and this is an aspect that, as we have already seen, was also to be explored by Earle Birney. But because he is a writer with a strong sense of political and economic trends and the materialist pressures of the period, Scott knows that history will soon catch up with this hitherto undeveloped space. He detects the forerunners of history in the first venturers into the area:

> The first cry was the hunter, hungry for fur,
> And the digger for gold, nomad, no-man, a particle;
> Then the bold command of monopolies, big with machines,
> Carving their kingdoms out of the public wealth.

He responds to the romantic remoteness of a wilderness 'with songs in its lakes / Older than love and lost in the miles,' but he has a shrewd suspicion that the future holds industry, exploitation, and the insidious dictates of global politics. The poem, based on the idea of a language which will articulate the silence, is full of words like 'technic,' 'productivity,' 'steel syntax.' Writing at a period of optimism at the end of the Second World War, Scott envisages a time when the hands of millions will 'turn this rock into children,' but even Scott can do little to alter the dominant image of northern inertness and inscrutability.

By and large, however, the later generation of Ontario-based poets exemplifies a remarkably similar pattern to that of the Ontario poets of Confederation. W.W.E. Ross, as I have indicated, wrote most of his deftly imagistic poems about the area in which he spent his summers on the shore of Lake Scugog. This is minimalist verse; once more, no geographical identifications are offered and it is therefore impossible to fix individual poems to specific locations. But he was clearly impressed by the 'northern-ness' of the whole of the province. The imagery he favours is that of the bare rock, lakes, and trees that northern and southern Ontario share. Whatever terrain Ross had in mind, the opening stanza of 'Rocky Bay' epitomizes for me the landscape of the far north:

> The iron rocks
> slope sharply down
> into the gleaming
> of northern water,

and there is a shining
to northern water
reflecting the sky
on a keen cool morning.   (78)

Ross, then, like Lampman, offers the northern landscape itself in its sharp and vivid specificity. Douglas LePan, who spent childhood summers on Georgian Bay, resembles Duncan Campbell Scott in exploring the impact of the north upon an expanding human consciousness. He can outdo the two Confederation poets with his lines of clinching, evocative northern description:

The slipway where titans sent splashing the last great glaciers.   (77)

Orchids along the portage, white water, crimson leaves.   (78)

lush raspberry-red of sumach's candelabra,
beds of wild raspberries, wild roses blooming,
rich cardinal-flowers in shadow.   (219)

He can also communicate a vivid sense of the wild life of the northern terrain:

                    And on
the sandbar footprints of other animals, firm pad
of a great black bear come out of the woods to fish,
the delicate track of mink, skimmings of sea-birds, sand-birds,
at the water's edge.   (218)

Most evocative of all is his recreation of the experience of encountering a moose

as you're paddling downstream and see it as big as a house
with a great hump at its shoulders to support its head and its antlers
but with spindly ungainly legs that splash through the shallows
as it gallops away into the bush.   (209)

Similarly, he can catch an equivalent in verse of the natural vigour that calls forth unusual physical energy in the human explorers:

      the canoe is catapulted out in a froth
of eddying foam (their flesh whipped too to froth)
down a wind-whipped lake where interlacing birch
and spruce lattice the lusts of animals coupling and killing.   (217)

But the last-quoted line opens up from primarily descriptive concerns to the contrast, which has struck most northern writers since Duncan Campbell Scott, between the conflicting suggestions of peace and violence.

When in 'A Rough Sweet Land' LePan describes this landscape as 'a whole wild dialectic of lakes and rivers' (217), the abstract noun sets the meditative intellectual tone. Because LePan is a thoughtful and well-informed man, he is aware of the various motives that attract human beings to the north. He knows in particular that the commercial imperative is strong. As he remarks in 'Canoe-Trip' (77–8):

> It is a good stock to own though it seldom pays dividends.
> There are holes here and there for a gold-mine or a hydro-plant.

A studied ambivalence is evident in such lines. Nonetheless, the overall tone implies a confidence on LePan's part that the landscape is stronger than the human greed for wealth and all the polluting side-effects that tend to accompany it:

> But the tartan of river and rock spreads undisturbed,
> The plaid of a land with little desire to buy or sell ...
> Let whoever comes to tame this land, beware! ...
> ... have no hope to harness the energy here.

What the north provides, he believes (romantically), is a haven for the jaded and distracted:

> here are crooked nerves made straight,
> The fracture cured no doctor could correct.

The last word is given to the unspoilt image of 'waterfalls curling like cumulus.'

The tone of 'A Rough Sweet Land,' though related, is more metaphysical. Part of the intimation of transcendence that is felt here derives from the sense of northern timelessness:

> The sun stands still. Two hundred years are nothing, nothing.   (218)

The poet is convinced that 'there is something still to find in all this welter' (218), and the 'something' in question seems remarkably close to D.C. Scott's 'Something [that] comes by flashes / Deeper than peace' in 'The Height of Land.' LePan defines it as 'balm, a breath of balsam, healing' (219). What for the earlier explorers, such as La Salle, was 'the

balsam of adventure' (73) is now the balsam of peace. But LePan realizes that even the northern landscape is less extensive than its mental
equivalent. He internalizes the north in 'Coureurs de Bois':

> But now
> That the forests are cut down, the rivers charted,
> Where can you turn, where can you travel? Unless
> Through the desperate wilderness behind your eyes,
> So full of falls and glooms and desolations.   (73)

Where D.C. Scott found the heart of darkness in the remembrance of
'vile water over viler mud,' LePan finds it in trees that are 'entangled
with menace' and realizes that 'The voyage is perilous into the dark
interior' (74). The 'wild dialectic of lakes and rivers' is transformed into
a dialectic of harshly conflicting human attitudes. Natural landscape
becomes human image.

Al Purdy continues the meditative strain. Of all the poets who have
written about northern Ontario he is perhaps the most conscious of his
status as an outsider. His handful of poems about the area runs the
gamut between images of tourist fancy – 'North of Kirkland Lake
raspberries are red earrings' (162), from a poem significantly entitled
'Tourist Itinerary' – to conflicting images of harshness and violence:

> traplines where the red-eyed weasel
> snarls in a wire noose
> and foxes gnaw their forelegs
> free from steel.   (121)

These last lines are from 'Watching Trains' and in this poem Purdy
interestingly reverses the process to which we have become accustomed
from Lampman and Duncan Campbell Scott onwards. Instead of viewing
the north from the perspective of a southern observer, represented here
by the 'schoolmarm passenger distributing / replicas of the new Canadian
flag,' he imagines the Indian boys at the wayside station dreaming of the
other world from which the passing trains come and to which they
depart. For them, Scott's inexpressible, elusive 'Something [that] comes
by flashes / Deeper than peace' is transformed into a world of unimaginable wonder projected on to the world of the trains:

> later in the snowbush
> with summer gone
> they hear a diesel hoot
> like blood that shrieks inside their toenails.   (121)

He even borrows Wordsworth's phrase from his famous poem about the daffodils by Ullswater, the 'inward eye,' and applies it to the Indian boys as they encounter the trains. This surprising perspective shocks the reader into viewing this northern landscape through new eyes.

After the train passes the settlements of Nakina and Sioux Lookout, only 'birds dispute the ownership of silence' (121). Purdy responds like his poetic predecessors to the sense of loneliness and stillness, but he does so in a characteristically original way. On one occasion he is driving north to take the Polar Bear Express from Cochrane to Moosonee, very much the traditional tourist, but as a representative of the later twentieth century he produces his own rendition of the already-quoted scene of Scott travelling down the Albany River:

> Driving north
> a bear crosses the road
> at his private pedestrian crossing
> the first animal we've seen
> and almost ask for his autograph.   (162)

At first the tone seems flippantly inappropriate, but it catches, in contemporary idiom, the same impression of overpowering solitude. Moreover, when Purdy eventually arrives at Moosonee, what strikes him most is the unknowability of the north. The poem is not called 'Tourist Itinerary' for nothing. While other less introspective tourists will return with a superficial confidence that they have 'seen' the north, Purdy knows that contact and understanding have been minimal:

> I know what the place looks like
> tasted the food and touched the land
> which is as much as any of us can do.

It is altogether characteristic of Purdy, however, that his most memorable poem about the northern area of the province should take for its subject the region's best known and most enigmatic work of art. In 'The Horseman of Agawa' (176–7) he attempts to convert the fixed pictorial image of the Indian rock-painting into fleeting, shifting words: 'I change it all back into words again for that's the best I can do.' Purdy and his wife visited this famous site on the cliffs close to Lake Superior in spring before the steel tourist-platforms had been re-erected, and they are deeply impressed as 'the rock horseman canters / by two feet from my nose forever or nearly.' He emphasizes the precariousness of this artefact that, fortunately preserved, creates a link between white and

Indian, past and present, life and art. He sees it as 'a signpost' (that is, a symbol) – 'a human-as-having-babies signpost / but also dammit part of the spirit.' It originally had a 'meaning,' which 'must be a four-day journey somewhere,' but now the immediate meaning, either lost or irrelevant, is converted into the resonant symbolism of art. It stands, inscrutable, amid the silence – the omnipresent northern silence – and Purdy pays a poet's sympathetic tribute to the heroic but generally doomed artistic attempt to create something permanent. He imagines the artist

> pitting fish eggs and beargrease against eternity
> which is kind of ludicrous or kind of beautiful I guess.

Poetry can confine itself to description and meditation; prose – especially prose fiction – almost inevitably finds itself dealing with human action and interchange. Moreover, in the north the interchange in question is generally between Indian native and white visitor or intruder. It is often violent; indeed, Allison Mitcham's chapter-title, 'The Violence of Isolation,' in her book *The Northern Imagination* succinctly sums up the matter. Nowhere do we find the violence of isolation more powerfully evoked than in the English writer Algernon Blackwood's short story 'The Wendigo,' set in the wilderness above Kenora (or, to give it its old name, Rat Portage). Here a young white hunter, a divinity student, is confronted with a terrifyingly alien spiritual experience when he is witness to an Indian Wendigo, defined by one of the characters in the story as '"simply the Call of the Wild personified, which some natures hear to their own destruction"' ('Wendigo' 102). Blackwood has neatly telescoped the Indian myth with the white phenomenon of being 'bushed.' Superficially a ghost story, a tall tale of the wild, it transcends its origins to become an unforgettable image of 'the Panic of the Wilderness' (89), an emblem of the unknown and the incomprehensible, a glimpse of 'the merciless spirit of desolation which took no note of man' (74).

In more prosaic terms, white intrusion into the northern wilderness is frequently in the interests of material wealth. Thus E. Brian Titley has recently shown how Duncan Campbell Scott's journey along the Albany River to negotiate another Indian treaty was motivated by the new discoveries of valuable mineral deposits in the north and the desirability of exploiting them without being subject to Indian property claims. The immediate result of this kind of interchange, alas, all too often led to violence, caused by the unnatural proximity of people with radically opposed attitudes and life-styles. Scott himself wrote a number of short stories set in the area and generally set in earlier parts of the nineteenth century. They were principally concerned with traders and their unhappy relations and rivalries with their assistants, whether white or Indian. The extended close – and often claustrophobic – contact over long periods of time, Scott implies, often led to paranoiac violence. Unfortunately, these stories are for the most part crude in conception, and rarely rise above the level of standard melodrama. Hugh Garner, in his frequently reprinted 'One-Two-Three Little Indians,' injects a strong element of social criticism into the subject by creating a plot which concentrates many aspects of racial discrimination and presents them from the viewpoint of the Indian victim. Rudy Wiebe's *First and Vital Candle*, set at the fictional 'Frozen Lake' in Ontario, also involves violence close to melodrama, though in this case the violence is imposed by the sinister and corrupt trader Bjornesen, who encourages the Indian population to drunken and sexual orgies. At the same time, through the development of the character of Violet Crane, an Indian girl inspired to become a teacher through the sacrificial example of the white heroine, Wiebe raises at least the possibility of peaceful co-operation rather than violent rivalry between the races.

If we are looking for an appropriate symbolic figure to embody the painful uncertainties of this human interchange, we shall find one in the ambiguous and enigmatic 'Grey Owl.' Born Archie Belaney in respectable middle-class surroundings in Hastings, England, he had become obsessed with the life of the Indian and what he was later to call 'the vanishing frontier' (his own title for his first book published eventually as *The Men of the Last Frontier*). Emigrating to Canada in 1906 at the age of eighteen, he found his way to northern Ontario, into the area of the Temagami where, a decade earlier, another Archibald, Lampman the poet, had been inspired on his wilderness trips. Belaney ingratiated himself into the Ojibway community on Bear Island, who taught him, in the words of Lovat Dickson, 'nearly everything he was to know about trapping, woodcraft, and Indian lore' (15). He saturated himself in their culture, learnt their language, and absorbed their attitudes.

Belaney arrived at a crucial period in the development of the north. Where Lampman found virgin wilderness, Belaney was first employed by a man who planned to build a tourist lodge on the lake. An intruder from outside himself, Belaney increasingly took over the role of defender of the north from the ravages of such intruders. He began as trapper and guide, as assistant to prospectors pouring into the area as a result of the discovery of silver at Cobalt in 1903. Later, however, he found work as a forest ranger, attempting to protect the North from the threat of destruction by fire that such an influx of people unskilled in the ways of the north inevitably brought in their wake. And eventually, of course, from being himself a trapper of beaver and other animals, he became the protector, the first conservationist of these 'pilgrims of the wild' whose very existence had been threatened. In order to accomplish his mission, he felt the need to become the voice and the conscience of the northern people: hence his transformation into 'Wa-sha-quon-asin' or Grey Owl.

Grey Owl was in many respects an incurable romantic. The dominant images of the north that I have already illustrated tremble, in his writings, on the verge of cliché. 'This is the most silent country on the face of the globe,' he wrote back to his school magazine in 1913, 'silent as death except for the booming of the ice on the big lake' (qtd in Dickson 91). And the opening words of *The Men of the Last Frontier* gather up all the romantic elements of our response to this landscape:

A deep slow-flowing river; silent, smooth as molten glass; on either bank a forest, dark, shadowy and mysterious.

The face of Nature as it was since the Beginning; all creation down the eons of unmeasured time, brooding in ineffable calm, infinite majesty, and a breathless and unutterable silence.   (1)

One side of Grey Owl, then, sounds suspiciously like the voice of the Hollywood travelogue. The height of land, for instance, is not merely a geographical phenomenon but 'a line of demarcation between the prosaic realities of a land of everyday affairs, and the enchantment of a realm of high adventure' (30).

But another side acknowledges the impossibility of the dream. In the same school-magazine article he can also write as follows:

It looks very picturesque and romantic to wear moccasins, run rapids, and shoot deer and moose, but it is not near as interesting as it seems, to be eaten up day and night by black ants, flies and mosquitos, to get soaked up with rain, and burnt up with heat.   (qtd in Dickson 91)

His mood can shift from page to page. *The Men of the Last Frontier* may be full of romantic evocation of 'the far-flung borderland beyond the fringe of Civilization' (6), but it is also an account of 'these degenerate days of traders, whiskey, and lost tradition' (154).

Belaney's own intellectual and psychological 'height of land' may be identified with the period of the First World War. He had spent most of the years between 1906 and 1912 in the Lake Temagami area, and had then moved west to Biscotasing where until 1914 he trapped in the winters and worked as forest ranger during the summers. He served in the war, and was wounded, and the experience appears to have had a profound effect upon him in revealing the extreme of human violence. When he returned to Bisco in 1918, he not only saw distressing changes in the north that he had come to love but now saw them through new and saddened eyes. To some extent, the dream persisted:

Far beyond the fringe of burnt and lumbered wastes adjacent to the railroads, there lies another Canada, little known, unvisited except by the few who are willing to submit to the hardships, loneliness, and toil of long journeys in a land where civilization has left no mark and opened no trails.   (*Men* 29)

But he was coming to the conclusion that so-called civilization was now leaving its mark everywhere. The 'burnt and lumbered wastes' extended further than the romantic part of him believed possible. This is made clear in the opening pages of *Pilgrims of the Wild*:

A disastrous bush fire had swept my hunting ground leaving it a barren area of cracked rock, burnt out stumps and tortured tree trunks, and I was bound North and East to the far off, supposedly fruitful ranges of the Abitibi district in Northern Quebec; a vast country which, so rumour had it, was little explored and was populated only by a few wandering bands of Ojibway Indians. Much of my route was through the country I had known. It was now almost unrecognizable. A railroad had been built through part of it. There were huge burns, areas of bare rocks and twisted rampikes, miles of staring desolation ... The change was nearly unbelievable.   (10)

Grey Owl's famous exploits with his beavers took place in Québec and Alberta, but his knowledge of the north and the foundations of his future fame were developed in Ontario. While his descriptions of the terrain are generally vague and over-romanticized, we get from him an invaluable picture of the mixed human community of Bisco in the early years of this century, a settlement with 'no roads whatever, and not a solitary yard of sidewalk' (*Tales* 170),

a collection of small wooden houses gathered, or scattered rather, around the rocky hillsides that enclose a sheltered bay of Biscotasing lake. In Summer the twinkling camp-fires of the Indians are visible at the edge of the forest that surrounds the clearing on three sides ...

About thirty houses, perched among the rocks, complete the toll of habitations, with two churches a short rifle-shot apart ...   (169)

The sketch comes from the essay 'Rivermen,' and it is here that we get the most vivid portrayal of the 'old-time canoemen,' inheritors of the traditions of the *voyageurs* and *coureurs de bois* of old, who (though 'very few today') still survived into Grey Owl's time (171): such men as Zeph, 'no zephyr, but a kind of human cyclone' (174); Baldy, who 'is convinced that the world was made for nothing but big men' and so 'carries enormous loads on every portage to prove that he is as good as any of them, even if he is below standard size' (174); Malogense, an Indian medicine man who 'once put out a forest fire by means of some incantations' (175); Red Landreville, with his inexhaustible stock of tall tales (who is also the subject of a separate essay) and many many more. These men demonstrate that the ideal human interchange of the north is capable of realization: 'White men, red-skin and half-breed, they belonged to that fraternity of freemen of the earth whose creed is that all men are born equal, and that it is up to a man to stay that way' (172). Above all, they stand for a coexistence and interchange between human beings and all the other creatures with whom they share the northern land.

But it is Fred Bodsworth who is the supreme writer of the Ontario northland – romancer rather than novelist, though his romance is of the traditional formal variety rather than the compelling but technicolor emotional romanticism of Grey Owl. Both writers, however, share a vision of the north. For Bodsworth, we might say, the north *is* the mixing of races – even if this means, for the most part, the enforced mixing of races. Astute enough to realize that the standard novel form, evolved for thickly populated and tightly knit societies, is ill suited to the primitive conditions and limited human contact of the north, he obviously feels the need, as an essentially didactic writer of fiction with an intensely private vision, to create his own distinctive form of narrative. His solution – to blend romance, pastoral, and animal story to produce a highly patterned, artificial, parable-like structure – may trouble the advocates of realism and alienate those for whom romance is a form that can only be approached condescendingly. It proves, however, remarkably effective for his purpose.

The non-realistic aspect of Bodsworth's presentation of the north is best illustrated by *The Atonement of Ashley Morden* (1964). Primarily it is a science thriller involved with research into germ warfare, though this is linked with the whole matter of moral guilt arising out of action in war. An anti-Nazi German doctor, whose wife died on the way to Auschwitz, survives with his young daughter and takes her to the most remote part of Canada he can find. In the wilds of northern Ontario he devotes himself to serving the local Indians and bringing up his daughter, Lilka, as far from human, especially male, contacts as possible. She develops into a figure not unlike W.H. Hudson's Rima in *Green Man-*

sions or Charles G.D. Roberts's Miranda in *The Heart of the Ancient Wood*, a symbolic figure who represents something close to the essential spirit of the wilderness: 'She melted unobtrusively into the forest and became a part of it like the deer and the whiskyjacks and all the other life that shared the forest with her' (347).

After her father's death, Lilka lives on her own in the remote haven he had planned for her, but – and here Bodsworth's allegorical consciousness becomes manifest – there is nowhere on earth beyond the reach of a defiling, post-Auschwitz humanity: 'the world had become too small and there was nowhere else for a man to retreat' (340). The novel's protagonist, Ashley Morden, is forced to bale out from a plane that contains mice potentially infected with a dangerous germ developed by military research. The disaster does not materialize, but Bodsworth's purpose is to instruct Morden, a twentieth-century moral Gulliver, on the awesome gap between human ways and those of nature. Lilka, who can read the wild like a book, shows him nature's way of dealing with rivalry and aggression. Her northern haven is a cold pastoral where important lessons for the southern human world are to be learned. The plot at this point involves violence (imported from southern 'civilization') and the expected hint of romance, but Bodsworth's serious emphasis is on the naturalness that still lingers in the north and its significance as a desperately needed moral resource.

Romance is also the dominant form in *The Strange One* (1959), but once again it is played out against a background of northern scenery and unnatural human prejudice. Structurally, the book depends upon an analogy between the mating of a European barnacle goose, blown off course by a storm, with a Canada goose in northern Ontario, and the love affair between Rory Macdonald, an ornithologist observing the geese, and an Indian girl he meets on the Polar Bear Express. Kanina Beaverskin is returning to her tribe after an unsuccessful attempt to learn and teach in the white world. She returns in bitterness, since she has lost her job as a result of anti-Indian prejudice, but events conspire to bring Kanina and Rory together. She sees the strange goose and reports it to Rory; he later establishes that it came from his own island of Barra in the Hebrides. In this way Bodsworth subtly complicates his story. This is not a matter of primitivism versus modern civilization, since Rory's origins are themselves northern and primitive (Indian and Scottish superstitions, for instance, are compared). The 'strange one' of the title applies to the goose, to Kanina, and to Rory, and the three are linked by means of the plot but also because of their common otherness. This is a parable about human and natural unity, and Bodsworth sets it in a locale that is itself an emblem of the unity.

The Sparrow's Fall (1967), based on Bodsworth's knowledge of the Indian settlements at Big Trout and Weagamow Lakes, is a novel in which all the main characters are Indian. A tale of endurance and rivalry and cunning in the muskeg terrain, its whole intellectual complexity derives from white intrusion. A Roman Catholic priest has converted two Indian lovers and married them without their parents' consent. But he has also taught them that God (or Manitou) 'sees even the little sparrow fall' and that 'killing when you don't have to is a bad thing' (14). The two have to live apart from their tribe and so fend for themselves; the priest's compassionate but imported message seriously interferes with their traditional Indian instincts and so imperils their survival. The exciting plot involves the triumph of intelligence and artfulness on the part of Jacob Atook over Taka, an Indian with designs on Jacob's wife, but Bodsworth is raising the whole issue of relative and conflicitng ideologies. Once again the traditional ways of those who live close to nature are contrasted with those who don't. *The Sparrow's Fall* elevates the issue on to a controversial religious level.

What unites all Bodsworth's parables is his insistence, regularly reiterated, that human beings sever their contact with the natural world at their peril. Of Joe Beaverskin, Kanina's father in *The Strange One*, he writes:

Joe Beaverskin was a simple unlearned man, but he understood intimately one basic principle of life that most white men, shielded behind their artificial civilization, have long ago lost sight of. He saw himself clearly as an integral part of the natural world ... His was a simple basic relationship of hunter and hunted.   (156–7)

It is the lesson that Lilka teaches Ashley in *The Atonement of Ashley Morden*:

'You are a part of all this, a part of this natural world, and it's a part of you, but you have forgotten ...
    ... We have lost that feeling of kinship with nature that Indians and simple peoples still have; we have lost our roots, and it hasn't been a healthy change, emotionally or mentally.'   (447, 448)

Similarly, the *Atihk-anashini* in *The Sparrow's Fall*, the Cariboo people to whom Jacob and Niska belong, are described as 'a part of their land in that vital, intense independent way that only primitive people can belong to the land on which they dwell' (8). In extracting quotations like this, I inevitably make Bodsworth seem oppressively didactic, but this is to do him a disservice. Rather, his books cohere impressively by virtue of the consistent vision which they embody. Canada has been described as 'America's attic'; if that is so, the north may be Canada's attic, and may well contain a store of neglected wisdom from which we can all benefit. Perhaps this is Duncan Campbell Scott's 'Something [that] comes in flashes / Deeper than peace.'

9 *Small-Town Ontario*

At the opening of Hugh Hood's *A New Athens*, as we have seen, Matt Goderich embarks on a walking tour along Highway 29, once known as the Victoria Macadamized Road. After observing traces of the older road-layer beside or below the surface of the modern highway, he comes upon the remains of what he ultimately identifies as an abandoned railway line. This is Hood's way, as a creative writer, of making the point Harold Innis had established a generation earlier: that, as a vast country with a relatively small and scattered population, Canada is particularly dependent for its economic and cultural survival upon its system of communications. As historians and geographers have noted, human settlements invariably develop along the main communication routes, and Ontario writers have not been behindhand in recording the phenomenon as it applies to their own province.

Stephen Leacock, who is an acknowledged influence behind Hood's work, and whose famous description of the train to Mariposa at the close of *Sunshine Sketches* will be discussed in due course, has offered an admirably clear and eloquent account of the process in relation to the development of small towns in southern Ontario:

The main railway ran through from Montreal to Sarnia-Chicago. But from the half-dozen little railway stations of the Toronto of early Confederation days, there radiated, like the fingers of a hand, half a dozen little railways with various gauges, reaching out north to the lumber woods – Huntsville, Coboconk, Haliburton – and north and west to the lake ports of Lake Huron and the Georgian Bay. Along the stations of these railway lines the horse and buggy and the lumber-wagon took up the traffic. General stores, each a post-office with a near-by blacksmith shop, arose at the cross-roads, and if there was also a river with a waterfall, there appeared a sawmill and a gristmill, and presently, as the farms multiplied, a village. Then the village became a little town, with not one [store] but rival stores, a drugstore, a local paper and a cricket club. In it were four churches and three taverns. One church was of the Church of England, one Presbyterian, while the Roman Catholics, Methodists and Baptists divided the other two ... The three taverns were one Grit, and one Tory, and one neither. Many things in Ontario ran like that in threes with the post-office and the mail-stage alternating as the prize of victory in elections. The cricket club is now just a memory, gone long ago. Thus the little Ontario town grew till the maples planted in its streets overtopped it and fell asleep and grew no more. It is strange this, and peculiar to our country, the aspect of a town grown from infancy to old age within a human lifetime.   (*Boy* 70-1)

This combination of accelerated growth and foreshortened history means that it is impossible to maintain the traditional distinction between 'village' and 'small town.' When in the 'town' of Hanratty in Alice Munro's *Who Do You Think You Are?* Milton Homer is referred to as the 'village idiot,' the narrator comments: 'They had never thought of Hanratty as a village. A village was a cluster of picturesque houses around a steepled church on a Christmas card. Villagers were the costumed chorus in the high school operetta' (193). But the terms obstinately overlap in literature. Leacock's Mariposa may qualify as the archetypal 'Small Town, Ontario,' yet Robertson Davies's Deptford, though referred to in the text as a village, clearly belongs in the same category. (At the other extreme the distinction between 'small town' and 'small city' is similarly vague; even Davies's Salterton retains many of the qualities of a small town, though I shall reserve these for consideration in the next chapter.) Here, 'small town' means any cohesive, distinctive, yet relatively compact human community.

It will be convenient to begin by constructing an overview or composite portrait before showing how individual Ontario writers have created a variety of equally individual small towns. While Leacock drew attention to the importance of church and tavern in the evolution of the average small town, Matt Cohen, in establishing his imaginary Salem as the focal point for a series of novels, has developed these contrasting structures into potent literary symbols:

At the southern end of these two streets, rising over and surveying the town and its inhabitants, was the Church of the New Age. In earlier eras it had been called Presbyterian, and then Methodist, but the name changes were only incidental, like new coats of paint. What stayed constant was the church's meaning, because it was placed at the edge of the stores as if to say: corruption – this far and no farther.

At the other end of the town, facing the farm and bushland to the north, was the town's other main institution ... It was the town's hotel and tavern. Its name also changed ... but its meaning too was consistent: a fortress of comfort that stood between civilization and the terrifying wilderness.

Between the poles of tavern and church Salem's inhabitants swayed or sometimes staggered. (*Flowers* 58-9)

Given the conspicuous Puritan inheritance of Ontario, this dichotomy between the respective homes of God and the devil is an appropriate imaginative device. In the main, however, perhaps because the tavern as a tempting if disreputable alternative to the pious and the domestic has become an almost hackneyed subject (Josh Smith's 'hostelry' in *Sunshine Sketches* is a relatively innocent example), writers have tended to concentrate on the refreshingly diverse inter-church distinctions and rivalries that seem to characterize traditional Ontarian life.

A recent writer, Isobel Huggan, has offered a general comment on this phenomenon that throws light on many Ontario small towns as well as on her own fictional community of Garten:

Religious affiliation was an important part of Garten life, not only for the women who ran the bazaars and sang in the choirs, but as social definition. It told as much about you as where you lived or what your father did or whether you went into commercial or academic in high school. You always had to know what people 'were'; it was like knowing their name or phone number, and when you met someone, it was one of the first questions you asked. (146)

In Garten itself, based on a community in the Waterloo area, it is interesting to note that Leacock's four-church pattern is seen as persisting well into the twentieth century. Earlier in the book, the narrator comments:

Except for the Roman Catholic Falconers on the corner, everyone on Brubacher Street was United Church or Lutheran, and the prospect of fundamentalist fervour on their doorstep [a proposed Pentecostal Church] made them nervous. (18)

Here, as so often, the recurrent suspicion of the old for the new, the respectable for the dubious, the restrained for the uninhibited, manifests itself in spiritual terms.

In *The Imperialist* (1904), Sara Jeannette Duncan emphasizes the gentler rivalries. Elgin (based on Brantford), though outdoing Leacock's norm by boasting no less than eleven churches (25), is presented as firmly Presbyterian, but Dr Drummond's sermons at Knox Church are sometimes attended by members of the congregation of 'St Andrews,

"Established" – a glum, old-fashioned lot,' and even, on occasion, by Episcopalians. However, the 'Established folk went on calling the minister ... "Mr" Drummond long after he was "Doctor" to his own congregation' (22). By the same token, Drummond himself would never think of going 'outside the congregation' when furnishing his house (23), and he is especially fond of spicing his conversation with Scotch stories 'at the expense of the Methodists' (39). While making strategic concessions to modern fashion, Drummond attacks Anglican saints' days and ceremonial in his Christmas sermon and Catholic practices and pageants at Easter (197). At one point, Duncan makes a comment that blends easily with Huggan's:

There was a simple and definite family feeling within communions. 'They come to our church' was the argument of first force whether for calling or for charity. It was impossible to feel toward a Congregationalist or an Episcopalian as you felt toward one who sang the same hymns and sat under the same admonition week by week, year in and year out, as yourself. 'Wesleyans, are they?' a lady of Knox Church would remark of the newly arrived, in whom her interest was suggested. 'Then let the Wesleyans look after them.' (61)

Rather surprisingly, given the references he makes elsewhere, Leacock has virtually nothing to say about congregational differences and rivalries in *Sunshine Sketches*, where the religious emphasis comes to rest wholly on the problems, more financial than theological, that beset the Church of England clergyman, Dr Drone. In Robertson Davies's *Fifth Business*, however, the familiar religious divisions (here expanded to five) are seen in their social *and* financial aspects. Dunstan Ramsay characterizes them as follows:

the Anglican, poor but believed to have some mysterious social supremacy; the Presbyterian, solvent and thought – chiefly by itself – to be intellectual; the Methodist, insolvent and fervent; the Baptist, insolvent and saved; the Roman Catholic, mysterious to most of us but clearly solvent, as it was frequently and, so we thought, quite needlessly repainted. (16)

This, of course, represented the situation before the amalgamation of various Protestant groups into the United Church of Canada in the mid-1920s. Munro, evoking a small town of the 1940s, records a different configuration. The Jordan family in *Lives of Girls and Women* are 'United,' and Del's account of her teenage religious experimentation reflects that emphasis so faithfully and so humanly that it deserves quotation at length:

The United Church was the most modern, the largest, the most prosperous church in Jubilee ... There were four other churches in town but they were all small, all relatively poor, and all, by United Church standards, went to extremes. The Catholic church was the most extreme. White and wooden, with a plain mission cross, it stood on a hill at the north end of town and dispensed peculiar services to Catholics, who seemed bizarre and secretive as Hindus, with their idols and confessions and black spots on Ash Wednesday. At school the Catholics were a small but unintimidated tribe, mostly Irish, who did not stay in the classroom for Religious Education but were allowed to go down to the basement, where they banged on the pipes ...

The Baptists were extreme as well, but in a completely unsinister, slightly comic way. No person of any importance or social standing went to the Baptist Church ... Baptists could not dance or go to movies; Baptist ladies could not wear lipstick. But their hymns were loud, rollicking, and optimistic, and ... their religion had more vulgar cheerfulness than anybody else's. Their church ... was modest, but modern and hideous ...

As for the Presbyterians, they were leftovers, people who had refused to become United. They were mostly elderly, and campaigned against hockey practice on Sundays, and sang psalms.

The final church was the Anglican, and nobody knew or spoke much about it. It did not have, in Jubilee, any of the prestige or money which attached to it in towns where there was a remnant of the Family Compact ... To be Anglican was therefore not fashionable as it was in some places ... However[,] the church had a bell, the only bell in town, and that seemed to me a lovely thing for a church to have.   (78–9)

I have quoted these passages not to suggest an overriding preoccupation with religious matters on the part of Ontario small towns, but to point up the paradoxical cohesiveness that operates within a context of various forms of exclusion. Select groups evolve in these communities through a series of affiliations that will be affected by social standing, ultimate national origin, specific shared interests, connections through marriage, as well as religious attendance (or, more recently, non-attendance). But such groups are also united through accepted distinctions that isolate them from groups with opposed attitudes or practices. Relations between groups may vary from bitter hostility to good-humoured acceptance, but boundaries are nonetheless maintained. There is interchange but within clearly established limits. A small town, then, is made up of a series of loose confederations that maintain a reasonable but sometimes strained coexistence. (This may explain why, in Canada, it comes close to qualifying as a national symbol.) But differing mixes, as writers are naturally quick to notice, produce differing overall characteristics. Some examples of the variations that can occur at different times and in different parts of the province will be presented in the ensuing sections.

Sara Jeannette Duncan's Elgin in *The Imperialist*, though it began as 'the centre of "trading" for the farmers,' is 'a thriving manufacturing town, with a collegiate institute, eleven churches, two newspapers, and an asylum for the deaf and dumb, to say nothing of a fire department' (25). It is a 'sunny little town' (13), thus anticipating Leacock's Mariposa, but it is by no means sleepy. Duncan presents it for us at the turn of the nineteenth and twentieth centuries, and she obviously regards it as both significant and representative at a time of momentous transition. As early as the second chapter, two of the prominent characters are discussing the fact of change, and both welcoming and lamenting it. '"We've seen changes, Mr Murchison. Aye. We've seen changes,"' says Dr Drummond (21). There has been heartening material progress; the 'prolonged "toots" of seven factory whistles' at noon are recognized with satisfaction as 'an indication of "go-ahead" proclivities' (26); at the same time, it is possible to be 'unnecessarily in advance of the times' (25), and the small number of drays moving through town to the Grand Trunk Station and the general lack of hurry on the part of the inhabitants look back to an earlier world. The Janus-faced quality of the town is represented architecturally by a 'pretentious red brick building with the false third story,' hinting that 'the line of legitimate enterprise had been overpassed,' and 'the solid "Gregory block," opposite the market, where rents were as certain as the dividends of the Bank of British North America' (25).

Yet Elgin is still seen – it still sees itself – as 'this little outpost of Empire' (21), and the two reminiscing citizens are both immigrants from 'the old country,' which still exerts its influence. '[O]bscure in the heart of each of them,' Duncan writes, 'ran the undercurrent of the old allegiance. They had gone the length of their tether, but the tether was always there' (22). On the other hand, the influence of the United States is everywhere apparent. Duncan makes the point imaginatively but pointedly in a scene in which the protagonist, Lorne Murchison, is welcomed home after his visit to London on a trade delegation, a visit that has impressed and inspired him with the importance of the British connection. But the details of the situation undercut these ideals:

'I suppose you had a lovely time, Mr Murchison?' said Mrs Williams, gently tilting to and fro in a rocking-chair with her pretty feet in their American shoes well in evidence. It is a fact, or perhaps a parable, that should be interesting to political economists, the adaptability of Canadian feet to American shoes; but fortunately it is not our present business. Though I must add that the 'rocker' was also American; and the hammock in which Stella reposed came from New York; and upon John Murchison's knee, with the local journal, lay a pink evening paper published in Buffalo.   (128)

Sometime later, when Lorne has become a political candidate campaigning on an 'Imperial Federation' ticket, he makes a speech that emphasizes the American threat to Canadian economic interests. The issues troubling an Ontario small town in the early 1900s can still produce a shock of recognition almost a century later:

'We often say that we fear no invasion from the south, but the armies of the south have already crossed the border. American enterprise, American capital, is taking rapid possession of our mines and our water power, our oil areas and our timber limits. In today's *Dominion*, one paper alone, you may read of charters granted to five industrial concerns with headquarters in the United States. The trades unions of the two countries are already international, American settlers are pouring into the wheat-belt of the Northwest, and when the Dominion of Canada has paid the hundred million dollars she has just voted for a railway to open up the great lone northern lands between Quebec and the Pacific, it will be the American farmer and the American capitalist who will reap the benefit.'   (232)

Elgin, like the rest of the province and the rest of the country, is forced to choose between traditional sentiment and contemporary practicality. The movement of the novel, from the parochialism of a spring fair to the far-reaching principles that affect the stability of nations and continents, is indicative of the representativeness – and therefore the significance – of Duncan's small town. 'Elgin market square ... was the biography of Fox County and, in little, the history of the whole Province' (73).

But another main emphasis of *The Imperialist*, and one that clearly harks back to the town's British origins, falls upon the 'social distinctions of Elgin' (14), the subtle 'lines of demarcation' (47) that the original settlers brought with them from the mother country. The Murchisons, the respectable middle-class merchant family at the centre of the novel, have established themselves in 'the Plummer Place,' an old house built on an ambitious scale, 'no doubt by one of those gentlefolk of reduced income who wander out to the colonies with a nebulous view to economy and occupation, to perish of the re-adjustment.' As a result, Mrs Murchison has 'an icehouse and a wine cellar, and a string of bells in the kitchen that connected with every room in the house.' It was, however, 'a negligible misfortune that not one of them was in order' (29). Duncan has a keen eye for this kind of placing detail, and is equally acute in her analysis of the process of adjustment and assimilation:

The little knot of gentry-folk soon found the limitations of their new conditions; years went by in decades, aggrandizing none of them. They took, perforce, to the ways of the country, and soon nobody kept a groom but the Doctor, and nobody dined late but the Judge. There came a time when the Sheriff's whist club and the Archdeacon's port became a tradition to the oldest inhabitant ... The original dignified group broke, dissolved, scattered. Prosperous traders foreclosed them, the spirit of the times defeated them, young Liberals succeeded them in office. Their grandsons married the daughters of well-to-do persons who came from the north of Ireland, the east of Scotland, and the Lord knows where.   (47)

By the end of the nineteenth century, these 'lines of demarcation' persist, but in varied form. 'Trade,' on which the prosperity of the town depends, is now respectable, but there are distinctions to be made among the trades:

Dry-goods were held in respect and chemists in comparative esteem; house furnishings, and hardware made an appreciable claim, and quite a leading family was occupied with seed grains. Groceries, on the other hand, were harder to swallow, possibly on account of the apron, though the grocer's apron, being of linen, had several degrees more consideration than the shoemaker's, which was of leather ... They were all hard-working folk together, but they had their little prejudices: the dentist was known as 'Doc,' but he was not considered quite on the medical level; it was doubtful whether you bowed to the piano-tuner, and quite a curious and unreasonable contempt was bound up in the word 'veterinary.' Anything 'wholesale' or manufacturing stood, of course, on its own feet; there was nothing ridiculous in molasses, nothing objectionable in a tannery, nothing amusing in soap.   (47)

Nowhere, of course, are the distinctions more delicate than in the matter of accent. The 'upper crust' of Elgin is represented by the Milburns – Mr Milburn is president of the Elgin Chamber of Commerce – and, Canadian-born, they attempt to keep up the displaced practices that are growing more and more anachronistic every year. Dora Milburn, the daughter, 'had been taught to speak, like Mrs Milburn, with what was known as an "English accent,"' though the customary Elgin accent (and here we encounter Duncan showing her hand between the dashes) 'was borrowed – let us hope temporarily – from the other side of the line. It suffered local modifications and exaggerations, but it was clearly an American product' (49).

The Imperialist is a complex novel. A fairly conventional romance plot (conventional, at least, until the climax) is well integrated with a shrewdly pointed political theme. Duncan writes out of an intimate knowledge of the inner social workings of her own small town of Brantford, and she treats her characters with a piquant irony that is tempered with genial acquiescence. Their foibles are pinpointed, but they are presented with wit and humour, and even with love. Although she initiates a whole tradition of Canadian small-town fiction, she has never been surpassed in the technical skill with which she combines the idiosyncrasies of politics, class, social behaviour, and religious observance with a clearsighted but kindly portrayal of fallible yet (for the most part) ordinary human beings.

Stephen Leacock's Mariposa is, of course, the epitome of the Ontarian (and Canadian) small town in the popular imagination. There must be countless non-readers who have never opened any of Leacock's works but who are nonetheless aware of Mariposa and have some inkling of its significance. It would seem reasonable to suppose, then, that *Sunshine Sketches of a Little Town* (1912) is one of those transparent, unambiguous texts that present no difficulties and yield clear meanings. In fact, however, no two literary-critical commentators seem to be able to agree in classifying the book, assessing its tone, or even establishing precisely what it is about. Many will argue about its genre: is it best categorized as irony, or satire, or pastoral? For some its tone is kindly and genial, for others, bitter – even virulent. For some it is a nostalgic recreation of a simpler past; for others it represents a searing revelation of the human capacity for deception.

This curious polarization of response was potentially present from the time of the book's first publication in 1912. The London *Spectator's* review asserted confidently that there is 'no bitterness in his laughter' (qtd in Curry 174), but the reviewer in question was several thousand miles away from Leacock's home-base. The inhabitants of Orillia thought differently (see Anderson 150-61, countering Curry 184). Later, as Leacock's best writings were recognized as more than mere ephemeral entertainment, as the complexity of his art became more apparent, the ambiguity of Mariposa loomed even larger. Individual critics may be found positioning themselves at the extreme ends of the spectrum, but the most useful commentary tends to come from those who focus on the fact of ambiguity itself, on the specific qualities of the text that can contain such diverging potential meanings. D.A. Cameron, for example, suggests that this ambiguity may be found in 'the town's simultaneous rejection of, and longing for, city values' (11); T.D. MacLulich argues that the sketches can be interpreted in two ways 'depending on whether they are read by our "city" or our "Mariposa" self' (168); Robertson Davies points out that we can be 'beguiled by the manner in which the book is written from giving too much attention to its matter' ('Stephen Leacock' 147).

Davies's approach seems to me to offer the most promising insight into the problem. The first word of the title prepares us for warmth and a pleasant brightness. 'There it [Mariposa] lies,' we are told on the opening page, ' in the sunlight,' and Leacock leaves us on the last page (after some disturbing – not to say tricky – changes of viewpoint and response) with the image of 'the Little Town in the Sunshine that once we knew.' The tone is established, and fulfilled; this is the frame, surely, through which we are invited to view the events that make up the body of the text (though sophisticated readers, geared for satire, may suspect a rhetorical trap). The first detail we are offered, also on the first page, is of the *Mariposa Belle* 'tied to the wharf with two ropes of about the same size as they use on the Lusitania,' and here the possibility of varieties of response may make themselves felt. If we are 'sophisticated' readers from the outside world, for whom travel on the *Lusitania* is imaginable (the Concorde jet might be an updated equivalent), the joke will seem obvious, non-threatening, genial, even 'cute.' For an Orillian, however, it may well appear condescending, 'superior,' deflating, reductive. The outsider, then, will respond to the tonal clues; the native will inevitably be more sensitive to the image presented to the rest of the world.

In his longer study, Davies cogently applies this principle to the rest of the book, and clearly demonstrates how two apparently contradictory readings can be applied to the same text:

Strip the book of its humour, and what have we? A community in which the acknowledged leaders are windbags and self-serving clowns, and where the real leader is an illiterate saloon-keeper; a community that sees financial acuity in a lucky little barber who makes a one-in-a-thousand killing in the stockmarket; a community that will not support a church, but will swindle an insurance company with a fraudulent fire; a community in which an election is shamelessly rigged ...   (*Stephen Leacock* 25)

One should not, of course, strip the book of its humour (and Davies would never do so as a general principle); at the same time, one needs to acknowledge that the book did develop out of a local matrix and that local susceptibilities should not be flouted. Leacock seems to have been either curiously naive or disturbingly cavalier in this regard. We cannot easily separate Mariposa from Orillia. When the contents of *Sunshine Sketches* originally appeared as serialized items in the *Montreal Star*, he employed comic names for his characters that were easily recognized as adapted versions of the names of well-known Orillian citizens, and several of these still survive in the text that we read today. This means, of course, that at the time of its first publication it would inevitably be read in different ways by outsiders and insiders. The whole incident reminds us that all writings based on local particularities are liable to a similar range of interpretations and reactions.

Hugh Hood, who shares with Davies a debt to *Sunshine Sketches*, has offered his own version of the central ambiguity of the book by characterizing it as 'a pastoral idyll treated satirically' (Struthers 'Interview' 26-7). In traditional pastoral (Shakespeare's *As You Like It* is a classic example), sophisticated characters from the city move temporarily into a bucolic setting and work out their personal problems within a simplified milieu. In *Sunshine Sketches*, this position is complicated by the fact that the narrator presents himself as an ex-Mariposan who has 'escaped' to the city and looks back with the double perspective of sophisticated outsider and nostalgic native son. Much of Leacock's humour derives from incongruous comparisons between large-city and small-town attitudes:

Of course if you come to the place fresh from New York, you are deceived. Your standard of vision is all astray. You do think the place is quiet. You do imagine that Mr. Smith is asleep merely because he closes his eyes as he stands. But live in Mariposa for six months or a year and then you will begin to understand it better; the buildings get higher and higher; the Mariposa House grows more and more luxurious; McCarthy's Block towers to the sky; the buses roar ...; the people move faster and faster; a dense crowd swirls to and fro in the post-office and the five and ten cent store – and amusements! well, now! lacrosse, baseball, excursions, dances, the Firemen's Ball every winter and the Catholic picnic every summer! and music – the town band in the park every Wednesday evening, and the Oddfellows' brass band on the street every other Friday; the Mariposa Quartette, the Salvation Army – why, after a few months' residence you begin to realize that the place is a mere mad round of gaiety. (3)

In such passages, one can see the city/rural contrast both presented and (in this case, good-humouredly) parodied.

Elsewhere, however, Leacock provides comparisons rather than contrasts between urban and rural. Just as we have decided that Mariposa is a pleasant retreat from the pressures of city living, he reveals his satiric aspect and (like Swift and Lilliput) shows that the delightful Mariposan oddities are reflections of urban values, amusing only because they are on a small scale and therefore neither threatening nor oppressive. Josh Smith's attempts to bring up-to-date city standards to the hotel business in Mariposa by introducing a 'caff' and a 'Rats' Cooler' (and proposing a 'girl room,' though this presumably involves a joke about linguistic transposition – a Freudian-slip-like version of 'grill room' rather than defiant strip-tease) are only the first of many instances. Others include Jefferson Thorpe's adventures with stocks, the imported fund-raising methods intended to clear the church debt, and Mariposa's microcosmic version of the Reciprocity election. And in the famous 'Marine Excursion of the Knights of Pythias,' Leacock plays with the age-old imagery of the ship of state; when the *Mariposa Belle* eventually returns to her dock to the strains of 'O Canada' after almost sinking, local (and, for that matter, Ontarian) application has been transcended. The town/country dichotomy disappears in satiric ambiguity when, on the failure of the 'whirlwind campaign,' bank manager Mullins declares that 'there were so many skunks in Mariposa that a man might as well be in the Head Office in the City' (77).

If, however, we look behind the humour, the satire, and the techniques by which they can be communicated, we find in Leacock the basic ingredients of the Ontario small town that we encounter elsewhere. The features he isolates in *The Boy I Left behind Me* (in the passage I quoted at the beginning of this chapter) are nearly all present here. Although he concentrates on Josh Smith's hostelry, we hear at one point of the 'three hotels' in the town (73) – presumably one Grit, one Tory, and one neither. The railway is also important, though here Leacock indulges in his characteristic love for exaggerated incongruity. The transcontinental railways 'run through Mariposa,' but the phrase is accurate in more than one sense of the words: 'It is true that the trains mostly go through at night and don't stop,' yet the 'joy of being on the main line lifts the Mariposa people above the level of their neighbours in such places as Tecumseh and Nichols Corners into the cosmopolitan atmosphere of through traffic and the larger life' (4).

As every commentator on *Sunshine Sketches* has noted, a change of tone occurs in the final section entitled 'L'Envoi: The Train to Mariposa.' This is partly explained by a change of location. Up to this point the narrator has been positioned in Mariposa itself, observing the small town from a somewhat detached perspective, since, as a visitor, he is able to compare it with other more populous and sophisticated parts of the world. Here, however, we are in the 'Mausoleum Club' of an unnamed city (which must in this context be Toronto, even if the equivalent Club in *Arcadian Adventures with the Idle Rich* draws upon Leacock's club-experience in Montréal). The reader is addressed colloquially and intimately, as earlier in the book, but here he (a male ambiance is obviously assumed) is hailed as a fellow Mariposan. Surprise is registered that the reader did not know of the existence of the daily train to Mariposa, 'though you come from the little town – or did, long years ago' (148).

This epilogue becomes, literally, a journey into the past, a past in which the absurdities and corruptions of the town are forgotten in a nostalgic glow. Imaginatively, we take the train home and witness with the narrator the way its character changes as it moves away from the city. At first a commuter train taking office workers back to their suburbs and patrons to the outlying golf clubs, it soon sheds them to reveal a hard core of Mariposans in 'last year's fashions' (150). But it is not only the passengers who change:

The electric locomotive that took you through the city tunnels is off now and the old wood engine is hitched on in its place ... [T]he trim little cars that came out of the city on the electric suburban express are being discarded now at the way stations, one by one, and in their place is the old familiar car with the stuff cushions in red plush (how gorgeous it once seemed!) and with a box stove set up in one end of it.   (150)

The train is a time machine (H.G. Wells's famous story had appeared seventeen years earlier), and we are back in the more leisurely Ontario of the late nineteenth century.

In this comic/satiric pastoral, it is appropriate that the pastoral patterns should be reversed, and that, instead of returning from the simplified green world to the city, we move in the opposite direction. The sight of farmsteads in the gathering dusk, 'the long muffled roar of the whistle, dying to a melancholy wail that echoes into the woods' (151), the first glimpse of the local lake, talk of 'harvest, and the late election ... and all the old familiar topics' (152) – all these prepare for the climax of arrival:

How vivid and plain it all is. Just as it used to be thirty years ago. There is the string of the hotel buses drawn up all ready for the train, and as the train rounds in and stops hissing and panting at the platform, you can hear above all other sounds the cry of the brakemen and the porters:
      'MARIPOSA! MARIPOSA!'   (153)

The tough-minded are likely to complain of sentimental indulgence at this point, and sentiment is certainly involved. But the mood doesn't cancel out the harsher side of the Mariposa that has already been presented, nor does it necessarily favour the positive side of the spectrum. This coda is best understood as a shrewd comment on the human tendency to idealize the past. A comparable kind of irony is now directed not at Mariposa itself but at people like ourselves always liable to forget the frustrations of schooldays, the mosquitoes and blackflies at summer cottages, the sadnesses of earlier years. Moreover, Leacock has a final, half-sentimental, half-comical trick up his sleeve. This last journey was, in fact, no more than a dream, a play of imagination. The vision fades and we are left, with the narrator, 'in the leather chairs of the Mausoleum Club, talking of the little Town in the Sunshine that once we knew' (153). You can't go home again; the pastoral ends conventionally in the contemporary city, after all.

Most of the presentations of Ontarian small towns employ the form of fiction or, as in the case of Leacock, prose with pronounced fictional elements. Since the writers generally look upon small-town people as somewhat prosaic (and even Leacock fits here, since his denials are offered ironically to convey the opposite of what is actually said) this is appropriate enough. James Reaney, however, represents an exception. His *Twelve Letters to a Small Town* (*Poems* 209–30) first appeared in 1962. Despite its title, it consists of a series of poems, and Reaney provides an essentially imaginative re-creation and transformation of the Stratford he knew as a child. This slim volume is perhaps the most original portrait of an Ontarian small town, since it has no clear antecedents; still, at least a slight connection can be made with the Envoi to *Sunshine Sketches*, since Reaney, like Leacock, is primarily concerned with the image of his town as it persists through the act of memory.

Reaney begins, in the splendid first letter, 'To the Avon River above Stratford, Canada,' not with the town itself but with the river that flows through it and upon which its existence originally depended. The retrospective narrative voice associates it with the traditional river-connected activities in small human communities – 'To skate upon, swim in / Or for baptism of sin' (211) – but he is also struck by a certain alien quality. He addresses it directly and asks about its Indian name 'For you do not flow / With English accents' (211). By contrast, in the second letter his figures, presumably an adult and a young child, are creating a model of the town out of ordinary available objects. Two sticks and two branches are arranged to form the 'spokes of an invisible wheel' and so represent 'The principal through streets of the town' (212). A green glass ball is placed at the end of one branch 'Because it fades into farms and fields and townships' (213). Berries are brought into use as houses ('Ripe gooseberries for red houses. / White raspberries for yellow brick houses' [213]), and, later, apples are placed to represent 'the business places' (213), potatoes to signify the Court House, the two principal churches, and the larger buildings, and finally 'a rather sharpside brick-coloured tomato ... to stand for the three towered City Hall' (213). It is even suggested that 'lady bugs' be dressed up to represent people. This whimsical game is interrupted by the town band, and the model is abandoned, presumably demolished, but the transition from childhood game to adult activity is seen archetypally as a 'Fall' when model becomes reality and the child is propelled into the actual community:

> Fall down! Fall down!
> Into our model of the town!   (213)

The band in question is apparently accompanying the July 12 Orange Day parade, the traditional Protestant festival which is the subject of the third letter. It clearly represents a child's first memory of a small-town happening. In the fourth letter the main features of town are listed and planted in memory as a child first notices them:

> Up here is the Water Tower, down there's the Sewage Farm
> Down there's the Old Folks' Home, up here's the Theatre.   (215)

Other details follow: the stone bridge, the market square, the cannon commemorating the Crimean War, the traditional farmers from Waterloo County 'with Amish bonnets and beards' (215), and, of course, the

> gold paper Christmas tree angels
> *In Kresge's dime store just after the war.*   (215)

The next letter, significantly entitled 'The Cloakroom at the High School,' symbolizes the next stage in the child's growth, and revives the whole ethos of the school – the radiators that 'teach the rule of monotony / Cheep cheep cheeping in the winter classroom' (216), the stuffed birds, the ninety-two traditional elements, and much more, but most insistently

> The insoluble mystery of the cloakroom
> And the curious question of the janitor.   (217)

The sixth and eighth letters may be treated together because both are set in old houses that conjure up the old-fashioned, unchanging, traditional

ways of living. In 'A House on King William Street,' the house in
question has become somewhat run down and shabby as the designs on
the fading wallpaper show:

> those behind the sofa
> Have kept their original blaze
> And these opposite the window
>   Have turned yellow.   (217)

That particular house was where the narrator boarded when he went to
school. The other, the home of the music teacher, is much grander. It is
a 'fantastic house' with 'huge green elm trees, red velvet curtains ...
marble fireplaces like Roquefort Cheese and much carved chairs' (220).
The cluttered hallway contains 'the Fathers of Confederation, the History
of the Dutch Republic, pictures of Greek Statues interestingly disfigured
and De la Motte Fouqué's *Ondine* gorgeously illustrated by Edmund
Dulac' (220) – a veritable museum of standard 'culture.'

But it is in the library, in the important seventh letter called 'Prose for
the Past,' that the child discovers his own impressionistic sense of local
history and attitudes. There he pores over old files of the town's newspaper, which make up 'a shaky fading paper rope into the darkness of
the past,' recording a time when Stratford was 'a small little embryonic
amoeba of a place' (218). He notes characteristic (because unfamiliar)
features: the coinage in pounds and shillings, fluctuations in the price of
grain and cordwood, forgotten tragedies such as two boys drowning in
the river, the coming of public gaslight and the railway, the overt class
distinctions. Yet even here historical record blends into imaginative
myth. The traditional figure of 'Granny Crick who every child has heard
about' (219) appears at this point. She is a favourite of Reaney's, mentioned in the early poem 'Winter's Tales' and in a separate poem called
'Granny Crick' from which part of this seventh letter derives; later, she
reappears in the play *Colours in the Dark*. But she is, of course, a traditional figure from British folklore, even making a brief appearance in
Dylan Thomas's *Under Milk Wood*. As so often in Reaney, the pattern
of legend here impinges upon the world of research, the romance of
libraries and half-forgotten lore.

The later letters concern themselves with various changes rung upon
the traditional aspects of small communities. The narrator indulges at
one point in an imaginative game of Happy Families – 'a seedsman
whose name was Seed,' 'Miss Bread and Mr. Bread,' who were bakers
(221). He remembers, as a 'Country Mouse,' his earliest memories of
town:

Terrifying sights: one's first nun!
   The first person with a wooden leg,
A huge chimney writing the sky
   With dark smoke.   (226)

The unique qualities of Stratford are celebrated in 'Shakespearean Gardens,' where a selection of Shakespeare's play titles are illustrated by observed or recorded events in the town's history, some tragic, some comic:

Titus Andronicus Young Mr. Wood to-day lost his right hand in an accident at the lumber yards.   (228)
...
Julius Caesar Antony wore a wrist watch in the Normal School production although he never looked at it during the oration.   (229)

But the final letter, 'The Bicycle,' devoted to an object that links the country boy with the town, ends on a positive note:

Between the highschool & the farmhouse
   In the country and the town
It was a world of love ...   (230)

For all its 'terrifying sights,' the town is at least a community; for all its injustices and sadness, it lacks for Reaney the oppressive monotony that he remembers in the isolated homesteads.

For most Ontario writers, the small town about which they write is a version – sometimes idealized, sometimes satirized – of the community in which they grew up. Even when they invent a number of small towns – Alice Munro, for example, has set her fictions in places named Jubilee, Hanratty, Logan, and more recently Walley – the basic features remain similar, and one gets the uneasy sense that they may in fact be interchangeable. Robertson Davies, by contrast, has created a number of communities which offer a remarkable range and diversity though unified by his conspicuous style and approach. He was himself born in Thamesville, which is generally recognized in his work under the guise of Deptford, but he has lived in other places, notably Renfrew, Kingston, and Peterborough, and has clearly put these experiences to good use by subsequently creating a set of distinctive villages, small towns, and small cities within his fiction.

Before we turn to his full-scale fiction, however, we should consider

Samuel Marchbanks, Davies's crusty *alter ego* created as a satirical persona and sometimes referred to as 'the Recluse of Skunk's Misery' (*Papers* 270n). The name, while memorable, exists in the Marchbanks material more as a comic effect than as a realized place, though Davies has recently insisted that it is not a comic invention but the actual name of a swamp near Thamesville (*Conversations* 262). Apart from a few stray references to an 'old homestead ... sunk rather far into the swamp' (*Papers* xii) and the ubiquitous weekly paper and barber's shop, it comes across (and here we may think of it as the obverse to Mariposa) as an archetypal place of unremarkable origins offered as a counter to the hackneyed rural myth. At one point Marchbanks refers (with a fine ear for clichés and stale conventions) to

my far-off youth in Skunk's Misery, before I was tarnished by the fetid breath of city life. I suppose everybody has these soft-headed spells, when they think it would be fun to live in a small town. They pass quickly, of course.   (*Papers* 192).

In terms of historical period rather than the chronological development of his own work, the earliest small town that Davies portrays is the turn-of-the-century Blairlogie in *What's Bred in the Bone*, though its clearest visual impression is provided by Simon Darcourt's description in *The Lyre of Orpheus* of Senator McRory's 'Sun Pictures' that preserve a 'record of a Canada gone forever' (257). Darcourt sees 'streets deep in mud, or snow, or baked by summer sun, with lurching, drunken telephone poles and cobwebs of wires, and in the streets were horse-and-rig equipages, huge drays laden with immense, unmilled logs drawn by four horses apiece' (256-7). Accompanying these are photographs of lumber-camps, loggers, and sawyers, and one realizes that Davies's Blairlogie, though very different in fictional terms and in the artistic quality of its presentation, follows in a direct historical line from the world of Ralph Connor's Glengarry.

In *What's Bred in the Bone* itself, Blairlogie is characterized initially as 'the Jumping-Off Place' (14), a once familiar phrase not unlike 'the end of steel,' representing the last point of civilization from which the intrepid plunged into the wilderness. By the time the action begins, however, it has developed, like Mariposa, into 'a town of about five thousand people' (14), and by the early 1930s, when Francis Cornish returns to his birthplace before leaving for Oxford, the resemblance continues, since his journey – in what is clearly a conscious allusion on Davies's part – parallels, though less sentimentally, the 'Envoi' of *Sunshine Sketches*:

From the excellent modern train ... he changed to a primitive affair in which an ancient, puffing engine pulled a baggage coach and one passenger coach at a stately twenty miles an hour through the hinterland. The passenger coach was old without being venerable; it had a great deal of fretwork ornamentation in wood that had once been glossy, but the green plush seats were mangy and slick, the floor was poorly swept, and it stank of coal-dust and long use ...

... Late in the afternoon the conductor tramped importantly through the car, shouting, 'Blairlogie! End of the line! Blairlogie!' as if some passengers could possibly have been in doubt about the matter.   (188, 189)

Once again, an emphasis on communications similar to Innis's (and Hood's) is paramount, though in the case of Blairlogie there is little impetus for its improvement. The roads are notoriously bad, yet 'Blairlogie saw no reason to be easily accessible' (20).

Unlike Mariposa with its predominantly Anglo-Saxon population, however, Blairlogie is a striking and socially differentiated ethnic mix. Davies's image of the town's wedding-cake structure is amusing but nonetheless telling, based as it is on an unabashedly materialist foundation:

The best of the town's money and business was firmly in the hands of the Scots, as was right and proper. [The narrator is here relaying the official – Scots – attitude.] Below the Scots, in a ranking that was decreed by money, came a larger population of Canadians of French descent, some of whom were substantial merchants. At the bottom of the financial and social heap were the Poles, a body of labourers and small farmers, from which the upper ranks drew their domestic servants ...

The town could have been represented as a wedding-cake, with the Poles as the large foundation layer, bearing the heaviest weight; the French, the middle layer, were smaller and central; the Scots were the topmost, smallest, most richly ornamented layer of all.   (20, 21)

Davies's blend of particularized delineation and representative social commentary is supreme here.

There is a reference late in the novel to 'Blairlogie harshness' (381), and the sensitive young Francis Cornish finds it a harsh place indeed, with the schoolchildren tough, cruel, and unforgiving. This is no 'Sunshine Sketch,' and the shadows are often dark. Even natural conditions are still primitive – 'when he was a boy a child had been eaten by a bear within three miles of Blairlogie' (316) – and social conditions no better. As Francis tells his Italian mentor Saraceni, in a passage that notably extends the picture we find in Connor:

'Where I grew up we had lots of incest. I knew one fellow, the son of a logger who was killed in the forest, and from twelve years of age onward he had to stand and deliver for his mother at least five times a week. When last I heard of him he had two brothers who were probably his sons.'   (260)

But hints of Gothic sensationalism are not confined to the traditionally disreputable classes. Francis discovers in the course of time a troubling secret within his own home and family, but before that the narrator has insisted that irregular actions and events are to be detected on every layer of the wedding-cake and that the dominant family (to which Cornish belongs) is the focus of rumour and speculation:

Whoever lives in the finest house of a small Canadian town dwells in a House of Atreus, about which a part of the community harbours the darkest mythical suspicions. Sycophancy is present, but in small store; it is jealousy, envy, detraction, and derision that proliferate. In lesser houses there may be fighting, covert abortions, children 'touched up' with a hot flat-iron to make them obedient, every imaginable aspect of parsimony, incest, and simple, persistent cruelty, but these are nothing to whatever seems amiss at the Big House.   (94)

Where 'Sunshine Sketches' end and 'Ontario Gothic' begins is not easily established; writers as diverse as Reaney, Munro, and Matt Cohen have emphasized the darker end of the spectrum. Davies offers hints at both ends, but in his best-known novel prefers the middle road.

For *Fifth Business*, the first book in the Deptford series, he chooses a historian for his narrator, and while offering an account of his own life Dunstan Ramsay is careful to set his own home town in its appropriate historical context. Moreover (with Davies, one feels, peering over his shoulder), he is concerned to put not just the historical but the psychological emphasis where it belongs:

Once it was the fashion to represent villages as places inhabited by laughable, lovable simpletons, unspotted by the worldliness of city life, though occasionally shrewd in rural concerns. Later it was the popular thing to show villages as rotten with vice, and especially such sexual vice as Krafft-Ebing might have been surprised to uncover in Vienna: incest, sodomy, bestiality, sadism, and masochism were supposed to rage behind the lace curtains and in the haylofts, while a rigid piety was professed in the streets. Our village never seemed to me to be like that. It was more varied in what it offered to the observer than people from bigger and more sophisticated places generally think, and if it had sins and foibles and roughnesses, it also had much to show of virtue, dignity, and even nobility.   (16)

Officially situated 'on the Thames River about fifteen miles east of Pittstown' (16), Deptford is easily recognizable as Thamesville, also on the Thames River and related in the same geographical terms to Chatham (William Pitt, the English prime minister, was Earl of Chatham). But its actual identification is far less important than its more general function as an average Ontario small town.

Davies gives us the usual vignettes of small-town life – the barber's shop, the school-yard, the Fall fair, etc – and instances of the loyalties as well as the rivalries that exist in such places. But it cannot be coincidental that all three of the Deptford protagonists who dominate the trilogy leave the town at the first opportunity. Boy Staunton has no intention of being even a large fish in so small a pond, and in later life 'did not like to be reminded of Deptford except as a joke' (180). Paul Dempster learns the full force of its meanness and cruelty; when in *World of Wonders* the theatrical company to which he is attached passes through Deptford by train many years later, he dramatically (albeit privately) spits at his native place. Dunstan Ramsay, who records the most disturbing manifestation of small-town (and, of course, of more than small-town) attitudes in the vindictiveness of the 'Hang the Kaiser' victory celebration after the First World War, feels the need to go elsewhere in search of large spiritual adventures. One of his complaints is that, though it 'contained much of what humanity has to show,' it lacked 'an aesthetic sense' (*Fifth Business* 25). Davies himself is both fascinated and repelled by what he calls 'those ingrown Canadian places' (*Conversations* 216); like his fictional creations, he insists on testing the microcosmic claims of these small communities by comparing them with the norms and standards of the larger world.

Although most authors who present accounts of small towns (like Duncan and Davies) present themselves as natives, as do their narrators (Leacock's and Davies's), they almost invariably write from a detached perspective. They have widened their own horizons and look *back* at the town in question with affection or amused irony or occasionally with disgust, but certainly from outside. Alice Munro is very much the exception here, and her most original contribution to the genre may well be that she presents the small town from a rural perspective and with total immediacy, conveying precisely what it feels like to grow up in such a place. In addition, her narrators frequently write from a child's perspective, and (rather like the view of Stratford we get in Reaney's poem) present what might otherwise seem ordinary and commonplace as amazing and surprising, a brave new – but often puzzling and frightening – world seen for the first time.

In 'Walker Brothers Cowboy,' for example, the narrator (who will later develop into the Del Jordan of *Lives of Girls and Women*) is excited when they move to a new town by 'the two movie theatres and the Venus restaurant and Woolworths so marvellous it has live birds in its fan-cooled corners and fish as tiny as fingernails, as bright as moons, swimming in its green tanks' (*Dance* 4). The slightly older Del in *Lives of Girls and Women* itself offers an enthusiastic, impressionistic list of memorable aspects of Jubilee, few of which have been noted by previous chroniclers of Ontario small towns:

I loved the order, the wholeness, the intricate arrangement of town life, that only an outsider could see [but an outsider from a smaller, not a larger community]. Going home from school, winter afternoons, I had a sense of the whole town around me, all the streets which were named River Street, Mason Street, John Street, Victoria Street, Huron Street, and strangely, Khartoum Street; the evening dresses gauzy and pale as crocuses in Krall's Ladies' Wear window; the Baptist Mission Band in the basement of their church, singing 'There's a New Name Written Down in Glory, And it's Mine, Mine, Mine!' Canaries in their cages in the Selrite store and books in the library and mail in the post office and pictures of Olivia de Havilland and Errol Flynn in pirate and lady costumes outside the Lyceum Theatre – all these things, rituals and diversions, frail and bright, woven together – town! (59)

This unqualified acceptance of small-town life will not last, of course; indeed, Del is writing her experience after she has grown out of and away from Jubilee. Yet the initial response, the wide-eyed wonder of it all, is vividly recaptured.

But there is another way in which Munro's perspective differs from those of her predecessors. They are, for the most part, middle-class in origin and attitudes; their perspective is that of the more prosperous members of the town. Del, however, comes from the wrong side of the tracks – or, to use the phrase which she employs in *Lives of Girls and Women* and Munro had significantly employed as the title of an early short story, 'the edge of town' (*Lives* 5). The view of Jubilee we receive at the opening of the book (Del and her mother ultimately move closer to the centre) is oblique, independent, unconventional, not quite respectable. 'The Flats Road,' we are told, 'was not part of town but it was not part of the country either.' It is the area of the idiosyncratic and the unsuccessful: 'There were no real farms ... Most people had one or two acres and a bit of livestock, usually a cow and chickens and sometimes something more bizarre that would not be found on an ordinary farm' (5). Close to the Jordans live the local bootleggers; two idiots also live on the road, and Mitch Plim's wife 'had once worked, though I did not know it then, in Mrs. McQuade's whorehouse' (7). Class distinctions, though generally criticized, are always important in Munro's writing. In *Who Do You Think You Are?* she makes a firm distinction between Hanratty, where 'the social structure ran from doctors and dentists and lawyers to foundry workers and factory workers and draymen,' and West Hanratty, where it ran 'from factory workers and foundry workers down to large improvident families of casual bootleggers and prostitutes and unsuccessful thieves' (4).

There is yet another way in which Munro's presentation of the small town differs from the earlier portraits I have examined. A supreme storyteller herself, Munro, as I indicated in the chapter about entertainments and relaxations, is acutely aware of small communities as places where stories grow and circulate. Rumour, gossip, anecdote, speculation: so often these provide the imaginative sustenance of small towns. Munro is conscious of her regional art growing out of a regional situation. In one interview, for example, referring to the small community in which she lives, she remarked that 'in places like Clinton, memory is always preserved in funny anecdotes. Even terrible things are presented as funny, because people have to live with it that way' (Connolly, n pag). Her stories are full of characters who themselves tell stories: it isn't accidental that one of her stories, which gives its name to the collection in which it appears, is called 'Something I've Been Meaning to Tell You.'

The special interest of *Lives of Girls and Women* derives in part from the fact that, as becomes evident by the end of the book, Del is a girl who intends to grow up and become a writer. What is more, she is going to write about her home town; indeed, we get the decided impression on the last page of the book that the next thing she will do is to sit down and write *Lives of Girls and Women* itself. Certainly, a significant part of the book is taken up with the question of how to attain accuracy, verisimilitude, fairness, authenticity, at any rate the illusion of what Del calls 'real life.' This is why her Uncle Craig's lifelong project of writing a local history of Wawanash County is so important. On the face of it, this is an unpromising subject; as Del remarks, the area 'had been opened up, settled, and had grown, and had entered its present slow decline, with only modest disasters – the fire at Tupperton, regular flooding of the Wawanash river, some terrible winters, a few unmysterious murders; and had produced only three notable people' (27). But for Uncle Craig 'it was daily life that mattered,' and his manuscript (which later gets destroyed in one of those regular floods) becomes 'a great accumulation of the most ordinary facts' (27).

Del will have none of this. When she is given the manuscript after his death, and is urged to complete it, she finds it 'so dead ... so heavy and dull and useless' (52). As she grows older, she projects a novel about Jubilee, but moves in the opposite direction – towards Gothic exaggeration. While basing her story on certain incidents in the life of the leading Jubilee family, she upgrades the head of the family from storekeeper to judge because 'in the families of judges, as of great landowners, degeneracy and madness were things to be counted on.' Similarly, their 'mustard-colored stucco bungalow behind the *Herald-Alliance* building' becomes 'a towered brick house with tiny narrow windows and *porte-cochère* and a great deal of surrounding shrubbery perversely cut to look like roosters, dogs and foxes' (203). When, however, Del is invited into that stucco bungalow and becomes more aware of '[t]he ordinariness of everything' (208), the Gothic trappings collapse, and she realizes that she must write in a different mode. What she wants, she realizes in the last pages of the book, is 'every last thing, every layer of speech and thought, stroke of light on bark and walls, every smell, pothole, pain, crack, delusion, held still and held together – radiant, everlasting' (210). Uncle Craig's 'facts,' then, but facts transformed by the creative imagination, the small town of Jubilee re-created in all its shabbiness and wonder and fascination and grotesquerie and monotony, its life rendered by means of art more real than real.

Attraction/repulsion, nostalgia/bitterness, love/hate. Responses to the Ontario small town – as well as small towns in other places (one thinks of Margaret Laurence's Manawaka) – tend to swing between opposing poles. Munro's fondness for paradox allows her to catch the sense of shifting attitudes in all its complicating vividness. Helen in 'The Peace of Utrecht,' returning to Jubilee after many years, recognizes 'a queer kind of oppression and release' (*Dance* 191). She is reminded of 'certain restrictions of life in Jubilee' and unforgettably evokes 'the quiet, decaying side streets where old maids live' (194, 196). Munro provides an inside view, but most of her characters, like Davies's, leave town at the first opportunity. Del Jordan is poised for flight at the close of *Lives of Girls and Women*; Helen here, Rose in *Who Do You Think You Are?*, the narrator of the frame stories in *The Moons of Jupiter*, have already left. Yet there is also a sense in which they never escape. They carry the imprint of their impressionable small-town years within their minds, and they nearly always return later to haunt their own pasts. The train to Mariposa is always available; Davies's characters usually revisit their small-town birthplaces; by the same token, Munro's protagonists continually return – if not physically, at least in memory.

Even Margaret Atwood's Rennie Wilford in *Bodily Harm*, who is continually making jokes about her 'background' and 'roots,' tries 'to avoid thinking about Griswold at all' (18), yet finds this increasingly impossible as the novel proceeds. One of her sardonic comments about small-town life – that domestic objects 'were considered important because they had once belonged to someone else' (54) – is intended as criticism, but it raises an aspect of the subject that should not be neglected, and it is one which Hugh Hood properly emphasizes: history, and what connects us with the past. Hood is preoccupied with a distinctive sub-species of the Ontario small-town situation in the area he designates 'the great southeast':

'The great southeast' was the local name for that bit of Ontario extending from, say, Deseronto and Napanee and Tweed to the Québec border, with Kingston as its acknowledged capital, a piece-of-pie-shaped region with a culture and speech of its own, intensely conservative and self-preoccupied in its politics, just as Québec was, but far less able to articulate its discontents. (*Motor Boys* 281-2)

These discontents stem from the never-fulfilled promise that seemed to be imminent in the first half of the nineteenth century. Hood divides his attention between Stoverville (= Brockville), one of 'the small river towns' (*Flying* 102), and Athens, representative of the inland centres inhabited by those not socially prominent enough to have a claim to any of the coveted river frontage. Both places have important historical backgrounds. Stoverville is full of rich houses built in the anticipation of a prosperity that never materialized. In *A New Athens*, the death of Flora Maclean in the early 1960s 'signalled the end of the long autumn of Stoverville's third generation of rich men and women,' and it becomes increasingly clear that economic currents have 'passed such places by' (180, 181).

Athens, by contrast, is farming country, although the land in question is relatively poor. Hood lays stress on the impressive architecture of the area, the handsome houses of stone and brick that bear eloquent witness to the rich continuities of family ownership. It is this area that leads Matt Goderich towards his lifelong preoccupation with 'an Ontario style' when he asks himself 'why Stoverville or Athens looked the way they did, what conditions of climate had affected that look, what materials were employed, what designs borrowed and followed' (*New Athens* 70). Above all, Athens is the community that changed its name from prosaic Farmersville in the late nineteenth century to commemorate its efforts to provide high-quality schooling for its children. The gesture sounds hubristic – or, in Matt's words, 'a ridiculous presumption,' but, as he goes on to realize, this is an unfair judgment: 'What they had done wasn't to insinuate that their village was as great, as central to culture as the city of Athens, but only that their schools were in the tradition of the Academy, that human culture is continuous' (59). No veiled sensationalism here, no incest, no oppressive monotony, and even a suggestion of that 'aesthetic sense' which Robertson Davies's Dunstan Ramsay found lacking. Hood's small-town world may veer towards the pastoral sunshine rather than the Gothic darkness, but it provides a salutary reminder that the very persistence of the small town as a focal point in the Ontarian literary consciousness is itself testimony to the continuity of all human experience.

10 *The Smaller Cities*

This will be a relatively short chapter for the simple but sufficient reason that the smaller Ontarian cities have not for the most part attracted the sustained interest of literary artists. This seems to be because they fall between the two stools of cohesive small town and multifaceted large city. All began, of course, as small towns and some remain so in character. To Norman Levine, for instance, Ottawa is 'still a small town,' a 'safe provincial place' (*Canada* 55). Those which grew tended to lose the congenial qualities of a closely knit community without attaining the diversity and sophistication of a large metropolitan centre. Expansion often produced a deadening sameness rather than an intriguing distinction. Their dilemma is nicely caught in the juxtaposition of casual comments by Frances Stewart and the poet Rupert Brooke. Stewart, writing late in life to a grandchild, observed: 'our own little Peterborough ... would be far nicer than Toronto if it were as old, and had the advantages that Toronto has had' (Appendix xxvii). Brooke's comment is more ambiguous: 'no Canadian city can ever be anything better or different. If they are good they may become Toronto' (84).

A further clue is provided by a passage in Robertson Davies's *Tempest-Tost*. One of the characters is searching for the home of another by venturing into a new and relatively poor area of Salterton that he had never explored before:

He walked slowly down one of those roads which are to be found in the new sections of all Canadian cities; rows of small houses lined both sides of the street, and although these little houses were alike in every important respect a miserable attempt had been made to differentiate them by a trifle of leaded glass here, a veneer of imitation stonework there, a curiously fashioned front door in another place, by all the cheap and tasteless shifts of the speculative builder. A glance at one was enough to lay bare the plan of all. (135–6)

Davies is arguing that newer developments, following the age of the bulldozer and the residential estate, impose a basic design that discourages all but the most superficial signs of human individuality. Distinctiveness is not impossible – Davies is about to introduce the novel's most idiosyncratic and colourful character, the musician Humphrey Cobbler, who is strong enough to triumph over his environment – but it becomes notably more difficult to achieve. Suburbia here is virtually identical with suburbia there. Writers can, of course, portray suburbia, but specific locality will not be an important ingredient. Certainly, there are plenty of novels recording Ontarian small-city life – David Helwig's, for instance, based like Davies's Salterton series on Kingston – but they convey a general sense of modern urban living and modern urban values rather than any conspicuously particular impression of a unique place.

Sometimes, indeed, as one finds early references to settlements that are later to develop into important cities, it is the incongruity between early description and later reputation that seems most noteworthy. Hamilton, for instance. As early as 1832 we encounter in *Authentic Letters from Upper Canada* a reference to 'a very pretty place called Hamilton' (Radcliff 77); at about the same time John Langton mentioned 'the pretty village of Hamilton' (26), and Patrick Shirreff called it 'one of the cleanest and most desirable places of residence in Canada' (104). Our post-Stelco perspective picks up these allusions and is intrigued by them, but little substantial follows. True, Sylvia Fraser's first novel *Pandora* (1972), a vivid and somewhat unconventional account of the first eight years of a rebellious girl's life in the period dominated by the Second World War, is set in Mill City, which is recognizably Hamilton, the author's home town. But the emphasis is more socio-political and psychological than topographical. Fraser is primarily interested in the working-class characteristics of her heroine's home, and there is an amusing but satirically telling section on behavioural standards in the area. Here is a specimen:

Standards of Dress: Housedresses, aprons, laddered stockings, are acceptable ... as far as the grocery store, but slacks, bare legs, bandanas, curlers, kimonos are not. A woman, who is going uptown, is expected to put on a hat or hairnet, almost run-less stockings, corsets and her earrings ... To point out that a woman wears mascara is to question her taste. To point out that she uses peroxide is to question her morals.   (33)

Although Fraser's main artistic concerns lie elsewhere, there is a suggestion here of Hugh Garner's Cabbagetown (to be discussed later). This is especially evident when we read that the local residents 'worry that more foreigners will move in from Mediterranean Avenue, though Mrs. Niobe is clean and quiet' (36). However, where Cabbagetown is presented as a unique area that has a character over and above its more general significance, Mill City is first and foremost a representative working-class community. The contrast between the prim and proper 'Paradise Park' and the more proletarian 'Civic Playground' (45–7) depends similarly on a class distinction that has more than local application. The identification with Hamilton is not ultimately integral, though Fraser's may well remain the most extensive fictional presentation of the city at the head of Lake Ontario. There is little else commemorative of Hamilton until we come to David McFadden's passing vignette of his birthplace in (oddly enough) his *Trip around Lake Erie*:

It's a dirty, dreary, burnt-out industrial city, a place covered by a perpetual black cloud, and it's not considered a great place to live. Yet I love its junkyards, its otherworldly skyline, the mysterious 1920ish architecture of its buildings glimpsed through the swirling clouds of soot.   (11)

The overall effect is unsentimental, even unflattering, but such is the dominant literary image.

Much the same, of course, might be said about Sudbury. Miriam Waddington has a poem entitled 'Dead Lakes' which refers to the environs of the city – 'those passive / unstirring waters / without splash / without fish / without waterbugs' (234), and goes on to mention how the 'slag fires / of Sudbury / spill molten metal / on summer midnights' (235). But the best-known literary comment on the city is undoubtedly Raymond Souster's memorable squib:

> '... But only God can make a tree.'
> (He'll never try it in Sudbury.)   (3.246)

Hardly an exhilarating portrait, yet once again this is the *image* of Sudbury that, for good or ill, has become the norm.

Other cities provoke other images. I have already referred to Stratford as the recipient of Reaney's *Twelve Letters to a Small Town*, written just as the Stratford Festival was establishing itself. The success of the festival has contributed to a growth that justifies its reconsideration as a city, but the literary reflection of this status, in Hood's *A New Athens* and Davies's *The Lyre of Orpheus*, focuses on the theatre rather than on the town itself. Other city settings are less specific. Reaney wrote a poem series entitled *The Dance of Death at London, Ontario* (*Poems* 231–50), but apart from a few rather perfunctory place-name references,

London seems to function more as a Canadian alternative to the British capital (and to Basle, home of an earlier *Totentanz*) than as a place with specific local qualities of its own. The emphasis falls on the dance of death as a universal symbol. Similarly, much of Marian Engel's novel *The Glassy Sea* takes place in a London convent, but the location is hardly crucial. There is little point in listing titles where cities play peripheral roles. Three exceptions to the general rule will therefore receive the bulk of our attention: Ottawa as the national (but not provincial) capital, which is a special case; Kingston, which failed in its bid to become the permanent capital of either province or country but which was fortunate enough to stimulate the comic-satiric vision of the young Robertson Davies; and, perhaps surprisingly, Sault Ste Marie.

The Sault Ste Marie of F.G. Paci, which appears as Marionville in his first novel but under its real name thereafter, seems less a city than an ethnic enclave. We get little sense of the city as a whole, but are confined – almost claustrophobically – to the area inhabited for a generation by the Italian community. His three novels, *The Italians* (1978), *Black Madonna* (1982), and *The Father* (1984), all play variations on a basic theme. A single family always provides the focus. In each case, the parents have emigrated from the Abruzzi region of central Italy just after the Second World War, and have settled in 'the West End.' Although they come to find a new life in a new world, they try to bring up their families as if they were still living in rural Italy. The result is forecastable, painful, but also moving.

Each novel becomes an elegy for a lost way of life as the second generation inevitably breaks away from ancestral customs, traditions, and attitudes. The Italian Catholics' God is forced to give way to the relentless principle of Mutability. Those who resist the process suffer, and their sufferings are presented as both sad and inevitable. Assunta, the 'black madonna' of the second novel, 'had never gone beyond short Sunday car rides to the outskirts of the Sault' (7); her son has lived all his life in the West End and complains: '"All I know of the outside world is what I see on television"' (92). He is amazed that his mother had lived over thirty years in Ontario and 'still hadn't learned English' (11). Hers is the extreme example of failure to change. That of Oreste Mancuso in *The Father* is more poignant. He attempts to run a small bakery business in the Italian fashion, but is inevitably overtaken by progress. He explains his philosophy of living to his children: '"the most important people next to your family are your *amici*, your friends in the community ... We all know each other here. We are friends. We help each other out'" (60). An admirable theory – which fails to work in practice in the Sault Ste Marie of the 1960s.

The process is described in *Black Madonna* from the viewpoints of both father and priest. In Adamo's words, "'The kids, they move out first ... As soon as they get enough money to buy a house in the East End. They move away from their parents. They don't want to do with their parents anymore, hey. They become *English*'" (66). Father Sorlo concentrates on the larger pattern when addressing "'You young people'" – "'You grow away from your mother tongue. You lose your culture and your heritage. And then you become strangers with your parents'" (158). Some escape through education to the university and an academic or professional life; others take the way of popular culture (hockey or rock music). With the exception of Aldo in *The Italians* – and even he comes perilously close to abandoning his vocation as a priest – they move away from their Catholic origins. One is seen initially as a pious altar-boy, but he soon lapses; another deeply offends his mother by marrying in a Protestant church. For Stephen Mancuso in *The Father*, the climactic moment comes at high school when he realizes that he can choose between the names of Stefano and Stephen; predictably, he chooses the latter.

The geography of these novels is more symbolic than topographical. It contains a small but carefully selected series of focal points. Firmly in the centre, of course, is the West End itself, a working-class area dominated by Italians but also containing 'pockets of Finns and French Canadians' (*Father* 125), though significantly they never appear. Dominating the landscape, however, are the steel-plant, with its 'large flaming A logo' (*Black Madonna* 20) and, later, the International Bridge. The plant is the most conspicuous employer. It was, we are told,

like a giant fortress rising squatly from a bend on the northern bank of the river. [Alberto] never lost his amazement at how such a structure could function, let alone exist, in the limitless expanse of snow and ice. Past the gate and administrative buildings its mills of dull red and turquoise formed a gigantic maze. (*Italians* 121)

Ultimately, however, it is the bridge, constructed in the 1960s, that has the most radical effect on the lives of the protagonists:

the erection of the International bridge joining the United States to Canada ... had spelled the end of the neighbourhood ... Once city planners saw what the American tourists were seeing as they came over the bridge, urban renewal came in and levelled the eyesores to make room for apartment buildings and old-age homes. (*Black Madonna* 20)

By the end of the decade, the West End 'was a dead neighbourhood with the heart ripped out of it' (*Father* 113).

The three novels, then, chronicle a relentless decline, a decline that is seen in terms of the physical landscape and in terms of the life and fortunes of the Italian community. The two combine in the following account from *The Father* of 'the devastation wrought by Urban Renewal' (133) as seen by the fate of James Street: 'Gone were the grocery stores and pool halls, the hardware and shoe stores, the barber shops and clothing stores, leaving huge gaps in the heart of the neighbourhood. Through the gaps [Stephen] could see the rust-coloured mills of the steel plant toward the west' (134). The West End is symbolically dominated by 'St. Mary's cross,' which 'had the reputation of being the largest free-standing cross in North America' (7). By the late 1970s it is 'unlighted and neglected' (7). At the end of the novel, we are told that it is going to be brought 'back into shape again,' but it is also revealed that, far from being an emblem of Catholic spirituality, it is owned by a 'group of businessmen' and is to be refurbished 'for the tourists' (177). Oreste's bread business has been killed by success: it is now a large organization that mass-produces its products by machinery. Even the tiniest details add to the general picture. The new doctor, for instance, though Italian by name, is second generation and speaks 'very little Italian' (*Black Madonna* 153). Paci's novels are significant, then, not for what they tell us of a particular city but for their insights into the immigrant experience, an experience that we shall see relived and resuffered, with variations, in cities as varied as Ottawa and Toronto.

Robertson Davies's first three novels, *Tempest-Tost* (1951), *Leaven of Malice* (1954), and *A Mixture of Frailties* (1958), are all set in the cathedral city of Salterton, which is clearly modelled so far as many of its basic physical features are concerned – the two cathedrals, a university, a military establishment, a prison – on Kingston. In many respects, despite the jump of a generation in time and the apparent expansion from small town to the dignified status of a city, the emotional distance between Salterton and Leacock's Mariposa is comparatively short. Although the narrator in *Leaven of Malice* echoes Paul of Tarsus by describing Salterton as 'no mean city' (77), it is 'not a large place' in *Tempest-Tost* (9), and Davies, who has clearly been much influenced by *Sunshine Sketches*, portrays it with a Leacockian doubleness that emphasizes its provincial narrowness as well as its old-fashioned charm.

When Davies wrote *Tempest-Tost,* he was brimming with wit and ideas but inexperienced in marshalling and controlling them. As a result there is a detailed description of the city in the opening chapter which is not fully integrated with the context in which it occurs. Nonetheless, it is especially suited to my purpose here in its vivid and concentrated presentation of the atmosphere of a small Canadian city at a particular moment in time:

People who do not know Salterton repeat a number of half-truths about it. They call it dreamy and old-world; they say that it is at anchor in the stream of time ... They say that it is the place where Anglican clergymen go when they die. And, sooner or later, they speak of it as 'quaint.'   (9)

But the narrator, temporarily taking over the tones of Saltertonian self-satisfaction, retorts that it seems quaint only to those 'whose own personalities are not very strongly marked and whose intellects are infrequently replenished' (9). Altogether, it is a tight little city, proud of its English associations, and reflects architecturally the kind of colonialism in which 'what had been done in England was repeated, clumsily and a quarter of a century later, in Canada' (11).

But Davies is at his most perceptive and amusing in his description of the religious attitudes that emanate from the two Salterton cathedrals:

The Catholic cathedral points a vehement and ornate Gothic finger toward Heaven; the Anglican cathedral has a dome which, with offhand, Anglican suavity, does the same thing. St. Michael's cries, 'Look aloft and pray!'; St. Nicholas' says, 'If I may trouble you, it might be as well to lift your eyes in this direction.' The manner is different; the import is the same.   (10)

Like Leacock, Davies is attracted to the genial anomalies of Salterton, where the social standards as well as the religious attitudes of a past age persist into the world of the mid-twentieth century. Mrs Bridgetower initiated her 'First Thursday' At Homes at the time of her marriage just before the First World War, and they continue in dwindling and decrepit fashion up to her death in the mid-1950s. Similarly, although Dean Knapp 'lived in Canada, in the middle of the twentieth century, his clerical ideals were those nineteenth-century clergymen in England who were witty men of the world, as well as men of God' (*Leaven* 60). Matthew Snelgrove, the lawyer, belonged more to the eighteenth century, displaying 'an enthusiasm for the *status quo* and a regret that most of the democratic legislation of the last century could not be removed from the statute books' (*Leaven* 73).

Tempest-Tost and *Leaven of Malice*, in particular, are concerned with the storms in teacups that tend to blow up in small, inward-turned communities, and Davies can laugh with his characters almost as much as he laughs at them. He is adept at isolating significant details, such as the 'strongly Ontario character' of parties in which 'all the ladies gathered in the drawing room, and all the gentlemen gathered in a small room behind it' (*Tempest* 165). One senses, however, that Davies found the intellectual boundaries of Salterton increasingly inhibiting as the series progressed, and as his own powers and ambitions developed. In *A Mixture of Frailties* its attitudes and pretensions are reduced to 'small-town stuff' (162), and Monica Gall, the protagonist, is allowed to escape the limitations of her birthplace and find a more artistically and experientially satisfying world elsewhere. As one character insists, '"Salterton can't be your measure of success or failure; what you think are its standards are just the standards of childhood and provincialism"' (301).

Superficially, then, Salterton gives the impression of the small-town life in Duncan's Elgin or Leacock's Mariposa or Munro's Jubilee extended in size but similar in character and atmosphere. The increase in numbers, however, allows Davies to highlight an element that is less conspicuous in smaller communities: the checks and balances of class. While class distinctions obviously exist in the smaller places – we remember the 'wrong-side-of-the-tracks' perspective in Munro – these are inevitably less rigid in communities where everyone is constantly meeting everyone else in the routines of everyday life. Salterton, however, has grown beyond such closeness and enforced intimacy, and Davies makes us aware, as we read, of the extent to which his characters represent a dominant class with dominating standards. Thus the Salterton Little Theatre in *Tempest-Tost* is a decidedly élite group; the professional director causes a minor crisis when she assigns an important role to a young man who is 'one of the stewards in the liquor store' and so may not be 'acceptable to the rest of the cast' (108). In *Leaven of Malice*, the social and cultural gap between the professional people who constitute the leading characters – Ridley the newspaper editor, Vambrace the professor, Snelgrove the lawyer, etc – and the lower-class world of Ridley's housekeeper and Bevill Higgin (ultimately revealed as the instigator of 'Malice') is considerable. Above all, in *A Mixture of Frailties*, the Bridgetower Trust is hard pressed and apprehensive when it finds itself having to name as its beneficiary an employee of the Glue Works with religious connections that are considered doubtful if not disreputable.

More is involved, however, than a mere sense of awkwardness and unease existing between groups of different social status, educational level, and economic position. The Salterton Little Theatre is not just an élite group in itself; it is controlled by an even more élite inner group. As Mrs Forrester explains, '"Professor Vambrace and I have to do all the real deciding, and get it through the committee, somehow, and then the committee usually carries the meeting'" (*Tempest* 29). The conduct of auditions for the production of Shakespeare's play is as revealing as it is humorous and realistically convincing; we see the inner group deftly manipulating events so that they obtain, at least for the most part, the results they desire. As the novel-series progresses, one gets the impression that the whole city is controlled in much the same way. Furthermore, the ways of Salterton take on a surprisingly close resemblance to the operations of the nineteenth-century Family Compact. Privilege and influence go hand in hand. Salterton, then, means many things for Davies. It is the appropriate historical and social setting for his plots; it is a half-loving, half-satirical fictional portrait of mid-twentieth-century Kingston and other small cities; but ultimately it serves as a microcosm – as a light-hearted but seriously intended commentary on the historical realities of both the province and the country to which it belongs.

Ottawa serves as a microcosm in a very different way, as we shall see. It is capable of provoking drastically opposed reactions. Earle Birney once wrote a poetic inquiry into Vancouver entitled 'Trial of a City'; if Ottawa were on trial, lengthy dossiers could be compiled for both sides. Let us begin, in typically Canadian fashion, with a series of extracts that would bolster the case for the prosecution. One of the most frequently quoted is a remark by Goldwin Smith in the nineteenth century: 'Ottawa is a sub-arctic lumber village converted by royal mandate into a political cockpit' (qtd in MacLennan 100). Davies's Samuel Marchbanks, a century later, is equally aware of its arctic quality: 'as I entered the city by train, and again as I left it, I was painfully struck by its resemblance to a foreign capital which I shall describe only as M-sc-w' (*Papers* 445). For Hugh Hood it is 'a city with no reason to exist except as the seat of a factitious government, with no real industry, commerce, or culture' (*Governor's Bridge* 68). And for the poet Raymond Souster it is condemned for its neglect of his fellow-poet Archibald Lampman:

> Ottawa,
> the city you worked in and died in,
> the city that has done exactly nothing
> for you its most distinguished citizen.   (*Collected Poems* 4.176)

This last reference reminds us, however, that Lampman himself, somewhat unexpectedly, is a prominent witness for the defence. In a prose tribute, he writes in praise of the city as 'a most picturesque and wholesome foundation for the dwelling of men' and goes so far as to forecast that 'Ottawa will become in the course of ages the Florence of Canada, if not of America, and the plain of the Ottawa its Val d'Arno.' Viewed 'at a distance of two or three miles,' he argues, 'it is one of the loveliest cities in the world' (*Mermaid* 255, 256). This point of perspective is, indeed, the key to Lampman's attitude. He would probably have been unhappy in any city 'begotten / Of the labour of men,' and is regularly wearied by 'The blind gray streets, the jingle of the throng' (*Poems* 17, 14). He hates the materialism of Ottawa and any other city – 'The curses of gold are about thee' – but the redeeming grace of Ottawa lies in the fact that the poet can also write: 'Thou art fair as the hills at morning' (215). Continually, in his gently appreciative poems about the landscape of the Ottawa Valley, a distant glimpse of the city adds to the sense of a beauty to which human beings can contribute. In 'September,' for instance, it is 'the wood-wrapt city, swept with light' (155); in 'Winter Uplands,'

> The far-off city towered and roofed in blue
> A tender line upon the western red.   (299)

In a late poem specifically called 'Ottawa,' it is presented as

> A city set like a star
>   Of stone on a soft grey hill.   (*Long Sault* 20)

For a native, indeed, Lampman is unusually positive. In the case of Ottawa, visitors have often outdone the Canadian born in their praise for the city. Thus Anthony Trollope, the English novelist, happened to visit Ottawa only four years after its being named as the Canadian capital. He saw it as a city 'still to be built' (65), but was clearly impressed by the fact that it was 'preparing for itself broad streets and grand thoroughfares' (66). Its geographical situation had 'great charm' for Trollope, if only because its rocky base precluded a grid-plan. While its position 'between two waterfalls' (66) is praised, he maintains that 'the glory of Ottawa will be – and, indeed, already is – the set of public buildings which is now being erected on the rock' (67). Trollope is not easily pleased, as will be seen in his comments on Toronto, so this note of approval carries weight. Half a century later, in 1913, Rupert Brooke was similarly positive. He had high praise for its general atmosphere: 'Ottawa came as a relief after Montreal ... the city seems conscious of other than financial standards, and quietly, with dignity, aware of her own purpose' (54). He later refines this impression by articulating 'an atmosphere of safeness and honour and massive buildings and well-shaded walks' (55). Despite being built in 'an unfortunate period' architecturally, the Parliament Buildings possess both dignity and beauty, and Brooke is not confined to tourist-like description; he remarks shrewdly that 'the rich and the poor ... live nearer each other in Ottawa than in most cities' (56). All in all, 'what Ottawa leaves in the mind is a certain graciousness' (57). But the most surprising outsider's report of all is that of Wyndham Lewis. In the middle of excoriating Toronto and all it stands for in *Self Condemned*, he judges Ottawa 'the finest capital city of the new world' (357).

Why these extraordinarily conflicting reports? They are partly explained, of course, by the city's curious history. Owing its existence to the development of the lumber trade during the Napoleonic Wars, and originally called Bytown after Colonel By, a soldier-engineer responsible for the building of the Rideau Canal, it became a centre for the shantymen and gained, in Max Braithwaite's words, 'a reputation as the roughest town in the country' (135). Queen Victoria, in proclaiming it the site of the nation's capital in 1857, was presumably advised of its strategic and diplomatic promise rather than of its moral character. The change in no more than a few decades from the wildness of Bytown to the comparative staidness of the Ottawa of Lampman and Duncan Campbell Scott is remarkable, but could hardly have been achieved without the occasional survival of the rough amid the smooth.

No one, I think, catches this ambiguous quality of the city better than Hugh MacLennan in his chapter on the Ottawa River in *Seven Rivers of Canada* (1961). Like Lampman, but three-quarters of a century later, he is conscious of the 'contrast between the settled and the wild' not only in the general area but within the city itself. The capital, indeed, becomes an appropriate microcosm for Canada as a whole:

There almost every influence in the country is visible and many of them are at odds with one another. Perhaps within twenty-five years' time the nation's capital will have become the beautiful, ordered thing the National Capital Planning Commission intends, but today its mixture of rawness and dignity reminds one of pictures of Washington at the time of the Civil War, except that the contrasts are all Canadian. (95)

MacLennan goes on to present this contrast in the imaginative-cum-documentary style that has become the hallmark of his novels:

Nobody can look at Parliament Hill, especially in the evening from the little park behind the Château Laurier, without being reminded of ancient France, of Westminster and of Edinburgh Castle. Yet that splendid composition stands isolated in the commonplace red brick of old Bytown, and faces across the river not only to the Laurentian wilds, but also to one of the biggest lumber stacks in the country. The last time I was in Ottawa there shone at night, on top of that hideous industrial congeries in Hull, in brilliant Neon, a huge advertisement for toilet paper.   (95).

After reading MacLennan, it is virtually impossible not to regard Ottawa as a symbolic city.

   Another potentially symbolic element, hinted at by Brooke's comment about the proximity of rich and poor, is the national capital's geographical and social division into Upper and Lower Town. Much of Upper Town, of course, is taken up with Parliament and all its associated public buildings and services. This aspect of the city makes various fleeting appearances in literature when, as in the case of some of Hood's novels, the plot requires a glimpse into the corridors of power, or when, in Jack Hodgins's 'Invasions '79,' a bittersweet story of doomed human intimacy is played out against an embassy setting. Socially, of course, Duncan Campbell Scott lived and belonged to Upper Town (Lampman moved between the two, though he had little to say about Lower Town in his writings). George Johnston deftly catches the official bilingual aspects of Ottawa in his poem 'Bicultural' (93–4), which itself intersperses lines of French and English. Johnston has fun with the bilingual versions of the city's name – 'Ottawattawattawa' becomes 'Outtaouttaouttaoua' – though, referring to the prominent French presence in the area, he describes how

> L'enfant éternal joue
> Dans les rues tristes de ton Lower Town.

He is more concerned, however, with parliamentary jargon –

> Words that are not what they seem
> ...
> Words that round the world resound
> With a House of Commons sound
> Noncommittal and profound –

and (inevitably) with the harsh climate, the wind

> that hunts all day
> And all night too, and searches out
> The shivers in our hearts.

The rest of Johnston's urban poetry has little *specific* reference, though he taught in Ottawa for many years, and the 'small suburban life' (23) presented in his first volume, *The Cruising Auk*, has been seen by the poet-critic D.G. Jones as reflecting 'the world of Ottawa – Lampman's Ottawa' ('Johnston' 85). The society presented, however, could be any Anglo-Saxon-dominated middle-class small town or small city. Nonetheless, its local associations once inspired Raymond Souster to announce:

> Ottawa for me, George Johnston,
> lies at the bottom of your street.   (*Collected Poems* 3.325)

There can be no doubt, however, that the writer who has in literary terms made Ottawa his own is Norman Levine – and Levine's Ottawa is decidedly Lower Town. His short stories inhabit a borderline zone between fictional construct and autobiographical memoir, as a comparison between a story like 'A Memory of Ottawa' and the equivalent narrative in his rather embittered *Canada Made Me* will show. Significantly, 'A Memory of Ottawa' begins in the lobby of the Château Laurier, where the narrator – as close to Levine himself as makes no difference – is waiting for an airport limousine. Impulsively, he decides to cross the Rideau Canal 'to go back to the places I knew as a child some twenty years ago' (*One Way* 174). This is a pattern – from Upper Town to Lower Town, from present to past – that recurs continually in his work; again and again the atmosphere of the modern capital is contrasted with the other Ottawa of his parents' generation to which he endeavours to return as a tentative and restless ghost.

When necessary, Levine can paint a vivid, impressionistic portrait of the tourists' picture-postcard Ottawa – 'the frozen canal, the trees like snakes, white snakes devouring the black' (*Canada* 37) or (a now vanished sight) 'red street cars like mechanical geese [that] swayed and clattered along the tracks' (*One Way* 174). Yet these are ultimately peripheral. For Levine, Murray Street, where his formative years as a child were spent, manifests itself as the imaginative centre of his early life and a focal point in his art. A whole section of *Canada Made Me* is devoted to the street. It immediately sparks off a sour nostalgia:

The same dull shabby boxes with wooden verandas and the walls so thin that you can hear every word that the neighbour says. The dungyards frozen hard in winter and crawling in summer with white maggots from the wooden manure boxes; the gloom from the warm smelling horsestables; the rats; the washing lines.   (44)

But Murray Street 'cuts right through Lower Town' and connects the various sections of the city. At one end is the Catholic section with two schools and a Bishop's Palace, and nearby 'a large barn, the end of a streetcar line,' where he is later to set his short story 'Champagne Barn.' 'At the other end of the street, past the synagogue, the Boulevard, are the wooden shacks, the poor French, the rough taverns ... And clustered near it is the centre of Ottawa the tourist knows: the Château Laurier, the Parliament Buildings, the By Ward Market, and the Basilica' (44–5). Here, then, Upper and Lower Town almost touch, but the part of Murray Street that Levine came to know as 'home' was further to the east, 'where most of the fruit and vegetable and rag pedlars of Ottawa lived.' Levine's father, who emigrated from Warsaw in early middle age and 'only knew a few words of English and a few words of French' (*Thin Ice* 31), was one of these. As a teenager Levine would sometimes accompany him on his rounds, and to this may be attributed his encyclopedic knowledge of the details of the city; in his own words, 'I doubt if there was anyone in the city who knew the streets of Ottawa physically as well as these men' (*Canada* 47).

Levine paints a memorable portrait in *Canada Made Me* of the Jewish and Catholic pocket from which he came. As a Jew himself, he remembers the 'drab houses, the rich food, the smells, the candles,' and an outside service by the river combining 'the Hebrew Chant, the sound of birds and frogs, bulrushes, leaves, sky' (47); as an outsider he recalls watching the Catholic procession through the street at Corpus Christi. The men in this community, he claims, were without ambition and apparently content with their humble life in this circumscribed area that seemed 'like a village.' But 'it was the wife who goaded on the man to give up the horse and wagon for a truck; to make money, to move away from Murray Street to a better district' (47). At all events the next generation, Levine's own generation, 'moved away from Murray Street and began to cover up their tracks' (48). The process haunts Levine. His short story 'In Lower Town' documents the complexities and tensions of this social mix. It was, he grants, 'a very democratic place' (*Thin Ice* 33), and as a schoolboy he was often invited to the homes of his richer classmates – one whose father was aide-de-camp to the Governor-General, another the son of a doctor who had his own boat to cruise along the Rideau Canal. But Levine couldn't reciprocate; he was ashamed 'of the house that smelled of the stable, and of parents who couldn't speak English.' He confesses:

I used to go to school day-dreaming that I had other parents, pretending I lived somewhere else. And wondering when I could get away from here. (33)

He got away, of course, but he has continually felt impelled to return:
'I find I am unable to stay away from it. It's become like a magnet'
(*Thin Ice* 34). But his later visits become, inevitably, a search for what
can never be recaptured. The past is past; Lower Town has changed.
His sometime companions, the self-made generation, have moved away,
and lack Levine's urge to go back. He cannot resist another sentimental
journey, but when he tells his mother where he has been she is unimpressed: '"I haven't been back there for over ten years," she said ...
"That's the old life – it's finished"' (36). She looks forward to a new era
of high-rises and motorways; he is resignedly aware of what will have
been lost.

In *Canada Made Me*, he could write that, though the fruit and rag
pedlars had died or moved away, 'Murray Street had not changed' (61);
now, however, like Paci's 'West End' of Sault Ste Marie, it is being
physically transformed — which means destroyed: 'The streets were
being altered, the wooden houses demolished and other houses had
doors and windows boarded up waiting to be pulled down' (*Thin Ice*
35). 'In Lower Town' takes on a tinge of elegiac sadness:

'They're knocking the wooden houses down,' I said. 'And changing the streets.
Soon there will be nothing left of the place the way it was.'   (36)

The story ends with the image of a Catholic convent on Rideau Street
being unceremoniously wrecked ('"You can't make a buck out of a
convent on Rideau Street"' [37]). It becomes, however, by extension,
the objective correlative of a deeply personal loss. The last sentences
read: 'It was all very tidy. Nothing to show that there ever had been a
convent there at all' (37).

All this may seem an exceptionally personal statement, and in some
respects it is. Yet, as we read, we come to understand his account in a
more representative way. He is insistent, after all, that Canada made
him, which means that Ontario and Ottawa's Lower Town made him. In
coming from Europe to create a new life in the New World, Levine's
parents were doing what thousands had done before them. The practice
of establishing themselves, and then watching their children break away
from their attitudes and ideals, is a sadly recurrent one. In focusing on
this pattern, in scratching the sores of his rootlessness, as it were, Levine
is indirectly analysing a profoundly significant process. That the recurrent
drama is played out on the streets of the nation's capital is disturbingly
appropriate.

Part Three:
'Famed Toronto Town'

11 *The Growth of Toronto*

At least two local ballads written to commemorate incidents during the 1837 Rebellion employ the phrase 'famed Toronto town' (Moir 2, 12). At that time, however, with the exception of an Indian encampment and the early small French fort, the area was less than fifty years away from uncleared forest, and had only been incorporated under its present name three years earlier. The provincial capital is, therefore, a city whose foreshortened and concentrated history involves rapid development and continual change. This change can be conveniently traced in the nicknames that have accumulated over the past two hundred years, nicknames which provide a potted history of the evolution I shall be tracing in the course of the next three chapters. What began as 'Muddy York' soon turned into 'Toronto the Good,' 'Tory Toronto,' 'The City of Churches.' An inevitable reaction followed, first through political and sectarian irony – 'The Rome of the Orange Order' or 'the Rome of Methodism'; then, by means of a kind of judgmental backlash, a perceived change in the city's reputation led to moral rejection – 'the Ontario Babylon,' 'Babylon on the Humber.' The tone of such nicknames can vary bewilderingly from 'Hick Town' at one extreme to 'the Queen City' at the other.

How did it all start? By a happy chance we are favoured with continuing literary impressions of Toronto from its very beginnings as an English settlement – even, indeed, a little before those beginnings. It is well known, of course, that a French trading post on the site was succeeded by the already mentioned log fort with its small garrison, and that this fort was burned when the French abandoned it in 1759. Not long afterwards, Jonathan Carver, who based his *Travels through the Interior Parts of North America*, published in 1778, on journeys undertaken in the previous decade, made the following comment: 'On the north-west parts of this lake [Ontario], and to the south-east of Lake Huron, is a tribe of Indians called Missisauges, whose town is denominated Toronto' (171). The site is mentioned again when Alexander Henry embarks from 'Toranto' on his journey back to Montréal from Michilimackinac (Henry 172). And a few years after that, in 1788, the first official survey and plans were drawn up by a captain of the Royal Engineers.

But it was, of course, John Graves Simcoe, first lieutenant-governor of Upper Canada, who was responsible for the choice and development of the site for the future city. We even have a description by Joseph Bouchette, another surveyor, recalling conditions immediately prior to the work carried out in 1793:

I still distinctly recollect the untamed aspect which the country exhibited when first I entered the beautiful basin ... Dense and trackless forests lined the margin of the lake, and reflected their inverted images in its glassy surface. The wandering savage had constructed his ephemeral habitation beneath their luxuriant foliage – the group then consisting of two families of Messassagas – , and the bay and neighbouring marshes were the hitherto uninvaded haunts of immense coveys of wild fowl: indeed, they were so abundant as in some measure to annoy us during the night.   (1.89n)

Possibly Bouchette had heard one of the two traditional explanations for the name Toronto, 'trees in the water' (the other, generally accepted one is merely 'place of meeting').

Because Elizabeth Simcoe, the lieutenant-governor's wife, was a diarist with a genuine if somewhat unorthodox feeling for English prose, the days of planning and founding are clearly and conveniently recorded. In her entry for 13 May 1793, while they were living at Niagara, she records how her husband returned from a visit to the area and how he 'speaks in praise of the harbour & a fine spot near it covered with large Oak which he intends to fix upon as a scite [site] for a Town' (95). Two months later, she accompanies him on a visit, and writes about the place with some enthusiasm. At this point the characteristic mixture of English and Indian names begins. She refers charmingly to 'the high lands of Toronto' and continues:

The Shore is extremely bold & has the appearance of Chalk Cliffs but I believe they are only white Sand. They appeared so well that we talked of building a summer Residence there & calling it Scarborough.   (102)

These 'high lands' are now known as Scarborough Bluffs. Similarly, like many another homesick traveller, she searches for resemblances to earlier landscapes: 'The Sands towards the lake remind me of the Sands at Weymouth' (102). As well as being a favourite haunt of George III, the Dorsetshire Weymouth was famous as a health resort, and Mrs Simcoe believes that this connection holds also: 'The air on these Sands is peculiarly clear & fine. The Indians esteem this place so healthy that they come & stay here when they are ill' (103). She returned again in October and mentions 'the firing when York was named' (108) – her husband favouring English over Indian names. The Simcoes left a further mark on the nomenclature of Toronto by building a cabin for their son Francis on the eastern side and playfully but permanently christening the area Castle Frank.

A generation later, Mary O'Brien recorded in her journal how her old German friend Balser Munshaw had been reminiscing about his early days as a settler within a year or so of the official founding: 'Then there was barely a road chopped through the forest, and York contained only two stores and not a single frame house' (93). Nonetheless, when the artist and writer George Heriot arrived in 1801, expansion had clearly begun:

The town, according to the plan, is projected to extend to a mile and a half in length, from the bottom of the harbour, along [the banks of Toronto bay]. Many houses are already completed, some of which display a considerable degree of taste. The advancement of this place to its present condition has been effected within the lapse of six or seven years, and persons who have formerly travelled in this part of the country, are impressed with sentiments of wonder, on beholding a town which may be termed handsome, reared as if by enchantment, in the midst of a wilderness. (1.138–9)

Such assessments, however, tend to vary dramatically in relation to the temperament and experience of the writers. Certainly Dr William 'Tiger' Dunlop was less impressed when he came to serve as military physician during the War of 1812. Reminiscing a generation later (by which time York had reverted to its Indian name), he remarks succinctly: 'Toronto was then a dirty straggling village, containing about sixty houses' (56). The town, such as it was, suffered a crippling setback at this time when its public buildings were burned by the Americans after their brief occupation during the hostilities. This may explain why the descriptions coming down to us from this period are almost invariably critical. John Howison, who spent two and a half years in Upper Canada, stayed in York only 'an hour or two' (57). He found the land around the town 'low, swampy, and apparently of inferior quality,' the trade 'very trifling,' and summed up: 'it is destitute of every natural advantage except that of a good harbour' (55). Edward Allen Talbot, who arrived in 1818, complained of the unfinished streets as, 'if possible, muddier and dirtier than those of Kingston,' and clearly did not share Elizabeth Simcoe's optimistic sentiments: 'The situation of the town is very un-healthy; for it stands on a piece of low marshy land, which is better calculated for a frog-pond, or beaver-meadow, than for the residence of human beings' (1.102). Frances Stewart, reporting five years later, agrees:

The town or village of York looked pretty from the lake as we sailed up in a schooner, but on our landing we found it not a pleasant place, as it is sunk down in a little amphitheatre cut out of the great bleak forest ... It is not a healthy town (fever and ague are common) ... a deadness hangs over everything. (15)

George Head was hardly more positive when he passed through in the early 1820s: 'On arriving at York, I was disappointed at the first sight of the capital of Upper Canada, which, although covering a large space of ground, was extremely straggling and irregular' (175). The future artist Paul Kane was brought to York from Ireland in 1818, and grew up there in the 1820s and early 1830s. He describes it as 'Little York, muddy and dirty, just struggling into existence.' In later life, however, he nostalgically remembered 'hundreds of Indians' visible in what he calls, inaccurately, his 'native village' and regrets that, in 'the City of Toronto, bursting forth in all its energy and commercial strength,' to which he returned in 1845 after spending almost a decade in the United States and Europe, 'the face of the red man is now no longer seen' (lxii). Other brief glimpses of the place that we catch from this period include some comments on its hostelries. Head found his inn 'not by any means prepossessing' (175), and at about the same time John Galt made his fictional character Bogle Corbet stay at the factual 'Steam boat Hotel,' which he describes as 'a raw, plank-built house' where the guests 'all mess at one common table' (54). He is struck by the 'taciturnity' of most of the company, and records his impressions in detail because it afforded him 'a view of habits and manners considerably dissimilar to those of England' (53). For Patrick Shirreff a few years later, this was 'an indifferent establishment in the sleeping department' (147). Such was Toronto, then, as the large wave of settlers from the United Kingdom was beginning to arrive.

Mary O'Brien (then Gapper) arrived in October 1828, just at the time when the future city was beginning to expand rapidly. It was now becoming the subject for frequent description and comment by settler and traveller alike. She had come via New York, and on first appearance this much smaller (and newer) York 'did not cut so gay an appearance as the Yankee towns, from the absence of the spires which always abounded there' (15), an interesting comment, since, within a generation or so, Toronto would become famous for its spires. Nonetheless, it is clearly beginning to take on the attributes of a city. As she comments somewhat sardonically in the same month, the inhabitants 'are making such rapid strides in civilization as to have had two murderers tried and condemned at the same assizes' (22). By early the next year, a pioneering equivalent of urban sprawl appears to be under way: 'The town of York ... seems to be all suburb. The streets are laid out parallel and at right angles to each other, and are formed by low, scattered houses. The shops are numerous but do not make much show ... [T]he town is so scattered that I hardly know where the centre may be' (34–5). She stayed with her brothers near Thornhill, then married and went to live at Lake Simcoe, so her visits to York/Toronto were occasional. (Before she even arrived, by the way, she wrote of York 'which ... either was or ought to be called Toronto' [7].) Later references regularly acknowledge its enlargement and improvement. As early as August 1829 the shops are found to be 'so much improved that it is hardly worthwhile to send for any common things from England' (70).

Once again, however, we encounter the pattern of local enthusiasm (based, doubtless, on the awareness of dramatic progress) dampened by the dour reactions of newcomers. In the *Emigrant's Guide* (1831), one George Henry had, to quote G.P. de T. Glazebrook, 'commented favourably on what he saw in York in 1831: Government House, Upper Canada College, the commodious hospital, the court house (then occupied by the Assembly) and "many elegant private residences,"' while the author of the *York Commercial Directory, Street Guide and Register* for 1833–4 had claimed that the future Toronto '"luxuriates in the solid evidences of a well-directed industry"' (Glazebrook 55, 43). By 1836, Mary O'Brien is further surprised: 'There is hardly anything left of the cabinet-maker order except a few old houses in the principal parts of the town. Large brick houses of three and four storeys are taking their place everywhere, and a complete new town is rising up about the government end' (248). But to Anne Langton's mother in the following year, the first view of Toronto (it is officially and permanently Toronto now) 'appeared flat and agueish,' and she continues in a spirit of depression: 'Our road to the Hotel, on a wooden foot-path with unpaved street, gave one at first a poor opinion of the Capital of [Upper] Canada, and our reception at the Hotel was most uncomfortable' (A. Langton 19).

The most intelligent as well as acid-tongued of the travellers in Upper Canada, Anna Jameson, had arrived between the time of O'Brien's report and that of Mrs Langton. She agrees with the latter. Though well aware of Toronto's short history, she is notably unimpressed by the strides purportedly made. *Winter Studies and Summer Rambles in*

Canada begins with a diary entry for December 1836 that reads as follows: 'Toronto, – such is now the sonorous name of this sublime capital, – was, thirty years ago, a wilderness, the haunt of the bear and the deer, with a little, ugly, inefficient fort, which, however, could not be more ugly or inefficient than the present one' (1.1). She had arrived by boat from Niagara, and her first impression was unfortunate: 'as I stepped out of the boat I sank ankle-deep into mud and ice' (1.11). Her lightning sketch of the place is vivid but the reverse of flattering:

A little ill-built town on low land, at the bottom of a frozen bay, with one very ugly church, without tower or steeple; some government offices, built of staring red brick, in the most tasteless, vulgar style imaginable; three feet of snow all around; and the grey, sullen, wintry lake, and the dark gloom of the pine forest bounding the prospect; such seems Toronto to me now. (1.2)

What she had not expected to find – but did find – was 'the worst evils of our old and most artificial social system at home, with none of its *agrémens*, and none of its advantages' (1.98). It is worth remembering at this point that she is writing within a year of William Lyon Mackenzie's attempt at rebellion. Her summing-up is damning: 'Toronto is like a fourth or fifth rate provincial town, with the pretensions of a capital city' (1.98).

At this stage in its development, Toronto is obviously going through a period of youthful uncertainty, subject to the enthusiastic prophecies of the optimistic but also to the chastening warnings of the sceptical. Elizabeth Simcoe, with her confidence in the health of the site, would have been shocked by Jameson's curt reference to the 'unhealthiness of its situation, – in a low swamp not yet wholly drained' (1.15). But Jameson is not completely negative. While she finds Toronto 'worse ... than other small communities' because 'it is remote from all the best advantages of a high state of civilization' and is 'infected by all its evils, all its follies,' she also finds it 'better' because 'besides being a small place, it is a *young* place' and 'it must advance – it may become the thinking head and beating heart of a nation, great, and wise, and happy; – who knows?' (1.105). For all her criticism – what she later calls her 'ill-humoured and impertinent *tirades* against Toronto' (2.4) – she is prepared to grant signs of progress.

A little later, however, Jameson surprises with the following remarkable passage:

There are ... good shops in the town, and one, that of the apothecary, worthy of Regent-street in its appearance ... Two years ago we bought our books at the same shop where we bought our shoes, our spades, our sugar, and salt pork; now we have two good booksellers' shops, and at one of these a circulating library of two or three hundred volumes of common novels. As soon as there is a demand for something better, there will be a supply of course, but, as I said before, we must have *time*.   (1.270-1)

I have described this passage as 'remarkable' not so much for its content as for its employment of those unexpected first-person plurals – as if Jameson, against her basic convictions, were being drawn into the society she elsewhere finds so irksome. Indeed, she goes so far as to speculate that she might even 'leave [Toronto] with regret' (2.4). In the event, she 'felt no sorrow' on departing (2.36), but her remarks about the fledgling city at least end on a note that allows for the possibility of change and growth.

Captain Frederick Marryat, in his time famous as the author of adventure stories about the sea, paid two brief visits to Toronto in 1837 and 1838, just after Jameson left, in the course of a more extensive visit to the United States recorded in his *Diary in America* (1839). Like her, he brings a critical outsider's view to bear on the growing town (he disdains to grace it with the word 'city'); the hotels and inns, for example, are judged to be 'very bad,' and in general he finds it, 'from its want of spires and steeples, by no means an imposing town.' The main interest of his account, however, derives from his determined comparison of Toronto houses with their equivalents in the United States, particularly in Buffalo:

The private houses of Toronto are built, according to the English taste and desire for exclusiveness, away from the road, and are embowered by trees; the American, let his house be ever so large, or his plot of ground however extensive, builds within a few feet of the road, that he may see and know what is going on.

Marryat goes on to generalize: 'You do not perceive the bustle, the energy, and activity at Toronto, that you do at Buffalo, nor the profusion of articles in the stores' (136).

Sir Richard Bonnycastle, in *The Canadas in 1841*, comments, like Jameson, on general cultural matters, but seems even less positive. 'The public amusements in Toronto,' he writes, 'are not of a nature to attract much attention ... A national Literary and Philosophical Society was by great exertion established; but, after being in a wavering state for about a year, it dropped' (1.168). A year later, however, Charles Dickens's report in *American Notes* (1842) is very different, and reads as if it might have been intended as a point-by-point refutation of Marryat:

the town itself is full of life and motion, bustle, business, and improvement. The streets are well paved, and lighted with gas; the houses are large and good; the shops excellent. Many of them have a display of goods in their windows, such as may be seen in thriving country towns in England, and there are some which would do no discredit to the metropolis itself ...

... the footways in the thoroughfares which lie beyond the principal streets are planked like floors, and kept in very good and clean repair.   (556–7)

Change and expansion, then, if not growth in the social and cultural sense of the term, seem the predominant features manifest in literary glimpses of Toronto in the 1840s. Politics, however, was another matter. Dickens wrote at this time to his friend and future biographer, John Forster: '[t]he wild and rabid toryism of Toronto is, I speak seriously, *appalling*' (Forster 275).

The most vivid, albeit semi-fictional account of mid-century Toronto is provided by 'Patrick Slater' (pseudonym for John Mitchell) in *The Yellow Briar*, a book not published until 1933 but based on the orally transmitted experiences of Mitchell's Irish grandparents. Part of the dramatic change in the city's character at this time may well be attributable to the notable influx of Irish immigrants; Glazebrook reports that by 1848 – that is, just after the disastrous Irish potato famine – 'more than a third of the people of Toronto had been born in Ireland' (108). At all events, old Paddy Slater first saw Toronto while he was still a boy, and it seemed to him 'a stirring, big town' full of bustling commotion: 'There were brawls a'plenty for the seeing, and startling street fires by night. Then, too, there were the public hangings. Adventure bunted into a fellow round any corner' (25). At the same time he offers charming vignettes of 'chivying the cows along Queen Street to a pasture field to the west' (28), and reports that, with a population of seventeen thousand, 'the little city had 136 full licensed taverns and 32 shops with liquor shop licences' (27). The days of 'Toronto the Good' are obviously far in the future.

A very different glimpse of Toronto at mid-century comes from the pen of Susanna Moodie, who – and this is a timely reminder of the barriers of distance before the age of the railway and the automobile – had lived for twenty years in southeastern rural Ontario before making her first visit to the expanding city. Her opportunity came in the eventual realization of a long-anticipated visit to Niagara Falls, the account of which forms the basis for *Life in the Clearings* (1853). Unlike modern visitors, but like several of the earlier travellers I have quoted (including Jameson), she approached Toronto by water: 'We rounded the point of the interminable, flat, swampy island that stretches for several miles in front of the city' (205). As so often with Moodie's enigmatic prose, it is not always certain precisely what effect she wants to communicate when she writes: 'A grey mist still hovered over its many domes and spires; but the new University and the Lunatic Asylum stood out in bold relief' (205). A satiric/symbolic juxtaposition? Uncertainty increases when we realize that she goes on to devote a whole chapter to the asylum but has nothing more to say about the university. In other writers (again including Jameson) acid irony might be assumed, but Moodie proceeds to offer a decidedly positive report on the city as a whole. Toronto 'exceeded the most sanguine expectations' she had formed of it at a distance, and she is impressed by its 'fresh, growing, healthy vitality' (206). She twice alludes to its 'handsome' public buildings, and, contrary to the fairly recent testimony of O'Brien and Marryat, observes that it is now 'very rich in handsome churches, which form one of its chief attractions' (208) – a feature often alluded to in the later decades of the century. King Street, she believes, may be regarded as 'the Regent-Street of Toronto' (208). Above all, she writes in praise of 'the beautiful trees which everywhere abound in the neat, well-kept gardens that surround the dwellings of the wealthier inhabitants' (206). One gets the sense of a city beginning to take pride in its distinctiveness.

Even at this time, however, comments range from enthusiastic praise to reserved coolness. The former is represented by Charles Horton Rhys, who embarked on a theatrical tour through North America. For him 'Toronto is the handsomest town we have yet seen. Wide streets, good shops, lovely gardens, handsome public buildings, churches rich in spires and traceried windows, spacious hotels and elegant equipages' (qtd in Kilbourn 38). That eulogy appeared in 1861. The following year, Anthony Trollope offered a counter-statement. 'Toronto as a city,' he wrote, 'is not generally attractive to a traveller.' He reports that the lake 'has no attributes of beauty,' and, while granting that the streets 'are better than those of the other towns, the roads round it are worse' (74). So far as Trollope is concerned, the newly built university (now University College) is 'the glory of Toronto' (73).

Nonetheless, different eyes take note of different features. Walt Whitman, passing through Toronto in 1880, in his turn contradicts Trollope: 'As we approach Toronto everything looks doubtly beautiful, especially the glimpses of blue Ontario's waters.' He praised the 'long and elegant streets of semi-rural residences, many of them very costly & beautiful,' remarking in particular that 'the horse chestnut is the prevalent tree – you see it everywhere' (qtd in Kilbourn 38). At about the same time, Stephen Leacock got his first glimpse of the city, and once again brought together the images of tree-lined streets and conspicuous recent church-building: 'Its streets were embowered in leaves above which rose the many spires of the churches' (*Boy* 69–70).

By this time, it seems as if the character of Toronto has changed once more. Such, certainly, is the impression one receives from Robert Barr's account in *The Measure of the Rule*. This is a rather tiresome novel which explores the less than absorbing topic of imperfections in the conduct of the Toronto Normal School (teachers' college). The setting is often more interesting than the plot. Although not published until 1907, it draws for its material on the author's own experiences as a young man in the early 1870s. The opening pages contain a vivid portrait of a Toronto we have not yet encountered. The protagonist, Tom Prentiss, had grown up in the country, and his adventures in the provincial capital often read like those of a nineteenth-century Lucky Jim. On his arrival, however, his wide-eyed naiveté seems close to Thomas Hardy's Jude with his sublime vision of Oxford/Christminster. From his first sight of 'the lofty canopy of the Union Station' (1) – not, be it noted, the present building – Tom is overawed by the wonders of the big city:

The streets presented all the splendour of an Arabian tale transported north; the shops were ablaze with light; the pavement thronged with an effervescent people. The street was musical with the tinkle of silver-tongued bells, and alive with the swift motion of spirited horses and gliding sleighs. This capital was a city of hilarious youth, with the riches of the world displayed behind sheets of plate-glass, transparent as curtains of dew. (8)

A little later, 'the taller Norman tower of University College' observed above the trees is described as 'the most magnificent [he] had ever seen' (9).

Tom arrives in Toronto in winter, and what he sees of the city's recreation at that time is as fresh for us as it was for him:

After lunch I wandered down to the Bay, and there, in the brilliant sunshine, saw an unaccustomed sight – three miles or more of dismantled shipping frozen in at the wharfs, as if they were all Arctic schooners that had lined up against the North Pole. But the Bay itself, with its glittering surface of clear ice, showed an animated scene in striking contrast to the frozen ships. Near the wharfs hundreds of skaters were disporting themselves, and even further out adventurous parties were gliding along the glare ice, a feat not without its dangers in spite of the expertness with which the swift ice-boats were managed. These ice-yachts, which seemed to consist of one huge white sail, flitted here and there at incredible speed, like dragon-flies, each a dragon-fly shorn of one wing and therefore kept from bearing aloft the dot of a body. The single wide-spread wing was out of all proportion to the tiny hull, and flying across the breeze these winter gulls shot through space at a rate considerably in excess of the wind ...   (37–8)

This is Toronto of the 1870s at play. But Tom also becomes aware of the fact that Toronto has a more serious and solemn side. As a hotel-clerk points out, '"We have more schools than taverns in this town, and I believe it's the only city in existence which totters under so unequal a balance of things"' (36). And a poor acquaintance introduces him to 'Church Street, the most godly of thoroughfares, said to contain more places of worship than any similar mile of road in the world' (54). *The Measure of the Rule* is, however, a less interesting novel than these extracts suggest, partly because it never finds a satisfactory way of reconciling the lighter, flippant aspects of its subject with the dour moral realities of 'Toronto the Good.'

Great strides have already been made in eighty years, but it would be a mistake to assume that Joseph Bouchette's '[d]ense and trackless forests' were wholly a thing of the past, or that the growing city covered anything like its present extent. We get a very different, balancing perspective of Toronto at this period from Ernest Thompson Seton in his autobiography. *Trail of an Artist-Naturalist* was not published until 1940, but Seton's memories take him back to the city of the 1870s. And what impresses him most forcibly is its accessibility to wilderness. By modern standards, his Toronto is still tiny: 'In those days, Wilton Avenue (near Dundas Street) was virtually the north boundary of the city, east of Yonge Street. North of that were open fields; then St. James' Cemetery; then a wilderness of ravines and thick woods, opening out on the Don Flats' (102). Urban and rural coexisted peaceably. Present-day Torontonians are all used to the squirrels, and many are aware of the surprisingly large number of rac-coons, while bird-watchers can compile an impressively long list of species regularly encountered within the city limits. Even so, Seton's recollections are striking. He claims to have seen, on about 20 April 1876, the last of the great flocks of doomed passenger-pigeons as it passed over the city (115), reports that '[e]agles of two species were quite nu-merous about Toronto in these early days' (93), and recalls, from as late as 1892, a wild fox living near Bloor Street not far east of Yonge (79). In 1881 a pigeon-hawk shot on Bloor Street became the subject for Seton's first bird-drawing (151).

Perhaps Seton's most evocative description of Toronto at this time is the following:

Not far, a quarter mile, from our home was Queens Park, one hundred acres of virgin forest preserved but little changed. Farther north were the grassy hills of Seaton Village and Wells' Hill where, not long before, a mountain lion had been killed. Then easterly was the Don Valley, a happy land of bosky dells and open meadows, abounding in bobolinks; and meandering down between, among them, was the winding River Don, vocal with sandmartin, flicker, kingfisher, peetweet, and occasional ducks.   (62)

The Don Valley, of course, became his wilderness haunt as a child – 'an uninhabited wonderland, that no one but myself had ever visited' (103). Here he finds his 'most glorious wooded glen' with its creek of 'purest water' that became his 'paradise': 'There was not a sign of man that I could find, and every proof that wild life here abounded' (103). As a fourteen-year-old in 1874, he built himself a cabin there, somewhere in the area now designated the Ernest Thompson Seton Park, and in the spring of 1875 'found unmeasured happiness in going there Saturdays alone' (105). Later that year, alas (a symbolic reminder of the other side of even nineteenth-century Toronto), his hideaway was discovered and polluted by tramps, but his brief interlude formed the basis for the story of 'Glen yan' told not only in *Trail of an Artist-Naturalist* but also in the early chapters of *Two Little Savages*. Moreover, a number of his animal stories, most notably the chronicles of Silverspot the crow and Redruff the Don Valley partridge, from *Wild Animals I Have Known*, found their origin in his early wanderings and observations in this area. (And here, I cannot resist recording my own experience of reading Seton seriously for the first time in a high-rise apartment on Cambridge Avenue in the mid-1960s and suddenly realizing that the story I was absorbed by was set within sight in the valley immediately below.)

Seton's rural Toronto in the late nineteenth century is supported from an unexpected source, the English writer Algernon Blackwood. In a memoir entitled *Episodes before Thirty* (1923), but looking back to a visit to Toronto a generation earlier, he records a parallel impression:

A pine forest beyond Rosedale was my favourite haunt, for it was (in those days) quite deserted and several miles from the nearest farm, and in the heart of it lay a secluded little lake with reedy shores and deep blue water. Here I lay and communed, the world of hotels, insurance, even of Methodists, very far away.   (50)

It is a charming but rather sad evocation of a lost world.

By the beginning of the twentieth century, then, Toronto had grown from 'Muddy York' into a city with its own individuality, potentially complex but still elusive. Just before 1914, the date that announced the effective end of the previous era, the city received one of the last of the English visitors making an exploration into unfamiliar territory and reporting back on what had been seen. This traveller was Rupert Brooke, of 'Grantchester' fame and so soon to be propelled into the equivocal role of sacrificial poet. Not, one would have thought, the ideal observer to sum up the personality of a fledgling Ontarian city, especially since *Letters from America* (1916) originated in articles, to quote Henry James's coy phrase from the preface, 'addressed, for the most part, to a friendly London evening journal' (xxxii), in fact the *Westminster Gazette*. This posthumously published volume, however, included a remarkably individual and multifaceted portrait of the early twentieth-century city.

The words 'individual' and 'elusive,' employed in the previous paragraph, are Brooke's own. He clearly encountered a challenge in finding the right tone and nuance to express the city's 'subtly normal ... indefinably obvious personality.' He begins breezily but somewhat unexpectedly:

Toronto (pronounce *T'ranto*, please) ... is a healthy, cheerful city (by modern standards); a clean-shaven, pink-faced, respectably dressed, fairly energetic, unintellectual, passably sociable, well-to-do, public-school-and-'varsity sort of city. (79)

At first, one suspects an outsider's selective superficiality, but it is soon evident that Brooke has a keen eye for paradoxes and contrasts. 'Toronto, soul of Canada, is wealthy, busy, commercial, Scotch, absorbent of whisky' (82), but he also notices 'the cheery Italian faces that pop up at you out of excavations in the street,' and realizes that, though 'liberally endowed with millionaires,' the city is 'not lacking its due share of destitution, misery, and slums' (80). His details are sharp, placing, offered without any attempt to smooth out and reconcile. He is fascinated by Torontonian anomalies: 'It is situated on the shores of a lovely lake; but you never see that, because the railways have occupied the entire lake front' (80). 'Entire' is, of course, an exaggeration, but one sees what he means.

On the one hand, he takes note of 'a few sky-scrapers in the American style without the modern American beauty'; on the other, he looks beyond these to 'the residential part, with quiet streets, gardens open to the road, shady verandahs, and homes, generally of wood, that are a deal more pleasant to see than the houses in a modern English town' (81). This may at first sight seem condescending, but is actually an honest compliment. We get the sense – and, surely, a legitimate sense – of a city poised on the brink of a problematic maturity. Brooke reports that Toronto 'has grown immensely of recent years' (80), but his final diagnosis is appropriately enigmatic: 'The only depressing thing is that it will always be what it is, only larger' (84). To test the accuracy (or otherwise) of that statement, we must look through the eyes of a new and primarily Canadian generation that portrayed the city as it emerged at the end of the First World War.

12 *Anglo-Saxon City*

When Rupert Brooke visited Toronto in 1913, he remarked on 'the wealthy interests, which are all-powerful here' (82). The western world was on the brink of a calamitous period of violence and challenge that called so many of the old ways into question, and writers who have portrayed Toronto in recent times tend to focus their attention on the less affluent inhabitants of the city. But the 'all-powerful' cannot be ignored – let alone dislodged – so easily. Their influence on Toronto's evolution was crucial. It is therefore appropriate to begin a literary tour of mid-twentieth-century Toronto with Robertson Davies's rendition of a society of wealth and privilege, since he provides the clearest account (set, however, within the key of an often sharp ironic comedy) of the influential and 'respectable' Toronto that established the various codes and standards against which other versions of life in the city can be judged and compared. I have already traced Toronto's physical growth from primitive trading-post to provincial capital, but the nineteenth-century literary evidence offered little concerning the human and social history of the group that both benefited from and helped to extend that growth. This is precisely what we find in the Toronto of Davies's fiction.

The Toronto that emerges from these novels is, almost without exception, firmly predicated on financial ease. In *What's Bred in the Bone*, Senator McRory, the protagonist's grandfather, recognizes the city's promise as a financial centre soon after the First World War. When asked by one of his cronies why he doesn't establish his trust company in Montréal, 'where the big money is,' he replies: '"Because there's other big money, and it's in the West, and Toronto will be the centre for that"' (142). As a result, we are soon initiated into the fine distinction between Old Money and New Money. The difference, we are assured, 'though subtle to the vast population which was No Money, was important' (151). Clearly, the Old Money in Ontario in the early twentieth century still carried with it a distinct whiff of the nineteenth-century Family Compact:

Old Money sought to conserve and strengthen whatever was best in the body politic and knew precisely where this refined essence was to be found; it was in themselves and all that pertained to them ... For them the nineteenth century had not quite ended. (151)

New Money, on the other hand, was Edwardian rather than Victorian in character. It 'aspired to be Big Money, and did not greatly care if the drawing-rooms of Old Money were not easily opened' (151). Davies is quick to insist, however, with characteristically suave elegance, that all this

should by no means be taken as evidence that Toronto's social and business communities were snobbish. They would assure you, almost before you asked, that they were pioneers and democrats to a man, or a woman. But they were well-connected pioneers and democrats ... (152)

The Senator succeeds because, though he represents New Money, he is canny enough to set up close diplomatic ties with Old Money. His brother-in-law, Gerry O'Gorman, acknowledges the subtle gradations between spiritual and commercial power and, on appearing in Toronto as the vanguard of the Senator's plans, proceeds to move strategically from Roman Catholic to Anglican allegiances. Similarly, and at about the same time, we may remember, Boy and Leola Staunton in Davies's earlier novel *Fifth Business* leave the Presbyterians for the more worldly Anglicans after moving from Deptford to Toronto at the beginning of Boy's political and financial career. If one wanted to lay up one's treasure in a sectarian Christian heaven, Anglican securities seemed a little more socially gilt-edged. By the same token, however, young Francis Cornish, the artistically inclined central figure in *What's Bred in the Bone*, soon becomes disillusioned by the 'middle-brow Anglicanism' of Colborne College: 'It was a religion well suited to Old Money and to the toadies of Old Money. It was a religion that Never Went Too Far' (156).

Davies's Toronto, then, may be a world of shrewd financial strategies, but it is also one in which 'gracious living' is more than a mere advertising gimmick. It is not, however, presented uncritically. The prevailing life-style is described graphically but perceptively by David Staunton, Boy's son, in *The Manticore*. The time is the mid-1930s.

We lived in an old, fashionable part of the city, in a big house in which the servants outnumbered the family ...

People who have no servants often have a quaint notion that it would be delightful to have people always around to do one's bidding. Perhaps so, though I have never known a house where that happened, and certainly our household was not a characteristic one. Servants came and went, sometimes bewilderingly. Housemen drank or seduced the women-servants; cooks stole or had terrible tempers; laundry maids ruined expensive clothes or put crooked creases in the front of my father's trousers; housemaids would do no upstairs work and hadn't enough to do downstairs; the chauffeur was absent when wanted or borrowed the cars for joy-riding.   (103–4)

Jocular, to be sure, and not offered as representative; nonetheless a recognizable and authentic way of life is conveyed.

The precise location of the Staunton home is never specifically identified, either in *Fifth Business* or here, but it is most probably Rosedale, the prosperous area associated, in literary terms, with the work of Timothy Findley. The Rosses, in *The Wars*, live on South Drive, and are seen in 1915 making their way 'down Park Road and up through the gulley of wild ravine to the other side past Collier Street to Bloor' (52) on their way to St Paul's Anglican Church. Findley is expert at portraying 'the category of what is known as the "professional" world,' the class that was able to live 'a life of absolute comfort supported by absolute money' (*Dinner* 16, 95). But he tends to paint this society in more extreme psychological colours than Davies. His books invariably lay stress on the emotional pressures of a claustrophobic privileged life in decline that manifests itself in alcoholism, violence, paranoia, and madness. They represent the epitome of what Margaret Atwood has succinctly described as 'Southern Ontario Gothic, Rosedale variation' (*Second Words* 295).

Nonetheless, the variety of life and attitude within Rosedale was, and is, remarkable, and the area can best be understood through a juxtaposition of various literary accounts of Rosedale houses. Hugh Hood was born into the poor fringes of north Rosedale ('the dormitory of the servants of the south' [*Swing* 23]), but his protagonist Matt Goderich's descriptions of what he calls '[u]nmitigated south Rosedale, redolent of fiscal power' (29) are unparalleled:

In south Rosedale a wholesaler's mansion might run to four storeys, here and there to 50 rooms. I have been in houses, though never as an invited guest and always by the side or back door, where the attic was the fifth floor, in whose recesses and at the top of whose depressing back stairs were long galleries of maids' rooms, walls the colour of inferior Ontario cheddar, a pale soapy yellow devoid of decorative impulse or effect, where now and then a cutout from a rotogravure, most often the *Star Weekly*, might droop from the slanting wall. These rooms were irregular in shape, tucked up under hipped or gabled roofing. One bathroom on the top floor. Short little bathtub. A good deal of danger from fire: these would have been difficult attics to escape from ... Seeing them now at 40 years' remove I guess these houses were meant to cow the paid police force, impress the casual passerby with opulence, house multitudes and encourage large families ...   (29)

In Findley's short story 'Sometime – Later – Not Now,' the son of 'an outrageously wealthy man' is portrayed as living in a house that was

the epitome of purchased taste. Most of the furniture was Empire and there was a lot of plum carpeting and velvet drapery everywhere. Rococo mirrors, Olympian paintings and Regency gew-gaws completed the picture. It had the charm of money ...   (*Dinner* 102)

Other houses were more modest. That inhabited in 'the old days' by Miss Marsalles in Alice Munro's short story 'Dance of the Happy Shades' was presumably closer to north Rosedale:

A narrow house, built of soot-and-raspberry-coloured brick, grim little ornamental balconies curving out from the second-floor windows, no towers anywhere but somehow a turreted effect; dark, pretentious, poetically ugly – the family home.   (*Dance* 213)

The inside decorations illustrate the lip service paid to a vaguely acknowledged 'culture' by including 'a picture of Mary, Queen of Scots, in velvet, with a silk veil in front of Holyrood House ... brown misty pictures of historical battles, also the Harvard Classics, iron firedogs and a bronze Pegasus' (214). More eccentric is the house inhabited in the early 1980s by Maria Theotoky's gypsy mother in Davies's *The Rebel Angels*. This is described as being

a handsome house, in the heavy banker-like style that prevails in the most secure, most splendidly tree-lined streets of the Rosedale district of Toronto ... Solid brick, white-painted woodwork, impressively quoined at the corners; a few fine trees, well attended by professional tree-pruners and patchers; a good lawn obviously planted by an expert, of fine grass without a weed to be seen.   (133–4)

Built, perhaps, by Old Money. Inside, however, this is a bizarre residence in the way that so many of Davies's settings are intriguingly and often profoundly bizarre, converted into apartments for a cross-section of eccentrics and oddities that neither Old nor New Money would have sanctioned. It is balanced, typically, by the house inhabited by Clement Hollier's mother, also in Rosedale. This was 'one of those houses stiff with Good Taste, and Mrs. Hollier ... was stiff with Good Taste too' (298). But all this is clearly a Rosedale in transition if not in decline, one that the denizens of half a century before would scarcely recognize. The earlier inhabitants are provided with a contemptuous epitaph in Findley's recent short story 'Bragg and Minna': '"Them as live in Rosedale," Minna had said ... "are them as keep their shit in jars"' (*Stones* 10).

For the poet Raymond Knister, unconsciously echoing Rupert Brooke, the Toronto of the late 1920s or early 1930s was 'a unique blend of English mannerisms and blood, pioneer Canadian puritanism, and American go-getter business tendency' (*Poems, Stories* 164). A later poet, Douglas LePan, grew up 'on a leafy / street in the Annex in Toronto' (16) – another comfortable though less ostentatious area – and he paints a scene of grace and cultured ease, recalling his parents'

> house on Walmer Road where, behind storm-windows,
> evening will bring music and laughter rising in bright
> arpeggios, higher and higher, like the pink and gold
> in the warm sunlight of a great Bonnard or Vuillard.   (17)

But this was, of course, a sheltered minority world. The majority of writers emerging after the First World War placed their emphasis elsewhere, concentrating on the meaner streets as well as on the modest and even desperate lives being lived there. The most prominent chronicler of this other side of Toronto is undoubtedly Morley Callaghan.

Callaghan, who began publishing in the 1920s, was the first writer of importance to make Toronto a central setting in his fiction. This fact has, however, been obscured. As is well known, the name of Toronto hardly ever appears in his fiction, and the standard explanation for this points to shrewd salesmanship. If he were to make a financial success as a writer, Callaghan needed to command a broad North American readership, but unfortunately the book-buying population of the United States was not at that time interested either in Canada or in literature that was set there. However, Callaghan was crafty enough to realize that, if he were to avoid specifically identifying his settings, American readers would assume that the city in question was in the United States. Such deliberate vaguenesses, apparently, made his books acceptable in the American literary market-place. All this may well be true; nevertheless, Ontario readers would have no difficulty in recognizing their provincial capital, since the main physical features and the names of streets, hotels, and public buildings are unmistakable. It is a city of bridges and ravines

– details Hugh Hood would later recognize as special Toronto character-
istics – with parliament buildings and a hill sloping down to the lake-
front. The specific references lay any possible doubts to rest: Hart House,
Sunnyside, the Don River, High Park, Bloor Street, Massey Hall, Queen's
Park, the Woodbine, the Park Plaza, Britnell's, the Sai Woo, the King
Edward, the York Club, the Royal York, Rosedale, Bay Street, Avenue
Road, and many more. The city is rarely described in any detail, but it is
evoked in a continuing litany of familiar names.

Although one character in *It's Never Over* remarks of the city,
'"Sometimes it's bright and sometimes it's shoddy"' (76), Callaghan's
Toronto is most notable for the latter impression, for its air of mildly
disreputable sleaziness. There is little sense of a 'great' city with dignified
architecture and a feeling of civic pride and achievement. More typical
is the description of Lou's rooming-house in *Such Is My Beloved* 'just by
the bridge, over the river and the railroad tracks. Across the bridge, on
the other bank, behind the factories, they could see the jail' (34). This is
a world of bootleggers, wrestling promoters, burlesque shows, hookers,
pimps, and the criminal underworld. We may meet judges, senators,
mayors, bishops, rich businessmen, but they find themselves involved,
for reasons of financial gain or sinful pleasure or (at best) social concern,
in a world of bar-rooms, police courts, cheap lodging-houses, shabby
hotels. A reference in *Strange Fugitive* to 'Elizabeth, the street of Chinese merchants, chop-houses and dilapidated roughcast houses used for
stores' (96) is typical.

In general, however, moral landscape takes precedence over realistic
topography. Especially in his early fiction – the novels, novellas, and
short stories written between the wars – the dominating image (and here
we become aware of Callaghan's strong Catholic preoccupations) is the
Cathedral. But it is less an indication of religious and ethical values than
a perpetual reminder of the conspicuous discrepancy between human
possibility and actual human achievement. The Cathedral is prominent
without being either spiritually or aesthetically inspiring. It was 'an old,
soot-covered, imitation Gothic church that never aroused the enthusiasm
of a visitor to the city. It had been in the neighborhood for so long it now
seemed just a part of an old city block' (*Such Is* 36–7). More often than
not there is something equivocal about its presence: 'The neighborhood
changed rapidly as [Marion] got close to the Cathedral, which was high
and splendid though surrounded by squat rooming houses and factories.
Its spire stuck up darkly against the light sky' (*Broken* 98). In *Such Is My
Beloved* it is 'always dirtied by city smoke' (15).

The Cathedral is important, then, not so much for its status as an
actual building existing in the world outside the fiction but as an emblem
that reveals meaning. In his first novel, *Strange Fugitive*, it is contrasted

with 'the Labour Temple, just across the road' (72) – a more deliberate (or, at least, more obviously symbolic) juxtaposition than Susanna Moodie's university and lunatic asylum! In the short story 'An Escapade,' it is conspicuously contrasted with 'the theatre' (*Stories* 124). In *Such Is My Beloved*, the story of an idealistic young priest who tries to save a couple of street-girls he discovers in his parish, it represents orthodoxy and uprightness in contrast to the cheap room in the cheap hotel where the girls live. *It's Never Over* provides an equivalent focusing image in the Don Jail. In *More Joy in Heaven*, which tells the story of a supposedly reformed criminal, an important recurring image is the bridge which crosses into 'a new country' (17) but also implies the darkness of a ravine into which it is possible to fall.

If Toronto is the ever-present but relatively anonymous background to Callaghan's work, it becomes – or, rather, a distinctive part of it becomes – foreground in Hugh Garner's *Cabbagetown*. This book had a curious history. According to an authorial note in the full-length text, it was 'published in a drastically cut 160-page version in 1950,' but was 'completely rewritten' before it appeared as a 415-page book in 1968. Garner had, one feels, more of a sociological than an artistic urge to produce this drab but memorable account of life during the Depression years. The central figure, Ken Tilling, grows between 1929 and 1937 from youth to manhood, making his initial encounters with employment (and unemployment), poverty, sex, politics, crime, and armed conflict (when the book ends he is in desperate straits at a climax in the Spanish Civil War). The plot is episodic though well sustained; nonetheless, only limited damage is done to the fiction as a work of art by discussing it in primarily documentary terms.

According to Bruce West, 'Cabbagetown' derived its name from the fact that 'the early residents of modest circumstances had planted cabbages on their front lawns as a way of stretching their meager grocery budgets' (248). For Garner (who grew up there), it was, in the years between the wars, 'the home of the social majority, white Protestant English and Scots. It was a sociological phenomenon, the largest Anglo-Saxon slum in North America' (vii). A firmly differentiated area on the eastern side of central downtown Toronto, it was bounded by Parliament Street on the west, Gerrard on the north, Queen on the south, and the Don River on the east. (The 1968 text reproduces a pleasant stylized diagram of the area on its title- and part-pages.)

Garner approaches the district with a sharp eye and a long memory for social injustice, but whatever their sociological impact his descriptions are impressionistic and essentially imaginative. They leave us with a sense of lived life, not with evidence and statistics. Thus, 'the prevailing smell,' he writes, 'was one of decay, of old wet plaster and rotting wooden steps, the smell of a landlord's carelessness and neglect' (7). At the same time, he rarely sentimentalizes, and never idealizes. 'The citizens of Cabbagetown believed in God, the Royal Family, the Conservative Party and private enterprise. They were suspicious and a little condescending towards all heathen religions, higher education, "foreigners" and social reformers' (6). The xenophobia alluded to here is shared by Callaghan's Harry Trotter, who lives close to the area in *Strange Fugitive*. As Robert Weaver has remarked, 'Harry Trotter doesn't like Jews or Italians, the two most visible groups of outsiders in the English-Irish-Scottish community that was the Toronto of his day' ('Introduction' ix). Garner's narrator makes a related point within his novel: 'The only "foreigners" around their neighbourhood were the Jewish storekeepers on Queen and Parliament Streets, and the Central Europeans who lived in a colony to the south of King Street' (306). And a little later Ken remarks: '"Down in our neighbourhood we still call Catholics dogans and micks. We also we call Jews sheeneys, and Central Europeans hunkies, Italians wops. They call us limeys, or more often bronchos. It doesn't mean much"' (374–5). That final sentence is a good example of Garner's complex balancing of criticism and charity.

Since the particular aspect of Toronto represented by the Cabbagetown of that time has long since passed into history (as a definable geographical area – doubtless its spirit still exists in increasingly isolated pockets), it is worthwhile turning at this point to a poetic rendition of the same phenomenon, Earle Birney's 'Anglosaxon Street,' written in 1942. Birney wittily offers a pastiche of the old English alliterative verse to provide a memorable picture of a shabby, declining outpost of Empire:

> Here is a ghetto   gotten by goyim
> O with care denuded   of nigger and kike
> No coonsmell rankles   reeks only cellarrot
> attar of carexhaust   catcorpse and cooking grease
> Imperials hearts   heave in this haven
> Cracks across windows   are welded with slogans
> There'll Always Be An England   enhances geraniums
> and V's for Victory   vanquish the housefly   (1.74)

Birney brilliantly evokes the shabbiness of the area ('blotching brick and blank plasterwaste') and of the people ('the bleached beldames / festooned with shopping bags'), yet manages at the same time to convey the pathos of stunted lives.

Hugh Hood's remarkably detailed memories of Toronto now extend back well over fifty years, and there is no better guide to the years immediately preceding the growth of the modern city. His own experience reflects a very different segment of Toronto, but family traditions preserve hints of a rarely documented community in at least geographical proximity to the areas I have been discussing. His short story 'Brother André, Père Lamarche and My Grandmother Eugénie Blagdon,' collected in *The Fruit Man, the Meat Man and the Manager* (1971), conjures up a distinctive area of Toronto whose origins extend back to the middle years of the nineteenth century. To be sure, this is fiction, but it is meticulously accurate fiction that depends for its effect on what Hood elsewhere described as 'super-realism,' and the authenticity of the history and atmosphere is not in question. Hood's mother, Marguerite Blagdon, was in origin French Canadian, and the autobiographical narrator records the combined religious and nationalistic tensions in an anecdote of the English-speaking neighbourhood children teasing her with the rhyme

> Marguerite, across the street,
> We can smell your dirty feet.   (60)

She grew up, then, as part of 'the Toronto French minority community, the world of old Sacré Coeur' (60). The parish lay in the eastern section of the city, the old church located 'just east of Sackville on King Street, around the corner from the House of Providence, and that's real authentic *old* Toronto, going back to around 1850' (62). More disturbingly, it is described as 'a parish where a minority in a hostile city flocked for protection in mutual solidarity' (63).

The district was not far from Cabbagetown, which, since Hood wrote the story as early as 1964, had not at that time been revived as a local household word through the influence of Garner's full-scale novel. The grandparents in Hood's story lived on Amelia Street, and this is described as 'separated from Cabbagetown by maybe six blocks and a pretty considerable status barrier' (65). It was a tightly knit area, whose South Pole was the old Sacré Coeur – 'now,' we are informed from the viewpoint of the 1960s, 'a Ukrainian-rite Church' in an area inhabited by 'speakers of the Central European languages' (62, 65). 'Almost everyone' his grandparents knew 'lived in the district, which was solidly middle class and perhaps upper middle class.' The narrator's verdict is firm and affectionate: 'pretty old-world and ingrown in those days; everybody in the French community knew everybody else and minded their affairs' (65).

Hood himself, as I have already indicated, was brought up in north Rosedale, and his *New Age/nouveau siècle* series, while presenting a panoramic view of eastern Canada in the twentieth century (as prelude to the actual 'new age,' which, we are assured, will be the twenty-first), offers fascinating glimpses of the city from the 1920s (as presented in *Reservoir Ravine*) up to the present day. Most detailed, perhaps, is the portrait of Toronto in the 1930s as remembered by Matt Goderich in the first volume in the series, *The Swing in the Garden*. This documentary narrative is packed full of loving detail, from architectural styles to dominant social attitudes to fashionable automobile designs to such minutiae as the colours and forms of transfers on the bus-and-streetcar system. On the level of social documentary, the book is without parallel for a sense of the everyday lives of a cross-section of middle-class Toronto at that time.

Yet Hood's particular images frequently open up to become intellectually representative. Matt's first memory is of watching the trains pass towards unknown destinations along the railroad tracks at the bottom of their garden. Hood insists that this is not merely a personal autobiographical memory but a deliberately inserted reminder, deriving from Harold Innis (and comparable with the intersection of road and railway at the opening of *A New Athens*, discussed in chapter 6), that communications are central to Canadian life. History is also invoked in the detail of the Lieutenant-Governor's carriage passing to his official residence nearby (now long since demolished), and Hood has a keen nose for the class gradations that were then more conspicuous because more generally accepted as part of the natural order of things. The Depression is not at the centre of Hood's concerns at this point (Matt, after all, is only a child at the time), but there is a definite sense of belt-tightening and a dim awareness of the darkening political shadows that lead to the outbreak of the Second World War at the end of the volume.

Hood, then, is acutely aware of the changes that accompany history, and is unsurpassed in his grasp of the gradual evolution of the city. At the same time, he is able to see Toronto, and the rest of human civilization, *sub specie aeternitatis*. The garden mentioned in the title of his first *New Age* novel is located on Summerhill Avenue, but it partakes of Eden; the child's swing is a tangible physical object, but it also records a continuous movement between innocence and experience. His Catholic world-view inexorably imposes a mythic (but not necessarily inaccurate) pattern upon his material, and this involves a sacramental view in which even the geography of Toronto is subsumed into a topographical imaginative scheme. It is almost as if Hood were building Jerusalem in Ontario's green and pleasant land. The physical features of the city are transformed through the application of religious imagery and allusion. Thus the hill which, as he says, is 'found all the way across Toronto,' the hill upon which Casa Loma stands, is seen as '[c]ursed' by the streetcar motor-men of the 1930s but as their 'promised land' by the child-protagonist and his sister (*Swing* 6–7). Even so secular (even profane) an event as a children's matinée in the Beverly Cinema is described in sacred terms: 'It sounded like Gehenna or Armageddon, or the awakening of the Divine Beast in the Revelation to St. John on Patmos' (56). The climax of this process is reached, perhaps, when 'the three islands (so-called) across the bay, Centre Island, Ward's Island and Hanlan's Point,' are recognized to be not 'wholly and distinctly and in every way separated' but as 'three in one' (171).

When Matt observes, 'I'm a Toronto boy and will be, I suppose, for ever' (*New Athens* 26), one suspects that he is close in sentiment to his creator. Both share a visionary attitude towards the city, and Hood expresses this directly, in his own person, in an article written in 1970, originally published as 'The Ravines and Bridges of Hugh Hood's Toronto' but later revised and retitled 'The Governor's Bridge Is Closed.' He establishes his creative writer's view of the city by remarking: 'I thought that the bridges and ravines were the most important imaginative properties on the Toronto scene. I still feel the same way' (*Governor's Bridge* 10). Not, perhaps, the first images that would spring to the minds of most of us, but, if I may speak personally for a moment, the more I think about them, the more valid they seem. And the more I read the literature that concerns itself with Toronto, whether by Hood himself or Morley Callaghan or Hugh Garner or Margaret Atwood or even Michael Ondaatje (in whose recent novel, *In the Skin of a Lion*, the Bloor-Danforth bridge over the Don Valley is a central image), the more I realize that Hood has here provided a crucial insight into an imaginative Toronto.

But he goes further: 'I still think that Toronto is a city where sooner or later you find yourself going down into a dark place in the ground' (9). The two main events in the article concern two of Hood's childhood memories: one, an almost fatal fall into some brick-workings in one of the ravines; the other, an eerie account of exploring (by climbing down into) a hole in one of the supports of the Governor's Bridge itself. Both are personal experiences that have a curious allegorical/symbolic suggestion, and one finds a similar quality about Atwood's fictional Toronto (especially, as we shall see, in *Cat's Eye*, where both bridge and ravine occur in a climactic sequence). But these intimations of higher significance only highlight the extraordinarily vivid realism of Hood's multifaceted presentation of Toronto life. As we read *The Swing in the Garden* and respond to the subtle and not-so-subtle distinctions that separate the children even within their relatively confined neighbourhood – the sour smell of dirt in the McNally home, the disdain of the aristocratic Bea

Skaithe when Matt remarks that he never sees her at the local cinema ('"Nobody on our street goes to the Beverly. It's just a *neighbourhood theatre*"' [87]), the religious rivalry between the boys from Our Lady of Perpetual Help and their Protestant counterparts at Whitney, a passing reference to 'the opprobrium often then visited upon too foreign character' (93) – we detect the touch of the snake within this childhood Eden and recognize our own world. Even his well-known documentary story 'Recollections of the Works Department,' in *Flying a Red Kite*, blends a transparent realism with a probing inquiry into contrasting assumptions and lifestyles. Hood's accurately observed Toronto and his imaginative or visionary Toronto are ultimately the same.

If *The Swing in the Garden* begins with an Edenic reference and ends (literally) with the ambivalent 'long fall' of 1939 (210), a different and less attractive kind of innocence is still evident in Hood's presentation of the Toronto of the war years in the alternating chapters of *Black and White Keys*. While in the odd-numbered chapters Matt's father is engaged in secret and dangerous missions in Europe, attempting to smuggle prisoners, including a distinguished philosopher, out of Dachau, in the other chapters Matt himself is attending school in a Toronto where the world war seems remote and unimaginable. There are, of course, signs of crisis – rationing, the controversy over conscription, etc – and *The Swing in the Garden* starkly records on its last page the death of one of Matt's older boyhood acquaintances in a raid on the Ruhr. But the image chosen by Hood for the essential detachment from the conflict of Torontonians (and, by extension, of Canadians in general) is a series of wrestling bouts at Maple Leaf Gardens, where the obviously phoney and corrupt emblem of simulated and manipulated conflict (complete with an absurd rumour that a masked combatant is Hitler himself) becomes an apt comment not only on the obscenity of war but on the ignorance, so far as many Torontonians were concerned, about the realities of war.

These chapters accurately catch an adolescent's impressions of the 1940s in Toronto, but, though they are appropriate enough for Hood's purpose, they are inevitably incomplete and make no claims to comprehensiveness. Adult memories of Toronto at the time were likely to be very different. Indeed, in novels set at this period whose protagonists and authors belonged to an earlier generation, the Second World War years and those immediately following come across as the least attractive in Toronto's history. At this period the city came in for particular criticism from outsiders, the most notable being the painter, novelist, and satirist Wyndham Lewis, who was stranded in Ontario for several of the war years. The fruits (if that's the right word) of this frustrating period were gathered together in 1954 in a novel entitled *Self Condemned*. Lewis's verbal portrait of the city, as angular as any of his human portraits in paint, is important as the viewpoint of a man who was as intelligent and perceptive as he could also be acerbic and often wrong-headed.

It must be made clear from the start, however, that Lewis's 'Momaco,' though based on his experience in Toronto, is highly exaggerated and, indeed, a demonstrable composite. (Lewis, with a smoke screen effect that may well have been intended as sardonic irony, specifically distinguishes actual from imagined city by naming both Momaco and Toronto within his text.) The clues lie within the fictional name. Momaco suggests Mimico, now a part of Metropolitan Toronto, but the first two letters posit an imaginative amalgamation of Toronto with Montréal (also mentioned specifically within the text), and Lewis's fictional city certainly contains a larger French-Canadian population than Toronto's and endures winters that seem excessively cold even by Montréal's standards. However, his assertion that 'Momaco was a city without a theatre' (224) was true of neither. The fact is that Momaco ultimately represents a more general portrait of Canada or North America or even the western world – it is described at one point as 'typically of the earth: and of the universe' (191). At the same time, Toronto unquestionably had the doubtful distinction of serving as its chief model.

Lewis's opening description recalls Anna Jameson's unsympathetic account just over a hundred years earlier. He writes:

This bush metropolis had the appearance of an English midland city, which had gone in for a few skyscrapers. Its business quarter, in spite of a dozen of these monsters, was mean. It even succeeded very successfully in concealing them; as if having committed itself to a skyscraper, it resented its size.

Momaco was so ugly, and so devoid of all character as of any trace of charm, that it was disagreeable to walk about in. It was as if the elegance and charm of Montreal had been attributed to the seductions of the Fiend by the puritan founders of Momaco; as if they had said to themselves that at least in Momaco the god-fearing citizen, going about his lawful occasions, should do so without the danger of being seduced by way of his senses.   (179)

The book is sometimes in danger or collapsing into an anthology of insults directed against the physical features of the city itself, against its inhabitants, and against the way of life that they create and maintain. The narrator speaks of 'the saddening and depressing sensations produced by the streets and alleys of Momaco' (181). It is 'the never-never land ... the living death, the genuine blank-of-blanks out of which no speck of pleasantness or civilized life could come' (214). A special contempt is reserved for the city's 'beverage rooms' and liquor laws, and the protagonist René Harding and his wife drink to 'Momaco suffering a similar fate to the Cities of the Plain' (226).

But what most appalled Lewis, naturally enough, was the level of Momaco culture. Harding decides that his employer, a Mr Furber, 'probably was the only man of wealth upon the Hill who knew the difference between Pericles and Petronius' (254), and even he displays his provinciality by attaching as great an importance to articles and reviews in Momaco newspapers and journals 'as if they had appeared in the *New York Times*, in *The New Statesman* or *La Nouvelle Revue Française*' (257). (This attitude, I cannot resist observing, still persists.) When Harding goes in search of 'hundreds' of reference-books that he needs to consult, he 'found perhaps a dozen in the Momaco libraries' (350). Moreover, the city's cultural emptiness is rivalled by its moral hypocrisy. Though it shows evidence of being a comparatively wealthy city, Harding discovers that 'people die every day from under-nourishment' (175). He sums it up ethically as 'the city of the Ten Commandments, all of which are so violently broken that they can never be forgotten, as they can in a place where no one pays any particular attention to them' (187). The last section of the novel is one long listing of 'the horrors of Momaco' (339).

This judgment on the fictional Momaco in *Self Condemned* tallies with the comments on the actual Toronto to be found in Lewis's letters. For him it was 'the most American of Canadian cities' but 'a mournful Scottish version of America' (*Letters* 283). It is 'not a good place to be an intellectual in' (291), and he speculates that 'if Bellini or Goya came to Toronto they would probably be regarded as "reds" or "bums"' (302). The chief enemies, he believes, are '"Methodism and Money"' which have produced 'a sort of hell of dullness' (327). Lewis was, of course, an embittered satirist who had turned his back on a Europe that he had also condemned. And the title of his Toronto novel suggests that he also condemned himself. Small wonder, then, that he should react so contemptuously to a Toronto that was unquestionably dull, parochial, and nervous of visiting intellectuals like himself. In his eyes it could only be described as 'that disgusting spot' (372).

Among Lewis's targets in *Self Condemned* were, forecastably, the Ontario liquor laws and, more peripherally, 'fortune-telling teacup-readers' (240). It so happens that both these topics recur in a now virtually forgotten anti-Toronto novel, Margaret Bullard's *Wedlock's the Devil* (1951), which deals with the immediately post-war years, though it was published three years before Lewis's book. There is, moreover, another connection. Lewis had written: 'If you criticize [the inhabitants of Momaco] you criticize the average population of Belfast, of Bradford and Leeds, and of Glasgow' (196). Bullard writes of Toronto under the name of 'New Glasgow.' Like Lewis, she reacts against ugliness – that of the city itself (only the unspoilt beauty of the ravines, she claims, redeems it from 'an otherwise unbearable dreariness' [16]) and especially of the inhabitants: 'was there anywhere in the world where the people were so diversely and uniformly ugly?' (110). Rachel Ambrose, a recent immigrant,

called to mind the average contents of a New Glasgow street car, the sallow-complexioned discontented faces, the nasal voices, the bad manners, the horrid clothes. People really ought not to be so ugly; it was rude, it was a deliberate insult, a social offence.   (110)

Wedlock's the Devil is, ultimately, an unsatisfactory novel, where an over-contrived plot and sardonic but often rather callow humour exist somewhat uncomfortably alongside virulent social jibes. Bullard is particularly shocked by what she calls 'the anti-Communist anti-Semitic hysteria of New Glasgow' (212). Philistinism, prejudice, and dullness appear to reign supreme.

These sour portraits from visitors are, of course, somewhat dubious. Not that there is any lack of evidence for what they report, but one suspects at the same time a superficiality as well as a preformed determination to dislike. Still, the attitudes of Wyndham Lewis are echoed by that other disillusioned European, Frederick Philip Grove. In his Ontario novel *Two Generations* (1939) we find the following exchange:

'Toronto is hideous,' Alice said. 'That's why we came away.'
[Ralph] nodded. 'In a sensible world there would be no justification for a place like that. It revenges itself on those who go there.'   (257)

This is also the period of Lister Sinclair's radio play 'We All Hate Toronto,' first broadcast in January 1946. This script has not in fact worn well, and its title is its chief claim to remembrance. But it contains a number of epigrammatic one-liners that are worth quoting:

... nothing is fun in Ontario.   (263)

if life's a play
Toronto's the censored scenario.   (263)

We *all* hate Toronto! It's the only thing everybody's got in common.
(277)

Humour can often be a more effective weapon than bitter diatribe, and the follies and foibles of Toronto in the immediate post-war years are most effectively portrayed by Robertson Davies – or, rather, by Davies's crusty creation Samuel Marchbanks. Marchbanks is a grouchy, witty commentator on 'things in general' whom Davies invented as a pseudonym and convenient *alter ego* in the 1940s in order to air controversial or unpopular opinions. His forthright judgments on Toronto at this time recall the responses of Lewis, Bullard, and Sinclair, but the focus is sharper, the criticism subtler. What is understated is often much more telling than exaggeration. Here, for instance, is a table-talk entry called 'A Modish Notion':

I see by the paper that a Toronto burlesque house offers a striking novelty – a dance of chorus girls who are shackled together in pretty imitation of a chain-gang. If I am not mistaken, the first appearance of this delicious new idea was in *The Beggar's Opera* in 1728, which includes a Hornpipe of Prisoners in Chains. Inch by inch Toronto is creeping up on modernity.   (*Papers* 216)

Marchbanks, of course, has his own individual views concerning the liquor laws. In one section, nicely entitled 'Of Ontario's Bacchic Refinement,' he remarks on the 'awesome hush' in the Cocktail Lounge of a Toronto hotel and notes the waiters at the door posted to refuse entry to the disreputable and the improperly dressed. Lewis's response would have been superior contempt expressed through enraged sarcasm. Davies/Marchbanks is indirect:

I approve of this sort of thing. It is very refined, and if there is one thing about which Ontario is particular, it is refinement. Fastidiousness was apparent everywhere in the Cocktail Lounge; all the men wore their coats, all the women wore gloves, and the only really loud sound was the silvery chinking of the waiters, as they ran to and fro with their pockets full of tips. My drink was not as good as I could have made it at home, but it was worth the money to sip it in surroundings of such mortuary restraint.   (260)

The last phrase conveys more than many of Lewis's paragraphs.

Toronto puritanism is a natural topic for Marchbanks. His account of a once well known incident in which the library controllers questioned the acceptability of Boccaccio's *Decameron* on their virtuous shelves begins as follows: 'I have a particular affection for the city of Toronto; the mere contemplation of its moral sublimity puts me in a good humour for days at a time' (352). His summing-up of the Toronto of this period clearly shows traces of Lewis's Momaco and Bullard's New Glasgow, but is an example of the kind of civilized and elegant wit that neither of the visitor-authors was prepared to acknowledge in the city:

I always think of Toronto as a big fat rich girl who has lots of money, but no idea how to make herself attractive. She has not learned to drink like a lady, and she has not learned to laugh easily ... she is dowdy and mistakes dowdiness for a guarantee of virtue. She is neither a jolly country girl with hay in her hair, like so many other Ontario cities, nor is she a delicious wanton, like Montreal; she is irritatingly conscious of her own worthiness. (268)

Such was the view of Toronto in the late 1940s and early 1950s from the perspective of an idiosyncratic adult with minority views, and it has become a standard verdict on the city at this period in its development. But this was also the period in which Margaret Atwood was growing up in the city, and in her novels *Lady Oracle* (1976) and *Cat's Eye* (1988) she has created narrators who look back from a later period to the Toronto of their formative years. In both books we are introduced to a superficially ordinary, unmitigatedly middle-class, suburban world. Joan Foster in *Lady Oracle* recalls 'the dark interior of upper Braeside [= Leaside?] Park... the trim, respectable, haunted fake-Tudor dwellings of [her] obese adolescence' (201), especially 'a bungaloid box near a Loblaws super-market' (48). In consonance with Hood's general view of the city, an important feature of the neighbourhood was the local ravine, and her recollections support his presentation of the mythology that they provide. When Hood published his article on the Toronto ravines, he received a number of letters from women who recalled how, as children, they had been warned by their mothers of dangers lurking there but always went anyway (*Governor's Bridge* 8–9). Joan Foster reports:

My mother was terrified of this ravine; it crawled with vines and weedy undergrowth, it was dense with willow trees and bushes, behind every one of which she pictured a lurking pervert, an old derelict rendered insane by rubbing alcohol, a child molester or worse. (49)

Typically, of course, the character whom Joan eventually encounters there is the decidedly equivocal 'daffodil man' – a rescuer who may possibly be an exhibitionist as well. In any event, he is less threatening than her sadistic and unpleasant girl-companions. The city is both ambivalent and equivocal. The overall impression is of 'dour Toronto and its gritty winter winds, its salt slush that decayed your boots, or its humid, oppressive summers' (100).

Because *Cat's Eye* covers much the same ground as *Lady Oracle* (including a traumatic confrontation in a ravine), while adopting a very different tone and presenting a different perspective, it shares many basic details with the earlier book. But Elaine Risley is destined to grow up to be a painter rather than a writer, and as a consequence her impressions are more imagistically visual. Thus she recalls spring in Toronto in the late 1940s as follows: 'On the lawns, as we walk home from school, we can see damp pieces of paper under the hedges, old dog turds, crocuses poking up through the grainy, soot-coloured snow' (59). Her painter's retentive eye is sharp. When, for example, a restaurant in the 1980s tries to exploit a taste for nostalgia by reconstructing a forties diner, she immediately recognizes its unauthentic elements, in part because 'it looks too clean,' showing that 'it's less forties than early fifties' (363). In both novels, however, it is the emotional atmosphere that ultimately proves more memorable than the physical features. For Joan Foster these include 'binges of approved sniveling' at the local movie-houses (*Lady Oracle* 79), attendance at church 'for social reasons' (103), a memory of the Royal York Hotel, 'that bogus fairyland of nineteenth-century delights' full of 'stodgy businessmen and their indistinct wives' (135, 136). Elaine Risley, by contrast, remembers 'foreign-looking' old ladies in streetcars, with 'dark shawls wound over their heads and around their shoulders' (*Cat's Eye* 4), the British influence represented by 'a large photograph of the King and Queen' in a classroom (79), the Happy Gang on the radio (138), the '[s]erious-minded good taste' of Simpsons with its 'sedate wood-rimmed glass counters' before they 'changed the whole thing over' (112). Throughout her work, Atwood creates her effects by means of this highly selective and disciplined literary impressionism. Here it evokes a vivid sense of vanished era.

The poet Raymond Souster is, however, the most wide-ranging literary guide to Toronto in the twentieth century. As he tells us in 'Earliest History,'

> I was born on Oakmount Road
> in the west end of sleepy Toronto
> January 15, 1921,   (6.183)

and with the exception of the war years he has made his home in the city ever since. Moreover, for decades he lived what might be called a double life – working as a bank clerk during the day, while writing verse, founding poetry magazines, and operating private presses during his spare time. He therefore bridges the literary and non-literary worlds; appropriately, a photograph of him with friends from the bank hockey-team is to be found in his *Selected Poems*. For Souster, poetry is a part of everyday experience and vice versa.

Virtually the whole of his life has been lived in the High Park district of the city, in the residential areas bounded by the Humber River on the west, King Street on the south, and the curving Dundas Street on the north and east. A representative Souster poem is likely to be set on a 'quiet, leaf-heavy street / of West Toronto' ('Armadale Avenue Revisited,' 3.87), and Michael Macklem, his publisher, has rightly identified a 'strong sense of *neighbourhood*' in his work (14). His 'local pride' (a phrase borrowed from William Carlos Williams to become one of Souster's book titles) is primarily a pride – tinctured with criticism and even hatred and disgust – for his native city. As a result, many of his poems consist of simple renditions of daily experience – watching the sail-skaters on Grenadier Pond, burying two young robins found dead on a driveway, a sudden revelation of the beauty of a neighbourhood poplar, the sight of a 'child's umbrella / lying inside out / on the winter pavement' (2.101). Such poems can run the gamut of emotions from the sardonic ('Bingo Comes to the Runnymede,' 4.68) to the near-sentimental ('The Roundhouse,' 3.66), but he is usually aware of the sentimental temptation in his retrospective poems. In 'Armadale Avenue Revisited,' for example, he describes himself as 'hooked on the past, / and a sucker for memories' (3.88).

Yet he is by no means a poet confined to the suburbs or the quieter residential areas. His most memorable poems, indeed, evoke the city centre in all its bustle and hectic speed. He is especially sensitive to the drastic contrasts which life in a metropolis provides. He observes

> the hurrying, branching crowds
> with laughing faces, hearts in the heavens,
> that quiet-eating acid despair
> etching many other faces, the hearts in darkness.   ('The Fond Desire,'
> 1.12)

And he is both fascinated and appalled by the inhabitants of the mean streets and the conditions under which they eke out a minimal existence. He is intimately familiar with the other side of Toronto, the Toronto of 'peeling store-fronts, settling houses, smelly alleys' ('Gerrard Street East,' 1.192). For Toronto can be 'the hated city' (1.86), a city to be assailed:

> Sleep city sleep
> push the last dead drunks into the cells of oblivion,
> chase the last chilled street-walker back to her rooming-house,
> bed the last derelict in the overnight cot of the mission.   ('Sleepy
> Toronto,' 1.159)

Souster is primarily an imagistic poet finding subjects for verse in the prosaic material about which Callaghan had written, and this aspect of the city is nicely summed up in the image of stale food left on the sidewalk that 'waits / its children of the shadows' ('Someone Has to Eat,' 2.260).

Although many of his poems are named after specific places in the city – 'Kensington Market,' 'In Mount Pleasant Cemetery,' 'Yorkdale Avenue,' 'Riverside Zoo,' 'Old Mill Bridge,' 'Along the Danforth' – he is ultimately more interested in Toronto's people than in its architecture or physical features. Poem after poem takes the form of a verbal snapshot, usually of the ordinary inhabitants – the lonely, the poor, the panhandlers. Souster's portrait gallery includes an old man who 'mumbles / only to himself / going down Bay Street' ('Old Man on Bay Street,' 2.92); the crippled seller of pencils not merely seen and described but imagined when at last 'they come for him, /... place him carefully in his basket, / then carry him away for the night' ('The Seller of Pencils,' 2.122); the junk man with a 'cardboard-box miracle' piled on his cart ('Junk Man on Front Street,' 2.268); the 'old geezer' with 'a few screws loose,' wearing dilapidated shoes, patched trousers, a frayed coat, and 'on his head the biggest, shiniest top hat / since Abe Lincoln' ('The Top Hat,' 2.127); the old lady crushed to death by a Bathurst streetcar with only 'one cent left in her purse' ('Death by Streetcar,' 1.307); the newspaper vendor who becomes the 'unshaved, / bleary-eyed, foot-stamping king' of his downtown corner ('Downtown Corner Newsstand,' 1.187); the '[p]ale butterflies of night' in 'Streetwalkers, Dundas East' (2.277); the down-and-out miraculously transformed into a 'battered Christ / of Yonge Street' ('Battered,' 3.232).

The city has many facets and many moods, and in the course of a long and prolific literary life Souster has recorded most of them. He is fascinated by the contrast between the noise of human crowds and the silence of the lake and wilderness that remain still surprisingly close. In 'Sunnyside Amusement Park' he lists the '[d]ark tunnel of love, the snaking roller-coaster,' the 'raw impact of faces, bodies .../ red lips, silk legs, cowboy hats, uniforms,' but is most struck by the contrast between 'this barker's hoopla world, this loud restlessness; and 'our great lake at the beach's end / stretching cool, stretching far into a saner night' (1.106). He is also interested, like virtually all subsequent writers on

Toronto, in the implications of change; moreover, he is conscious of having watched the city change while he has himself changed. A surprising number of poems identify themselves even in their titles with the fact of demolition: 'Wreckers' (2.78), 'Shea's Hippodrome Coming Down' (2.120), 'Demolition' (2.184), 'Wrecking-Ball' (3.72), 'Demolition in August' (3.310), 'Wreckers' Progress' (3.339), 'Last Sad Day of Our West Toronto Station' (6.177). Another cluster of poems develops a tradition of change-poetry from Wordsworth's Yarrow poems to Charles G.D. Roberts's famous meditation on Tantramar; so we find 'Kew Beach Revisited' (1.203), 'Humber Valley Revisited' (2.45), 'Armadale Avenue Revisited' (3.87). Most often, of course, the change involves degeneration. This is especially evident in 'Kew Beach Revisited.' In 1940 the beach was 'very nice then, / wide with the sand white and clean'; in 1952 it is

> now half gone
> with the high lake level,
> stink from the open sewer
> of Ashbridge's Bay indescribable
> when the wind's blowing right,
> litter strewn everywhere.   (1.203)

And in a now discarded poem remembering the war years ('The Arcade: Wartime') he writes a moving elegy for

> another landmark gone in a changing city – like
> Sunnyside, Shea's, the west bank of Humber
> below Bloor Street – buildings, pieces of ground tied so closely
> to my life and my time, all gone now, only the memories left.   (*Local Pride* 30)

But Souster is not confined to documentary realism. If he is prepared, like Thomas Hardy, to take a full look at the worst, this is because he has a surprising, resilient capacity to find beauty and even magic in the shabby and the drab. In 'Yonge Street Bar,' for example, he portrays a 'phony ... clip-joint of watered drinks, cheap women, rummy playboys,' yet is entranced by the light on the bottles:

> Really, there's something almost beautiful,
> almost good, almost child-like,
> the way these bottles seem to glow
> like so many blue fairy lights!   (1.166)

Remarkably often, the cheap and seemingly repellent is suddenly transformed into something wondrous:

> City, while the night rides high,
> the stink, the filth is forgotten
> what the sewers run with, what the hospitals throw in the garbage,
> what the stockyard breathes, is transformed as if by magic ...
>
> ('Night-Town,' 1.20)

Sometimes, this apparent magic merely proves deceptive. In 'Lower Yonge Street,' 'the flashing neon, / the red, green banners of the city's magic,' are soon revealed as 'trick deceivers of the unwary' (1.88). More often, however, Souster places emphasis on the warmth and vitality of a people's yearning for wonder, surprise, colour.

In one of his rare panoramic long-shots, looking down from Casa Loma, Sir Henry Pellatt's eclectic early-twentieth-century castle-folly, he observes the 'shower of lights at a roadside carnival' ('Shake Hands with the Hangman,' 1.109). A sense of carnival and colour is continually breaking through what would seem to be the habitually drab. Thus the staid downtown offices are lit up by the 'saucy every-colour- / of-the-rainbow coats and hats' of professional working girls ('First Spring Day in the Canyons', 1.293), while the blacks and greys of buildings are suddenly splashed with colour when, in 'Fruit Stand, Adelaide and Bay' he notices the 'loud sun-glare of bananas, / tree-greens of ripe apples, / dark blood of the plum' (2.266). A similar effect is to be found in 'Shopping Notes from China Village' where his eye is caught by

> that white turnip called lo pak ...
> gou-toy looking like dark-green grasses,
> the narrow shape of bitter lemon
> with its light emerald leaves
> ... and a gleaming purple vegetable
> resembling a long, thin cucumber ...   (6.163)

He also pays tribute to the colourful contribution to the life of the once Anglo-Saxon city provided by the many immigrant peoples – for example, the 'live, earnest people' who create 'this part of Toronto called Little Italy' ('A Roomful of Immigrants,' 2.104–5), or, more recently, the exotic figure wearing giant wings in 'Caribana Parade, University Avenue,' who is imagined climbing up and flying 'as far south as his beloved Trinidad' (6.164). Indeed, it is this sense of imaginative miracle that provides some of the most memorable moments in Souster's verse.

Best known, perhaps, is 'The Flight of the Roller-Coaster,' where the circus-ride amusement at Old Sunnyside Beach breaks clear from its tacky setting, rising into the air 'like a movieland magic carpet, some wonderful bird,' and is last seen

> heading leisurely out above the blue lake water
> to disappear all too soon behind a low-flying flight of clouds.   (1.316)

In Souster's Toronto, for all its dinginess, prejudice, stuffiness, hints of violence and heartbreak, the capacity for miracle and splendid metamorphosis is always latent.

13 *A Changing Toronto*

Between the end of the Second World War and the late 1960s, Toronto changed more conspicuously and more drastically than at any other period in its history after the early nineteenth century. Few communities have made the jump from Victorian primness to contemporary trendiness (however desperate, however self-conscious) with such dizzying rapidity. In a single generation the reputation of the city was dramatically transformed. The process has been neatly summed up, as usual, by Margaret Atwood while looking back at the mid-century of her undergraduate years from a perspective in the mid-1980s. 'In 1960,' she has observed, Toronto 'was not then known as People City or the Paris of the Northeast, but as Hogtown, which was not an inaccurate description' ('Great Unexpectations' xiii).

The writers who have chronicled this change most perceptively are Atwood herself and Hugh Hood, both of whom began their creative lives within this period. The matter is faced most directly by Hood – or, to be more circumspect, by one of his narrators, Tony Goderich – in *Tony's Book* (1988). He traces the beginnings of this change in a passage so central that it must be quoted at length:

I grew up in Toronto at precisely the wrong time in the city's modern history, between 1948 and 1954, the worst time in history because those were exactly the years when the old Toronto[,] ... the provincial capital with the quiet leafy streets, the thousands of profoundly independent homeowners, the total absence of visible minorities, the branch banks on every corner, a city that had gone on existing in much these terms for a hundred and twenty years, was passing out of existence to be replaced over the next two decades by an entirely different collection of folkways: gay lib and CHAT, two dozen highly visible and vocal minorities, a huge population increase, arrival on the scene of an enormously vigorous communications industry, a shift in economic and financial

power from Montréal to the newly transformed Toronto, the status of a potential world capital, like Los Angeles, perhaps, or Osaka, though not one of the
hideously ugly metropolitan cancers like Mexico City or Sâo Paulo ... (114–15)

This change is later encapsulated verbally in the distinction made between '"the Queen City," which is how the old Toronto thought of
itself, and "Queen City," aspiring centre of a new lifestyle' (115).

An image of the old Toronto, just before the change, is caught like the
proverbial fly in amber by Hugh Garner in *The Silence on the Shore*,
published in 1962. Garner has moved across the city from pre-war
Cabbagetown to post-war Annex, the area immediately above Bloor
Street between Bathurst and Avenue Road where, as we saw in the
previous chapter, Douglas LePan had grown up in the 1920s. (The street
names in Garner's novel are rather tiresomely scrambled – Admiral,
Bedford, Bernard, and Lowther appearing under the coy disguises of
Adford, Bemiral, Bertha, and Leonard – but even without this less than
impenetrable smokescreen the area is readily identifiable.) Garner seems
drawn towards residential areas that are coming down in the world.
There is a sense of once-refined seediness about his setting. The lodging-
house which is central to the novel is impressively representative, and
its description beautifully catches the atmosphere of the Annex at this
period (as the present writer remembers, since the landlady mentioned
in my introductory chapter – albeit wholly different from Garner's –
belonged to this neighbourhood):

It was a detached three-storey building, its Victorian gingerbread gone from its
wooden porch, but its age and former social position still apparent in its stringy
lace curtains, old-fashioned looking on a street that had long ago embraced the
genteel drape ... The house was like its neighbours, a tall austere old family
dwelling, probably with steep staircases for skivvies to climb. It was a house
that had grown too big for the families of the present, and too private in its
shouldered intimacy with those beside it for the modern suburbanite.   (1)

It retained, however, a backyard that was 'strangely beautiful' and had
remained 'a semi-rustic symbol of a day long past' (4). The loose plot of
The Silence on the Shore is not especially memorable; what stays in the
mind is the sense of a distinctive area caught in a moment of time – a
moment now lost in history, since, like Cabbagetown though not so
drastically, the Annex, for all its rash of university fraternity-houses, has
undergone a commercially profitable face-lift in recent years.

The particular interest for our purposes of Atwood's first novel, *The
Edible Woman* (1969), is that it is set at this very moment of radical

change both physical and moral. The uneasy tension between old and new is initially located in the conspicuously different atmosphere and surroundings of her hero and heroine (to employ traditional but, in this context, incongruous terminology). Marian McAlpin, the central figure, is living in lodgings which are consonant, in terms of historical detail though not of exact geographical location, with Garner's boarding house; she inhabits 'the top floor of a large house in one of the older and more genteel districts, in what ... used to be the servants' quarters.' Atwood goes on to provide a vivid description of the two flights of stairs with

the line of pioneer brass warming-pans strung on the wall ... the many-pronged spinning wheel on the second-floor landing ... the ragged regimental flag behind glass and the row of oval-framed ancestors that guard the first stairway ... the rubber-plant on one side and the hall table with the écru doily and the round brass tray on the other. (12–13)

Surely an unsurpassed portrait of a traditionalist lodging-house that works up to the entrance of the archetypal but anonymous landlady referred to throughout the novel as 'the lady down below.' The sense of period is superb.

But this evocation of the old Toronto is set into sharper focus when it is juxtaposed with her boyfriend Peter Wollander's apartment in the vanguard of development in a 'run-down area, nearly a slum, that is scheduled to be transformed over the next few years by high-rise apartments' (56). Marian describes it herself:

All summer whenever I went to the apartment I had to thread my way through piles of concrete blocks near the entrance to the lobby, around shapes covered with dusty tarpaulins on the floor inside, and sometimes over troughs of plaster and ladders and stacks of pipes on the stairway going up; the elevators weren't in order yet ...

Structurally the building was complete, except for the finishing touches. They had all the windows in and had scrawled them with white soap hieroglyphics to keep people from walking through them ... Inside, the shining surfaces – tiled floors, painted walls, mirrors, light-fixtures – ... had not yet begun to secrete themselves. The rough grey underskin of subflooring and unplastered wall-surface was still showing, and raw wires dangled like loose nerves from most of the sockets. (57)

The older Toronto is passing; the new is rough and unfinished. Marian's dilemma is that she finds herself out of sympathy with both extremes.

Atwood seems in this first novel to follow in the footsteps of Morley

Callaghan, since the name of Toronto is never used in the book. Nonetheless, Torontonians will readily recognize certain well-known features of the city, including the 'gold-mosaicked dome,' 'spiral staircase,' and 'incongruous totem-pole' of the Royal Ontario Museum (182), as well as more general references to the subway and streetcar system, and Toronto's unique atmospheric combination of the stuffily conventional and the determinedly up-to-date. Most characteristic of all, however, is the use of the ravine as a crucial if symbolic element within the plot. Atwood published *The Edible Woman* a year before Hood's seminal essay on Toronto's bridges and ravines first appeared, and she employs them in a similar way. After Marian's sexual adventure in a cheap hotel with the enigmatic Duncan, he takes her down into one of the ravines that on the one hand is realistic in the sense of being topographically accurate (reference is made to the readily identifiable 'familiar bridge with subway cars moving on it' [265], the Bloor-Danforth bridge across the Don Valley), and on the other hand conjures up an eerie sense of a mysterious subterranean city with awesome features. The brickworks mentioned by Hood are pointed out, and Duncan refers to 'a prison down here somewhere, too' (262). It is a wintry landscape with unmistakable suggestions of a country of the dead, and an appropriate setting for Marian to come to an important decision about her future life. When she makes her way out of the pit, she returns to a very different life – for our purposes, a very different Toronto – from the one in which we found her as the novel opened.

Life before Man (1979) similarly presents a Toronto that is at one and the same time highly realistic and effectively symbolic. The action takes place in the 1970s and traces the complex and often desperate interrelationships of three main characters who are associated with significant aspects of the city. All three are, in their various ways, trapped. Elizabeth is trapped in an oppressive home and a failing marriage. Most of the time we find her within enclosing rooms in her own house, but, like Marian in *The Edible Woman* (though the emotional tone is very different), she must make her personal journey into the underworld, and in one sequence, on a 'grey bench in the Ossington subway station,' she senses a 'chasm opening in herself' (87). She gets into conversation with a man sitting beside her, and later arranges a sordid and abortive assignation with him that begins 'in the underground gloom of the Pilot Tavern' (206). Both subway station and tavern are authentic locations, yet they exist also in a Dantesque landscape of the doomed. By contrast, Nate, Elizabeth's ineffective husband, is a jogger seen running around and around Queen's Park and the Parliament Buildings, a sardonic emblem of the modern Ontarian citizen. He is there early in the novel

(39), and that is where we catch a last glimpse of him, trying to pull himself together, but able to envisage no more than a regular, recurring schedule: 'Same time every day, on and on forever' (287).

The third character, Lesje (the significance of whose ethnic origins will be discussed later), is a paleontologist working, like Elizabeth, in the Royal Ontario Museum, a building which is clearly the imaginative centre of Atwood's Toronto and one that appears continually in her work. In a comparatively early poem, 'A Night in the Royal Ontario Museum' (*Animals* 20–1), the protagonist is portrayed as trapped in the museum, wandering hopelessly within the labyrinth of history, 'looking for the EXIT sign,' but realizing, with Sartre, that there is no exit. In this surrealist fantasy the speaker finds herself locked 'into this crazed man-made / stone brain,' lost 'among the mastodons / and beyond.' The museum is also a world of the dead in *The Edible Woman*, where her mentor brings Marian to the Mummy Room and confronts her with daunting images of 'Mutabilitie' and death. In *Life before Man*, however, the museum provides Lesje with material not for thoughts of entrapment or mortality but for escapist fantasy. She can imagine herself 'wandering in prehistory ... uninvolved' (10), indulging in what she recognizes as a regressive daydream 'left over from her childhood and early adolescence' but a haven when 'thinking about men has become too unrewarding' (11). We follow her sporadically into the world of dinosaurs, and are thereby offered an alternative time-scale to Toronto's puny two-hundred-year history. Similarly, while the children are visiting the Museum, Elizabeth goes to the adjacent Planetarium where, rather like Thomas Hardy's characters in the observatory in *Two on a Tower*, she sees the rapidly changing Toronto skyline' ('the Park Plaza squat now compared to the Hyatt Regency beside it; BRITANNICA to the east; Sutton Place, the weather building, the CN Tower' [65]) against the pitiless context of outer space.

In Atwood's other novels set, at least in part, in Toronto, we find the modern city from the late 1960s onwards presented through her characteristically sharp and satiric eyes. No significant detail, however small, seems to escape her. In *Lady Oracle*, as soon as Joan Foster publishes her book of enigmatic poems, she is whirled into the hoopla of the new 'artsy' world and finds herself associating with an avant-garde artist who has made a reputation by constructing collage-sculptures out of the bodies of dead animals run over by cars and displayed in freezers. He calls himself The Royal Porcupine, is advertised as 'Master of the CON-CREATE POEM,' and has a show entitled 'SQUAWSHT' (241). This is the new, swinging, but aesthetically uncertain Toronto of the late sixties. In *Bodily Harm*, the process has developed further. The opening image of the novel is of an intruder in the protagonist's apartment who leaves a coiled rope in her bedroom: symbol of increased metropolitan violence and danger. Rennie Walford herself is a popular journalist specializing in articles on the latest trends, often 'trends that didn't really exist' but which are copied from her column by people who would 'do anything not to be thought outmoded' (25). One is on 'the Queen Street renaissance,' which covers 'the conversion of hardware stores and wholesome fabric outlets into French restaurants and trendy boutiques' (24–5). Another, on pornography, turns serious (and so is never written) when she is faced with the realities of the subject in a police exhibition of confiscated objects. In *Cat's Eye*, Elaine Risley walks along this 'new' Queen Street and finds 'art galleries and bookshops, boutiques filled with black clothing and weird footgear, the sawtoothed edge of trend' (19). We have come a long way from the dullness of Toronto the Good – or have we? Elaine is not so sure. But we shall return to this question, after sampling other presentations of the new Toronto, at the end of this chapter.

Hood also presents his view of the new Toronto. In the opening sentence of a short story entitled 'Cute Containers' he focuses on an incongruous juxtaposition in the Yorkville area: 'From where they were sitting you could look right across the street at Love Handles, the sex boutique, and beside that the Angel Gabriel Nursing Home' (*August* 48). Characteristically, this seems 'a type or abstract of the structure of human life' to the protagonist. Hood introduces us to a gaudy world of electric signs and vibrating stripes of colour, and he also catches the accompanying economic ironies by taking note of the surviving 'tiny cottages, storey-and-a-half constructions of great antiquity built no later than the 1870s,' that find themselves 'at the centre of the post-Yorkville real-estate boom' (50).

But Hood is more interested in dramatizing the psychological effects of this rapid change in the city's character than in merely recording the conspicuous details of the change itself. He achieves this effect supremely in the strangely moving eleventh chapter of *Reservoir Ravine* (1979) where, after the detailed evocation of Toronto in the 1920s in the first ten chapters, we are suddenly propelled into the late 1970s. Matt Goderich decides to walk to the Reservoir Ravine, which he had not visited for decades. The geographically specific directions (which can be followed on a street map) gradually give way to the account of an emblematic journey: 'Why am I always walking under bridges,' he asks himself, 'seeing things high overhead, trains, angels?' He sees himself as Dante: 'Here I am in the middle way' – not in a dark wood but in a 'misty ravine' (209), and he gradually makes his way up 'the steep angle of ascent' to where he expects to look down on the reservoir. He prepares himself for 'the vertiginous effects of recollection' (210), but when he comes 'over the top' he gets 'a bad shock':

They've closed over the water. Somebody has covered in the reservoir. It's gone, gone, the open water ... I'd been picturing it to myself, looking forward to it. But there was nothing visible. Simply a wide range of browned grass, nothing to what I'd hoped for, flat, uninteresting, with clumps of yelling children roving across it, some involved in ball games, others tumbling and fighting and generally carrying on. (211)

This is more than just a fact of inevitable change, like the telling detail in *The Swing in the Garden* where, by means of a sudden flashforward, a funeral parlour of the 1930s is transformed into a unisex boutique (17). The reservoir and all its subsidiary elements had grown into his 'stock of private imagery,' and it is deeply disturbing to have 'all this ripped out of place in an instant' (211). At the same time, Hood has prepared his readers to comprehend the scene as one more example of continuity within change. Where Matt had played by the water as a child, other children now play ball games. The reservoir is still there, invisible but enduring beneath the surface of the contemporary reality. The past, by implication and extension, survives under the present. Yet for the aging, realization of the extent of change can be traumatically disorienting. As various subtextual allusions make clear, Hood in his novel series is investigating similar tricks and effects of time that have been portrayed in earlier novel-series by Marcel Proust in France and Anthony Powell in England. Toronto has been written into this larger context.

We speak of 'Toronto,' but there are – and have been throughout the twentieth century – so many coexistent Torontos. Frequently separated in space, almost invariably differentiated by class, often distinguished by the national or racial origin of their principal inhabitants, they are not uncommonly seen to exist independently, unaware of each other's special qualities. It is readily understandable, then, that a character in one of Hood's short stories should be presented as having 'no knowledge whatsoever of other kinds of lives lived in other parts of the city'; each of her office acquaintances resided in 'some distant region which her imagination could not penetrate' (*None Genuine* 16, 17). Like most cities, Toronto has had its distinctive areas – its Chinatown, its Italian sections, its Greek enclave – for many decades. I have already referred, among others, to Findley's Rosedale, Garner's Cabbagetown, and the old French community recalled by Hood. One difficulty in identifying and tracing these distinctive areas is the fact that they regularly change over the years, one group moving out as another takes over. This process is well illustrated, during the pivotal period at mid-century, in *The Silence on the Shore*. As so often, religious differences are an underlying factor in what Garner here describes as 'a once-Protestant city':

A member of the congregation had told [Paul Laramée] that St Sulpice's had originally been an Irish church, situated in a neighbourhood that between both world wars had become largely Jewish. After its early Irish parishioners had died or moved away, and the Jewish immigrants and their children had prospered and moved north into a new residential section, a new congregation had moved in, mostly Italian but with many immigrant Polish, German and Hungarian families.   (92)

The instance is fictional, but the general pattern has repeated itself constantly in different parts of the city.

Hood's Tony Goderich referred to 'the total absence of visible minorities' in the Toronto of earlier days. A strong emphasis falls, of course, on the word 'visible.' It was not until the 1960s that an already developing ethnic diversity became a conspicuous element in the general awareness of the city. With the appearance of 'multiculturalism' as a sociological term, the fact of Toronto's multicultural inheritance became evident. Furthermore, as writers emerged from these divergent backgrounds, using English as their prime medium of expression (a development that makes its own significant and potentially distorting contribution to the historical pattern), the general attitudes towards these separated areas changed dramatically. What had once seemed 'alien' suddenly became dynamic, exotic, different, interesting – even (alas) fashionable. The distinguishing words themselves took on subtle nuances. The key term has gathered around itself all sorts of new and self-conscious meaning by the time Andy Wainwright can refer in a poem to

> spadina ave.
> and all that ethnic.   (n pag)

As might be expected, Margaret Atwood is the writer who has shown herself most keenly sensitive to this development. In *Life before Man*, as I have already indicated, one of the three central characters is Lesje Green (the surname changed from Etlin), whose mixed parentage includes Ukrainian and Lithuanian-Jewish. She is herself obsessed with this intricate background, and it is a not altogether pleasant revelation when she discovers that her archetypally Anglo-Saxon boy-friend (whom she nicknames William Wasp until she realizes 'that he found it a racial slur') considers her 'impossibly exotic' (20). Characteristically, Atwood extracts the maximum complexity out of her creation. Lesje's difficulty is not ethnicity itself but a bewildering mixture of ethnicities. There is a comic yet at the same time pathetic moment when she visits the Odessa Pavilion during the Caravan Festival in the hope of finding her roots, but encounters only 'songs she couldn't sing' and 'dances she'd never been taught' (81). When her Jewish friend refers to fashionable clothing as '"too goyish," ... which is her word for tacky taste' (79), Lesje is acutely reminded of 'her own hybrid state,' though the friend tries to reassure here with the statement, '"Ethnic is big these days"' (80). But Lesje cannot forget the power struggle between her grandmothers: how the Ukrainian had once given her 'one of the untouchable decorated eggs kept on the mantelpiece along with the family photos in silver-plated frames' (56), an egg which the Jewish grandmother had smashed. Ironically, her childhood had been culturally deprived by the rivalry, since, in an essentially negative compromise, she 'hadn't been allowed to go either to the golden church with its fairy-tale onion dome or to synagogue' (81). Her life interest in palaeontology, however, was accidentally stimulated by Grandmother Etlin's taking her to the Museum instead of a synagogue on the Sabbath for the prosaic reason that 'it was cheap and out of the rain' (83).

In 'Loulou; or, The Domestic Life of the Language,' a story from *Bluebeard's Egg*, the physical aspects of so-called ethnic areas are spotlighted. The name character is visiting her income-tax accountant, himself second-generation Czech, on Queen Street:

Because of the section of the city she's going to, which is mostly middle-European shops, bakeries and clothing stores with yellowing embroidered blouses in the windows and places where you can buy hand-painted wooden Easter eggs and chess sets with the pawns as Cossacks, she's draped a black wool shawl over her head. This, she thinks, will make her look more ethnic and therefore more inconspicuous.   (56)

A similar passage from *Cat's Eye* shows the central figure, returning to Toronto after many years away from her birthplace, registering with her artist's eye the tell-tale details of this particular aspect of change:

I hit the corner of King and Spadina, walk north. This used to be where you came to get wholesale clothing, and it still is, but the old Jewish delis are disappearing, replaced by Chinese emporia, wicker furniture, cutwork tablecloths, bamboo wind chimes. Some of the streets are subtitled in Chinese, multi-culturalism on the march, others have *Fashion District* underneath the names. Everything is a district now. There never used to be districts.   (43)

To be accurate, of course, there were always districts; but there never used to be perceptive artists of the calibre of Margaret Atwood to record and so, in terms of print, to preserve them.

If Tony Goderich is accurate in identifying 'two dozen highly vocal and visible minorities' (not to mention other distinguishable areas), it is clearly impossible to isolate and discuss all of them here. Moreover, some (including the Chinese and Greek communities) have not become prominent in imaginative literature in the English language. Others have not merely changed but have been transformed out of all recognition. Garner's Anglo-Saxon slum of Cabbagetown is an example. Even when he published the full text in 1968, he felt the need to include a preface which acknowledged that it remained 'only a memory to those of us who lived in it when it was a slum' since, after the Second World War, most of the area 'was bulldozed to the ground' (vii). Garner returned to the area for the setting of a later novel, *The Intruders* (1976), by which time 'old Cabbagetown' had become 'the Regent Park Housing Development' (18). Most of the original inhabitants have departed, and most of those who remain are resentful. As one character expresses it to a representative intruder who seemed 'too well-dressed for the neighbourhood' (16): '"My resentment is due to the fact that you people pay crazy inflated prices for houses that were rented at reasonable rents by my people, who then had to move out"' (86). Another, himself one of the intruders who is in a position to flourish as an interior decorator, reveals the change in attitude by observing that now '"Cabbagetown has a nostalgic ring, like Vancouver's Gastown"' (289). Yet another, in perhaps the most troubling statement in the book, even questions whether the architectural gutting and redesigning have made any essential difference: 'They'd torn down old Cabbagetown, a slum neighbourhood of stinking lanes and back alleys filled with bug-ridden row houses, then in South Regent Park they'd built apartment blocks that soon became a slum of their own' (31).

Elsewhere, on the sideroads rather than on the more prominent main arteries, the ordinary middle-class lives of descendants of the Anglo-Saxon city – or those who have long assimilated with it – continued (and continue) much as before. Douglas Lochhead, an Ontarian by birth though a Maritimer by adoption and inclination, records a year's stay in the Davisville area in his Souster-like *Millwood Road Poems* (1970). The traditionally 'poetic' and 'non-poetic' are alike recorded. Lochhead catches the curious beauty of residential Toronto in the image of an elm that 'flings wide through air / its branches / in deft curves / of motion / the Chinese would also / respect" (37). At the same time he observes how 'Two secretaries / in bathing suits / lie down to sun / on stretched out towels' (39). It is an area of tree-lined lanes and an appealing neighbourhood park where

> my children race the clouds,
> overtake and wrestle them to ground
> like steers. (38)

Nothing, however, is constant:

> In the evenings
> at the picnic tables
> the new Canadians sit
> studying their grammars,
> the way into the new world. (49)

The existence of other areas is indirectly signalled in a casual-sounding but significant poem that heralds inevitable change of more than one kind:

> We might be in Rome,
> for Italian voices
> tell us it is seven-thirty,
> a cold morning in December.
> They are the wreckers
> come to demolish the next-door houses ... (41)

'We might be in Rome.' The Italian community in Toronto has long been prominent in numbers, though only recently has the impact of Italian culture made itself felt in literary terms. It has recently done so in the poetry of Mary di Michele, though she has concentrated not on 'Little Italy' or the world of '"doferin e san cler,"' in Joseph Pivato's words (81), but on the uneasy relationships between the young who are eager to assimilate and their parents who are not. She catches, then, like F.G. Paci in Sault Ste Marie, the schizophrenic quality of ethnic life, writing of those

> with one bare foot in a village in the Abruzzi,
> the other busy with cramped English speaking toes
> in Toronto. (*Bread* 33)

This particular generation gap is well articulated in 'Pièta '78':

> Between my mother and me the spaces are long and filled
> with other things: TV, a companion, the moka, in its
> jet rush, the pouring of espresso, the passing of sugar,
> the clicking of spoons. (43)

Nowhere are the tensions of Italian-Torontonian life better expressed than in the long poem 'Mimosa' from *Mimosa and Other Poems*. It begins with an impressionistic portrait of Vito as

> a sad man,
> all Sunday afternoon finds him rocking
> in the brighton rocker, in the backyard
> of the house he's earned, under the sky he's created
> of green fiberglass. (1)

We follow 'a walk of broken tiles through the well trimmed grass / leading to a vegetable patch, fenced and carefully tended' (1), and we are told of his attempts 'to improve the English he learned in classes / for new Canadians by reading the daily papers' (2). But we are also told of 'the estrangement like a border crossing / between himself and his children.' Subsequent sections consist of the monologues of Martha, the daughter who has obediently but resentfully remained at home, and of Lucia, who has broken away. The family bonds are all too obviously disintegrating. 'I know they've made their sacrifices,' Lucia admits, but adds bitingly: 'they tell me so often enough' (13). Most of the time, she observes, 'I can't even talk to my father' (13), and the only human bond that can be acknowledged is the minimal realization that 'we love each other in that country / we couldn't live in' (16). This is, of course, a historical drama being played out in many areas among many nationalities, but di Michele gives it an especially poignant local habitation in the Italian districts of the city where a hitherto unquestioned traditionalism comes into conflict with distressingly insistent new ways.

As far to the west of downtown Toronto as Cabbagetown was on the east lay the Jewish district, the heart of which is defined by Shirley Faessler in her collection of stories, *A Basket of Apples* (1988), as 'the area bounded by College and Spadina, Dundas and Elizabeth' (21). The leading character in Henry Kreisel's *The Rich Man* (1948) is presented as living here in the 1930s, when he worked in the well-known clothing area around the southern end of Spadina. There the Jewish section is merely described as 'one of the poorer districts of Toronto' (14), but in Faessler's fiction, the full-length *Everything in the Window* (1979) as well as her short stories (some of the same characters appear in both), a focal point is Bellevue Avenue and the Glicksman home which Sophie refers to bitterly as 'that dump of a place she had come from' (*Everything* 49).

Much of the action in Faessler's work takes place in the 1920s and 1930s, during the times of Prohibition and Depression. The main difference between the two books is that *Everything in the Window* is a straightforward linear narrative whereas *A Basket of Apples* looks back at the earlier period from the perspective of the sixties and seventies. We see the Jewish immigrants seeking a new life in North America after the privations and pogroms of Europe. They begin modestly – the Glicksman family live at first in 'two rooms and kitchen above a synagogue' (*Basket* 46) – and we watch the men attempting to make their living as pedlars and later (more dangerously but also more profitably) as bootleggers. The women of this generation, however, remain fixed in a circumscribed world of home and immediate local district. Sophie's stepmother Chayele, for example, had lived in the city for 'umpteen years' but had 'only learned to speak a dozen words in English' (*Everything* 43).

Faessler can project a very real sense of human community with all the tension and bickering that tend to accompany this. In a manner recalling di Michele, she chronicles the relentless decline of traditional ethnic ways over the years as her younger characters drop away from the beliefs and practices of their forebears. Chayele, the stepmother, is religious but illiterate, her husband aware of Jewish history but an atheist. When Sophie marries a gentile, however, he insists on his becoming a Jew and undergoing the rite of circumcision. On the death of her husband, Chayele refuses to move in with her stepchildren because 'neither of us kept a kosher table or observed the dietary laws' (*Basket* 154). There is much traditional Jewish humour here, but it invariably contains a tinge of sadness, since incongruity arises between what is officially accepted and what is actually professed; it is a humour of subterfuge, of hypocrisies exposed and deceptions revealed. The sense of lives lived close together is deftly and impressively evoked, but the area itself is one from which, in later years, the successful become eager to extricate themselves. Their motives are vividly recaptured in Rick Salutin's *A Man of Little Faith* (1988) with a reference to 'musty houses and tenements, where Yiddish accents cling to the wallpaper in the halls like mildew' (87).

The original Jewish district is an area which, as we shall see, was infiltrated by Austin Clarke's 'Wessindians' in the 1960s, by which time the more affluent Jews were looking 'north into what was fast becoming the Ghetto, the area of success' (Clarke, *Meeting Point* 108). Not only 'the Ghetto' but, as Salutin reminds us, 'the gilded ghetto' (87) – another example of a radical change that paradoxically contains the seeds of continuity and recurrence. The process is illustrated by a casual reference to a peripheral couple in *A Basket of Apples*: 'the business prospered and in no time they were living in a house Up the Hill (north of Eglinton) with wall-to-wall broadloom, a maid and a big car in the garage' (152).

Significantly, the last three stories in Faessler's collection are set in the comparatively recent past. They are all concerned with women's poker games. There are no topographical references; the women in question move to and fro in taxis, and win or (more generally) lose sums of money that would have been considered vast riches by the previous generation. We get a strong impression of material advance, but concurrently of spiritual and moral decline. Beneath the veneer of sophisticated tough-minded humour lies a disturbing sense of emptiness, of that special boredom that accompanies prosperous decadence.

Whereas Faessler devotes most of her space to the old district, Salutin emphasizes the new – the stretch of Bathurst immediately above St Clair: 'Temple and synagogue, hill and dale, liberal and orthodox; the duplexes and triplexes; the bridge over the ravine. The side streets peeking east into Forest Hill Village and west into more modest Cedarvale, all home to Jews who escaped Christie Pits and Kensington Market, fleeing north from downtown' (10). Oskar, the chief character, is described as 'dybbuk' of Bathurst (260), and Salutin is clearly fascinated by the paradoxes that exist within contemporary Jewish culture, but his 'man of little faith' is still a God-intoxicated man even if he is unsure of His existence. Faessler's gambling women, though their language is spiced with Jewish allusion, have become part of an assimilated rootlessness. When one character dies of a heart-attack after just missing 'the 250-dollar prize at the Knights of Columbus giant bingo game' (*Basket* 155), Faessler so complicates her readers' responses that they do not know whether to laugh or cry.

The reference to Christie Pits, the scene of a notorious Fascist and anti-Semitic demonstration in the 1930s, reminds us, like Earle Birney's 'Anglosaxon Street,' of the ever-present danger of prejudice. This is exacerbated, of course, with the appearance of large numbers of immigrants with a conspicuously different skin-colour. Writers have frequently drawn attention to human responses, whether of interest or unease, to this new phenomenon. Aunt Muriel, in Atwood's *Life before Man*, is riddled with prejudice: 'She is now saying that Toronto is not what it was ... The Pakis are taking over the city ... A shopgirl (implied: foreign, dark skinned, accented, or all three) was rude to her in Creeds just last Wednesday' (108). But the matter can be troubling to people of less obviously entrenched racist biases. A leading, reasonably sympathetic character in Marian Engel's *Lunatic Villas* (1981) is acutely conscious of the 'degree to which the city is increasingly non-Anglo-Saxon, to say the least' (83–4). She notices 'prim-voiced ladies in saris, turbanned Sikhs looking wary, slouching or preening in their confusion at having become the new Jews; and the stout, winter-sallow Mediterranean people' (84), and remarks: 'It's hard ... not to think of us and them' (85). In contrast, however, another character 'drools at the black babies encased in shocking-pink artificial fur, in snowsuits that would be vulgar on pasty white ones but are luscious against brown skin until they've been two or three times to the laundromat' (84). Similarly, Raymond Souster gives thanks to God in 'Milk-Chocolate Girl' for the Caribbean beauty who has lit up

> the darkness
> of this lunch hour for us
> with a turn of your head,
> a single flash from your eyes. (3.153)

These are some of the ways in which established Torontonians view the new immigrants; how do these new immigrants view the established Torontonians? The fiction of the Barbadian-born novelist Austin Clarke is of particular interest because he provides a complex answer to this question. By happy accident, Clarke himself came to Toronto with the first wave of West Indian students in 1955 to study at the University of Toronto. In those days, the narrator of *Storm of Fortune* recalls, 'Huron used to be the international street' (188). The following decade saw the arrival of considerable numbers of immigrants from the Caribbean in search not only of education but of employment and material advance. Clarke catches so many of the dramatic and pathetic human qualities that result from this new development. He is skilled at evoking the curious juxtaposition of Ontarian and 'Wessindian' speech, and is also sensitive to what he calls 'racial fall-out' (*Meeting Point* 21). In his trilogy consisting of *The Meeting Point* (1967), *Storm of Fortune* (1973), and *The Bigger Light* (1975) he follows the fortunes of a handful of such immigrants – especially Bernice Leach and her sister Estelle, and Boysie and Dots Cumberbatch – as they proceed to carve out new lives in a strange and often harsh city. In addition, he has written short stories about West Indians in Toronto gathered into volumes such as *When Women Rule* (1985) and *Nine Men Who Laughed* (1986).

The importance of Clarke's contribution to the literary history of Toronto is twofold. Not only does he present the world of Caribbean immigrants from their own viewpoint; he also presents a fresh and challenging perspective on the richer areas of Toronto – Findley's Rosedale and Salutin's 'gilded ghetto,' for instance – as seen through the eyes of these same West Indians working in menial occupations such as office cleaning and domestic service. Early in *The Meeting Point*, for example, we are introduced to 'this cadillac-and-fleece-lined, suede-coat-and-fur-and-sable-reinforced section of Forest Hill Village' (5) where his protagonist Bernice works as maid. '"There's money on everybody' [sic] face and clothes, up here in Forest Hill!"' she exclaims, and her friends Dots 'said the same thing about Rosedale' (6). Clarke's newly arrived Barbadians are continually amazed by aspects of Toronto life that long-term Torontonians take for granted. To take an innocent example, Estelle, Bernice's sister, is catapulted from the Caribbean into a Canadian winter and cannot understand 'why steam was coming out of their noses and mouths, whenever words came out' (67). Bernice herself wonders 'how these people could laugh at jokes about Jews, when they were all Jews themselves' (10) – not realizing that, along with her Barbadian friends, she is constantly making comparable jokes about West Indians. Her friend Dots has sharp eyes for the amatory habits of Torontonians: '"you have no idea of the amount o' sinning, fornicating, and adultering that takes place in this Toronto. But when it happens in the white man's corner o' the world, I think they calls it by another name"' (192). At the same time, for Estelle '"Toronto is a cruel place"' (*Storm* 35).

Clarke brilliantly juxtaposes the working days of his Barbadians, which inevitably bring them within the purlieus of the older Anglo-Saxon city, 'the suburbs of wealth and loneliness, and long hard work' (*Meeting Point* 103), and their leisure hours when they seek a home away from home. In the earlier parts of the trilogy Bernice finds this primarily in the area around Shaw Street (to the west of the city centre) where her church is located:

It was a community of immigrants: immigrants who were not Anglo-saxon. Like her, these immigrants had suddenly realized they were lost in a foreign land. And like her, and her West Indian friends, they came together like seaweed on pieces of drifting wood, in a sea with a current that went no way ... Dots had said, once, about this street, 'This is the only street in this place, this Shaw Street, where people talk and walk in a million and one different nationalities and languages, and nobody doesn't stop talking the moment I walk by, or you walk by. And one thing on this street I notice: nobody don't look at you with wonder and scorn.'   (*Meeting Point* 101)

To which Bernice adds: '"I don't feel that I am either a black person or a white person. Not on this street. This is like home in Barbados"' (101). Some years later, Boysie has a similar experience 'on Wells, a street jammed with West Indians who went about their business with the easy pace and the silent dreamlike manner as if they were still walking under the sun' (*Bigger* 204).

'Loneliness' is a recurrent word and theme in Clarke's work. Bernice complains: "'It is too lonely here. And people don't speak to you on the street car.'" Colour prejudice is, of course, suspected, but a fellow Barbadian remarks that "'the Jewish fellar who lives in the room next to mine, he tell me they don't speak to him, neither'" (*Meeting Point* 70). Which may merely enlarge the extent of prejudice, or suggest Canadian restraint or Anglo-Saxon formality seen from the other side. But Clarke is interested at least as much in the human and psychological as in the sociopolitical aspects of prejudice. He is concerned with what happens to people, black or white, within a situation where the possibility of prejudice is ever-present. Thus Bernice, an open and loving person, 'grew to hate Mrs Burrmann [her employer] even more than she hated winter and the snow' (*Meeting Point* 7). The conditions of her life cause her to swing drastically from positive to negative attitudes. "'Canada, Mississippi, Alabama, South Africa, God, they is the same thing! ... As far as a black person is concerned.'" But the narrator points out that she was, 'in a sense, as happy on Marina Boulevard, as she could be (as a black woman) anywhere else in North America' (95). Alas, the parenthesis is crucial. At the same time, Clarke refuses to confuse black and white skin-colour with black and white moral judgments. One of the most poignant moments in his books occurs in a scene on the subway where a small child, to the embarrassment of his mother, points to Estelle and says: "'Mummy! *Look!*'" (202). The narrator informs us that the child is impressed by her beauty, but Estelle herself understandably interprets it as a critical racist reaction. Again, Clarke notes that neither prejudice nor moral right is a prerogative of one side. Boysie remarks at one point, "'All white people is bitches, if you ask me,'" but adds: "'And we, as black people, ain't much different, neither'" (*Storm* 238).

But circumstances change in the Caribbean community, as in any other. In *The Bigger Light* and some of the later short stories, Clarke paints a picture of his West Indian characters settling into a Canadian life-style with a sad blend of loss and gain. For an aging Byosie in the process of transforming himself into the more respectable-sounding 'Bertram,' Barbados is 'no longer in [his] plans,' and he is more concerned 'to live here [i.e., in Toronto] in the best way' (*Bigger* 39). He begins to think about moving to a 'better' district, since Ontario Street 'was not the place to live when he was striving so hard for appearances' (67). He is no longer blaming either Canada or Toronto: 'the country was good to him. It was all those noisy West Indians whom he had learned to tolerate but who were not good for the country, his country' (271). The pathos of assimilation is supremely caught here. Boysie 'had everything he wanted in life in this country. He was solvent, his business showed a profit, his clothes were new and expensive, and he had the car of his dreams' (228). But he is not happy, and when we see him for the last time he is not so much 'moving up' (98) as moving on, a latter-day example of the traditional Canadian pioneer who becomes dissatisfied as soon as he has changed his status from nothing to something. Yet even this is not the final irony for the 'Wessindians' in Toronto. This is to be found in 'The Discipline,' a story from the collection *When Women Rule*. A black father is accused of assaulting his son. He is embittered because the son '"can no longer understand the way I speak"' (132). The climax comes when the son says to him: '"You're a damn old-fashioned West Indian. I was born here, man. I'm a Canadian"' (133). Success and failure are no longer distinguishable.

The dour and dull Toronto of the Second World War period, excoriated by Wyndham Lewis, gave way in the sixties to a bewildering but exciting and exhilarating new city. In the closing years of the century, however, that revised image of Toronto is in turn giving way to something more equivocal. The variety and cosmopolitan vibrancy remains, but some disconcerting shadows are becoming visible. The trendy has now become the established and in the due course of things is being challenged in its turn. Of course, for the earlier generation of writers – those who came to artistic maturity before mid-century and have survived as active commentators on the new Toronto – the changes have been painful as well as stimulating. The older city may have been oppressive and in need of invigorating challenge, but for those who had grown accustomed to the old ways, the danger of degeneration rather than improvement was always present.

In his later novels written after 1970, Morley Callaghan duly registered the physical changes (which often imply moral changes), though the new atmosphere is skilfully presented within a context of human continuity. In *A Fine and Private Place* (1975), for example, one of the characters walks north up Yonge Street into 'the neighborhood of hamburger joints, bars with naked-breasted girls, bars with naked-bottomed girls, dance halls, horror movies, dirty-book stores, Oriental shops and bazaars, and on the corner, the hookers and pimps. Down the street in single file came eight young Buddhists in saffron robes and shaven heads chanting "Krishna, Krishna"' (101). A similar impressionistic vividness conjures up an unnamed but clearly recognizable Yorkville:

Moving slowly in the crowd, Jake and Lisa passed little boutiques in battered old houses and new expensive restaurants, and there, that most quixotic spot, the old folks home, where elderly people sat on lounging chairs watching the new life flow by. Some people in town were proud of the neighborhood of hippies, junkies, and discontented, bored, high school girls. The people who were proud said the little neighborhood showed how the town was in close touch with the restless boredom of the outside world.   (141)

Such generalized commentary is somewhat rare in Callaghan – it recalls Hugh Hood, who published the first of his *New Age* series in the same year, and later, as we have seen, set his story 'Cute Containers' in the same area and employed many of the same details. Callaghan's juxtaposition of 'little boutiques in battered old houses' with 'new expensive restaurants' shows how the old contrasts in class and prosperity continue in new guise. Later, however, Callaghan's view of the city grew darker. Of the 'downtown core,' the narrator in *Close to the Sun Again* (1977) comments: 'The neighborhood was deteriorating. It was impossible to control the deterioration, with loudspeakers permitted to blare out the attractions of body rubs and porno shops. This pimp's paradise. This hooker's haven' (39). The new Toronto clearly has its shadow side.

   Robertson Davies's contemporary response is wittier and more elegant, but the message is similar. When he reprinted his earlier Samuel Marchbanks books in the 1980s, he acted as if he were a historically minded editor, commenting in his own name on the attitudes and opinions of his crusty persona. This creates an additional complicating effect. For example, in 1947 Marchbanks had recorded the following account of the area just described by Callaghan:

Riding up Yonge Street in the trolley, past all those postage stamp stores, dress-suit renters, used car bazaars, pants-pressing ateliers, bathtub entrepreneurs and antique shops specializing in leering china dogs, my heart was heavy. This, I thought, is Canada's answer to Bond St., to Fifth Avenue, to the Rue de la Paix.

Davies, commenting on the passage in 1985, observes: 'The area so described is now called The Strip, and its transvestite population alone rouses the envy of Hamburg, Copenhagen and other foreign sin centres' (*Papers* 31). And so the whirligig of time brings in his revenges. Davies makes a similar point, lightly but unequivocally, in a later note: 'Times have changed. Toronto is now the soignée enchantress of Canadian cities, wearing her necklace of murders and crimes of violence with an air of international chic' (269). Babylon on the Humber once again.

Margaret Atwood herself is an eloquent reminder that a younger generation of writers can be no less satirical of contemporary excesses. The writer of this period who has offered the most probing critique of Toronto as a modern human centre is, however, the poet Dennis Lee, who was an almost exact contemporary of Atwood as an undergraduate at Victoria College, University of Toronto. Both share an unease about the dizzying period in which they grew up, but, where Atwood articulates her concern in satirical presentations of absurd extravagance, Lee becomes more brooding and meditative. For him, the specificity of place is a habitual starting-point for intellectual exploration that takes him beyond the local. And the place is always Toronto. He has poems with titles like 'Brunswick Avenue,' 'High Park, by Grenadier Pond,' 'Sibelius Park,' 'When I Went Up to Rosedale,' and these evoke concrete or at least relevant images that conjure up the experience of city living in general and Toronto living in particular. So Brunswick Avenue suggests this:

> Outside, the rasp of a snow shovel
> grates in the dark
> Lovely
> sound, I hang on to it.   (11)

And High Park, this:

>   in front of us the
> path makes stately patterns down the slope to Grenadier and all the
> random ambling of the couples hangs
>   like courtly bygones in the shining air.   (13)

Or Sibelius Park, a small park in downtown Toronto, this:

> Across that green expanse he sees
>   the cars parked close, every second license yankee, he thinks of
> the war and the young men dodging.   (23)

For Lee, these varying spirits of place bring out respectively a unique sense-experience, an awareness of the interrelatedness of past and present, and the bitterness of the concerned citizen. It is this last response that becomes dominant.

Civil Elegies (1968, revised 1972) is unquestionably Lee's major poem.

It takes the form of nine meditations set in Nathan Phillips Square in front of the newly built and once controversial City Hall, and in the vicinity of Henry Moore's abstract sculpture *The Archer* ('that big dinosaur's knuckle-joint,' as Al Purdy later called it [qtd in Kilbourn 181]):

> I sat one morning by the Moore, off to the west
> ten yards and saw though diffident my city nailed against the sky
> in ordinary glory. (33)

A microcosm of the Toronto population of the late 1960s is to be found there: 'the shoppers, hippies, brokers, children, old men dozing alone by the pool' (52). The scene spurs Lee into an anguished consideration of the complex social and political problems of the time: the euphoria of the Canadian centenary not quite able to mask the nation's indirect involvement in the Vietnam War, the increased separatist tension in Québec, the threat of foreign (especially American) ownership of Canadian resources, and not least the growing pains of a nation beginning to become aware of its international role. All these are primarily national (rather than exclusively provincial) problems; Lee is in many respects a spokesman for that outgoing Ontarian viewpoint – here paired with an intense moral conscience – that sees itself as the region of the centre.

Lee's tone in *Civil Elegies* is muted and generally dour. He has a keen eye for 'the acres of gutted intentions ... the concrete debris ... parking scars' (33), for 'asphalt panaceas,' and 'the itch for new debentures, greater expressways' (35), and an equally keen nose for political corruption – he is aware that 'Heavy developers / pay off aldermen still' (35). He is also conscious of a modern sense of cushioned pointlessness; in the final poem, 'The last few tourists pass by the Moore and snap their proof that they were also alive' (55). But the willed sense of modernity seems strangely deadened. In the 'Sibelius Park' poem, he had recalled his earlier Christian zealousness and its failure ('what broke at last was the / holiness' [24]), and in *Civil Elegies* one feels – and is furthermore aware that Lee also feels – the impulse of an Old Testament prophet without any divine mandate. Deeply influenced by the thinking of the philosopher George Grant, Lee feels drawn to a superior past but is at the same time suspicious of a retreat into sentimental reaction. He recalls sardonically the almost farcical collapse of the 1837 Rebellion, recognizes it as a recurrent pattern, and gives vent to a sense of helplessness. Nonetheless, the shade of an ideal remains, and he dreams, though without much conviction, of a possible, positive citizenship:

> to furnish, out of the traffic and smog and the shambles of dead
> precursors,
> a civil habitation that is
> human, and our own.   (36)

Perhaps the most memorable feature of *Civil Elegies* – its affirmation achieved, as it were, against the grain – is not so much the portrayal of Toronto at a crucial stage in its growth, but rather the fact that Toronto can be used as the basis for a profound meditation on the course of the twentieth-century western world.

It would be inappropriate, however, to leave a literary portrait of Toronto with the hermit-like figure of Dennis Lee pondering corruption in Nathan Phillips Square. This is a city of conspicuous contrasts, well exemplified by Minna Joyce, a rebel exile from 'the depths of Rosedale' (50) in Timothy Findley's short-story collection *Stones*, who escapes the unbearable respectability of her birth to live 'on Foxley Street in Parkdale ... centred in the dark of Crazyland' (56). This is close to Queen Street West, which, as we have seen, provides Atwood with an ambiguous image of the contemporary city. Minna finds work in the Morrison Café (which she christens, significantly, 'The Moribund Café' [29]), 'just across the road' from the Queen Street Mental Health Centre (30). Indeed, Rosedale and the Mental Health Centre (known for generations as 999 Queen Street West, though now listed less dramatically as 1001) become the extreme points of Findley's Toronto. On the one hand, the decadent rich; on the other, 'the rummies and drugged-out kids, the schizoids and the dead-eyed retainers' (31). Here we find the twentieth-century equivalent to Susanna Moodie's University and Lunatic Asylum (see p. 199 above).

It is also a city of restless movement, and any conclusion should involve a walk through the jostling streets and an exploration of the dizzyingly shifting districts. This can be provided through a return to Margaret Atwood's *Cat's Eye*, where Queen Street West is once again prominent. Elaine Risley, a painter returned for an artistic retrospective, makes her own peace with the city in which she grew up by retreading its streets, which in turn spark off her individual remembrance of time past. A novel that concerns itself with Time, relativity, and the relentlessness and inevitability of change necessarily comments on the changes that have overtaken its principal setting. These are architectural, cultural, and psychological; they are expressed through a preoccupation with transformed life-styles and the grotesque vagaries of fashion. Elaine finds herself plunged equivocally into the lost world of her childhood:

Once it was fashionable to say how dull it was ...

Now you're supposed to say how much it's changed. *World-class city* is a phrase they use in magazines these days, a great deal too much. All those ethnic restaurants, and the theatre and the boutiques. New York without the garbage and muggings, it's supposed to be ...

And I can't believe it's changed ... Underneath the flourish and ostentation is the old city, street after street of thick red brick houses, with their front porch pillars like the off-white stems of toadstools, and their watchful, calculating windows. Malicious, grudging, vindictive, implacable.   (13–14)

Like Hood's Matt Goderich at the turfed-over Reservoir Ravine, like Garner's cabbagetowner contemplating a yuppie slum, like Salutin's recognition of a 'gilded ghetto' in North York, Elaine discovers the changelessness of change.

Yet, as she walks along the familiar downtown streets, the changes are startling:

I head north, then east along Queen Street, which is another place we never used to go. It was rumoured to be the haunt of grubby drunks, rubby-dubs we called them; they were said to drink rubbing alcohol and sleep in telephone booths and vomit on your shoes in the streetcar.   (19)

Now it's a place of trendy art and trendy fashions, the area summed up in the already quoted phrase, 'the sawtoothed edge of trend.' Some of these physical changes are profoundly indicative of changes in human attitudes and priorities. She walks up past the Parliament Buildings into the haunts of Elizabeth, Nick, and Lesje in *Life before Man*, and comes upon the Church of the Redeemer:

I cross the street, cut in behind a small church, left stranded here when they redeveloped. Sunday's sermon is announced on a billboard identical to the kind for supermarket specials: *Believing Is Seeing*. A vertical wave of plate glass breaks against it. Behind the polished façades, bouquets of teased cloth, buffed leather, cunning silver trinkets. Pasta to die for. Theology has changed, over the years: *just deserts* used to be what everyone could expect to get in the end. Now it's a restaurant specializing in cakes. All they had to do was abolish guilt, and add an S.   (312)

This is more than mere literary impressionism. These are found symbols as potent in Atwood's fictive vision as in the painterly vision of her protagonist.

Even more disconcerting is her visit to Simpsons, the long established and seemingly timeless department store. But here, as elsewhere, contemporaneity has triumphed:

I become lost immediately. They've changed the whole thing over. It used to be sedate wood-rimmed glass counters, with gloves in standard patterns, appropriate wristwatches, accent scarves in floral prints. Serious-minded good taste. Now it's a cosmetic fairground: silver trim, gold pillars, marquee lights, brand-name letters the size of a human head. The air is saturated with the stink of perfumes at war.   (112)

Elaine gets the uneasy impression that she is 'jumping time' (113).

And so, in the process of reading *Cat's Eye*, do we. Not just in the description but in the attitudes. 'The fact is,' Elaine records early in the book, 'I hate this city. I've hated it so long I can hardly remember feeling any other way about it' (13). This may spark off a memory of Raymond Souster's poem 'The Hated City' (1.86) or the apostrophe, 'Strange city, / cold, hateful city' in 'The City Called a Queen' (1.239). Or Lister Sinclair's insistence: 'We *all* hate Toronto!' (227). But that stretches back over half a century, and love has interspersed with hate many times since then. Souster's hate, we remember, is balanced by 'a local pride.' The continuity calls attention to the change, and vice versa. The fact of change bears testimony to a living city, one that will change, unceasingly, in the future.

Indeed, by the time these words are read, Toronto – and Ontario – will have changed again.

Epilogue: The View from Wells Hill Park

I began this book with personal reminiscences of immigration, worked back to the early European settlers battling with omnipresent trees, and end with accounts of a rapidly changing contemporary Toronto. Now I lay down my pen, move to my window, and look out over the leafy expanse of green to Wells Hill Park from the house in which I have lived for over twenty years. Toronto, the natural world, change. It was in this area that, according to Ernest Thompson Seton's memoir of the late nineteenth century, a mountain lion had been killed not long before. About the time we moved in, at the close of the 1960s, I read a news item about a stray and starving wolf recently shot within the boundaries of Metropolitan Toronto. No mountain lions, no wolves here now, but Works Department concrete has not yet wholly replaced the earth and the green and the living.

Once, some fifteen years ago, when I had occasion to leave home at earliest dawn, I flushed a killdeer while crossing this tiny, block-square park. Every spring and fall, migrants on their way to and from the northern coniferous forests pause for a day or two to rest in the blue spruce on our front lawn. Just this last May, I looked out one morning and there was a male black-throated blue warbler resplendent in his spring plumage. A little earlier I had watched myrtle warblers and golden-crowned kinglets. Yet change has affected the bird population also. When we first moved in, the occasional gull would appear during bad weather; now there is a resident and vociferous colony of ring-billeds, an offshoot of the population at the Leslie Street spit. More recently, a pair of house finches, the latest immigrant colonizers, marked out their territory; throughout May we watch for the flash of red, listen for that bubbling, narrow-registered, strangely endearing song.

The human population that uses the park has also changed. In the early days, an elderly, dark-clothed Italian widow was to be seen there constantly, sitting on one of the municipal park benches, watching the children at play. Dead now, perhaps. Certainly, the gossiping, eccentric odd-jobs man died a few years ago. He had added a vivid dimension to our private mythology of the area by warning the previous owners of our house of the depredations caused by moose: 'They come up out of the ravine!' My predecessor spoilt the potentiality of the story by inquiring whether he was confusing moose and raccoons: 'Ah yes, raccoons.' He is gone now; the story, the non-literary and deceptive image, lives on. Those who come to the park in the early 1990s reflect the new multiculturalism: black children cavorting in the paddling pool, babies in the sand box tended by young women who are, I suspect, the children of Vietnamese boat-people; a sprinkling of Indian men from a recently opened hostel. All of them enjoying the summer, so it would appear, in reasonable harmony. In the early morning, orientals are not uncommonly seen performing Tai Chi exercises in silent unison. At lunch-time last year, a young man of Caribbean origin regularly came here to practise his golf-strokes. Males of all shapes and sizes play touch football; young girls skip; people of both sexes and all ages and colours exercise with frisbees or skate in winter on the hastily improvised rink. But I must not get sentimental. A couple of years or so ago, a rape case was reported from this same park – a circumstance undreamt-of earlier; the new patterns of living create their own problems and dangers.

Why mention all this here? Because it indicates my own perspective, my idiosyncratic interests, the personal aspects that must have affected all that I have written in this book. As an immigrant, a British immigrant, and for most of my residence in Ontario a Torontonian, I bring my own quirks and biases to the subject. Ontario is vast, and large areas of it I have never seen. The literature is also vast; though here I can claim to have read quite widely, I am aware of many gaps it could take the best part of my lifetime to plug. Over the last few years, friendly colleagues and chance acquaintances, hearing of my work on this book, have been prodigal with advice: 'Have you read this?' 'What about that?' I have been grateful, yet at the same time somewhat stubborn. This is *my* book, *my* vision, *my* Ontario. Someone who lived in Belleville, or Smith's Falls, or Sarnia, or Sudbury, or Sault Ste Marie, or Hearst, or Manitoulin, or Kenora would inevitably have written a different book. So would any writer whose cultural background is different from mine. Even as I write, other voices are beginning to be heard – Indian voices, eastern European voices, voices of those whose roots are in the process of digging deep, have already dug deep, into the Ontario soil. (Only a fortnight ago, I met a Chinese who could trace his family – within Ontario – almost back to Confederation.) I make no apology for my unique, necessarily limited viewpoint. This can only be my book, selective, imperfect; but no one can write a comprehensively adequate book about Ontario.

Ontario changes, and so does the literature that encompasses it. Had I written only a few months later, the text and the whole balance of the book might have been different. I have just been reading Thomas King's much-discussed collection *All My Relations: An Anthology of Contemporary Canadian Native Fiction*, published after I had completed my main text. Many of the authors come from and write about Ontario; they present a perspective likely to become more prominent in the immediate future. Then there is Al Purdy's recently published first novel, *A Splinter in the Heart*. Based on his own memories of growing up in Trenton, it would have filled in one more comparative blank on the literary map. At about the same time, Hugh Hood's *Property and Value* appeared, with its extended comparison between Toronto and Venice – a provocative linkage absurd to some, stimulating to others. By the time these pages see print, other books will have added new images and qualified others. This is an ever-changing kaleidoscope caught in its shifting pattern at an arbitrary moment in time – or, more appropriately, a dense literary forest where it is difficult, as the saying goes, to distinguish the wood from the trees.

Even the trees around Wells Hill Park, trees that seemed so permanent, are changing. A day or two ago, a flyer from the local residents' and ratepayers' association announced that the Norway maples lining Hilton Avenue, the street on which I live, are reaching the end of their lifespan: 'The number of trees in Hillcrest has been declining over the last decade or so. The area used to be the site of a large native stand of oaks dating back 150 years or more.' Through the remaining foliage, I catch brief glimpses of St Clair Avenue. I am reminded, appropriately, of the concluding poem in Margaret Atwood's *Journals of Susanna Moodie*. Throughout the book, Atwood has scrutinized Moodie as an equivocal, infuriating, but unique and necessary ancestor. The nineteenth and twentieth centuries, so superficially different, blend as Atwood attempts to look through Moodie's eyes and also imagines the reverse process. Finally, in 'A Bus along St Clair: December,' she presents the image of a resuscitated Susanna Moodie as an old lady in a St Clair bus, a wraith not confined to the perspective of the present, one for whom the Toronto of the 1830s and that of the 1970s are not to be distinguished. She speaks – to me, to all of us – from the bus window:

> Turn, look down;
> there is no city;
> this is the centre of a forest   (61)

The sound of a powerful revved engine comes to me. Almost certainly a bus moving to or from the St Clair West subway station. A characteristic Torontonian, Ontarian sound. But I cannot quite see it for the surviving, intervening trees.

Works Cited

Anderson, Allen, ed. *Remembering Leacock*. Ottawa: Deneau 1983

Atwood, Margaret. *The Animals in That Country*. Toronto: Oxford University Press 1968

– *Bluebeard's Egg*. 1983. Toronto: McClelland and Stewart–Bantam 1984

– *Bodily Harm*. Toronto: McClelland and Stewart 1981

– *Cat's Eye*. Toronto: McClelland and Stewart 1988

– *The Edible Woman*. 1969. Toronto: McClelland and Stewart 1973

– 'Great Unexpectations: An Autobiographical Foreword.' In *Margaret Atwood: Visions and Forms*, ed. Kathryn VanSpanckeren and Jan Garden Castro, xiii–xvi. Carbondale: Southern Illinois University Press 1988

– *Journals of Susanna Moodie*. Toronto: Oxford University Press 1970

– *Lady Oracle*. 1976. Toronto: McClelland and Stewart–Bantam 1977

– *Life before Man*. 1979. Toronto: McClelland and Stewart–Bantam 1980

– *Second Words: Selected Critical Prose*. Toronto: Anansi 1982

Barr, Robert. *The Measure of the Rule*. 1907. Rpt. Toronto: University of Toronto Press 1973

Bartlett, William Henry. *Canadian Scenery*. London: Virtue 1842

Belaney, Archie. *See* Grey Owl.

Birney, Earle. *The Collected Poems of Earle Birney*. 2 vols. Toronto: McClelland and Stewart 1975

Blackwood, Algernon. *Episodes before Thirty*. London: Cassell 1923

– 'The Wendigo.' In *Windigo: An Anthology of Fact and Fantastic Fiction*, ed. John Robert Colombo, 65–112. Saskatoon: Western Producer Prairie Books 1982

Bodsworth, Fred. *The Atonement of Ashley Morden*. 1964. Toronto: McClelland and Stewart 1977

– *The Sparrow's Fall*. 1967. Scarborough: New American Library of Canada 1969

– *The Strange One*. 1960. London: Sphere Books 1979

Bonnycastle, Sir Richard S. *The Canadas in 1841*. 2 vols. London: Henry Colburn 1841. Rpt. Wakefield, Yorks: S.R. Publishers; New York: Johnson Reprint Corporation 1968

Bouchette, Joseph. *The British Dominions of North America*. 2 vols. London: Longman 1831. Rpt. New York: AMS Press 1968

Bourinot, John George. *Our Intellectual Strength and Weakness*. Montréal: Foster Brown 1893. Rpt. Toronto: University of Toronto Press 1973

Braithwaite, Max. *Max Braithwaite's Ontario*. Vancouver: Douglas and McIntyre 1974

Brooke, Rupert, *Letters from America*. London: Sidgwick and Jackson 1916

Bullard, Margaret. *Wedlock's the Devil*. London: Hamish Hamilton 1951

Burwell, Adam Hood. *The Poems of Adam Hope Burwell, Pioneer Poet of Upper Canada*. Ed. Carl F. Klinck. London: Lawson Memorial Library, University of Western Ontario 1963

Callaghan, Morley. *A Broken Journey*. New York: Scribner's 1932

– *Close to the Sun Again*. Toronto: Macmillan 1977

– *A Fine and Private Place*. 1975. Toronto: Macmillan 1983

– *It's Never Over*. New York: Scribner's 1930

– *More Joy in Heaven*. 1937. Toronto: McClelland and Stewart 1960

– *Morley Callaghan's Stories*. 1959. Toronto: Macmillan 1967

– *Strange Fugitive*. 1928. Edmonton: Hurtig 1970

– *Such Is My Beloved*. 1934. Toronto: McClelland and Stewart 1957

Cameron, D.A. 'The Enchanted Houses: Leacock's Irony.' In *The Canadian Novel in the Twentieth Century*, ed. George Woodcock, 1-14. Toronto: McClelland and Stewart 1975

Campbell, Wilfred. *Selected Poetry and Essays*. Ed. Laurel Boone. Waterloo: Wilfrid Laurier University Press 1987

Carver, Jonathan. *Travels through the Interior Parts of North America in the Years 1766, 1767, and 1768*. London: privately printed 1778. Rpt. Toronto: Coles 1974

Clarke, Austin. *The Bigger Light*. Boston-Toronto: Little, Brown 1975

– *The Meeting Point*. Toronto: Macmillan 1967

– *Nine Men Who Laughed*. Markham: Penguin 1986

– *Storm of Fortune*. Toronto: Little, Brown 1973

– *When Women Rule*. Toronto: McClelland and Stewart 1985

Cohen, Matt. *Flowers of Darkness*. Toronto: McClelland and Stewart 1981

– *Night Flights*. Toronto: Doubleday 1978

Colombo, John Robert. *Mysterious Canada: Strange Sights, Extraordinary Events, and Peculiar Places*. Toronto: Doubleday 1988

Connolly, Kevin, Douglas Freake, and Jason Sherman. 'Interview: Alice Munro.' *What* [Toronto] (September–October 1986), n pag

Connor, Carl Y. *Archibald Lampman, Canadian Poet of Nature*. Montréal: Carrier 1929. Rpt. Ottawa: Borealis Press 1977

Connor, Ralph. *Glengarry School Days*. 1902. Toronto: McClelland and Stewart 1975

– *The Man from Glengarry*. 1901. Toronto: McClelland and Stewart 1980

Crawford, Isabella Valancy. *Collected Poems*. Ed. J.W. Garvin. Toronto: William Briggs 1905. Rpt. Toronto: University of Toronto Press 1972

Curry, Ralph. "Stephen Leacock and His Works." In *Canadian Writers and Their Works. Fiction Series. Volume 3,* ed. Robert Lecker, Jack David, and Ellen Quigley, 163–212. Toronto: ECW Press 1988

Davies, Robertson. *Conversations with Robertson Davies.* Ed. J. Madison Davis. Jackson: University of Mississippi Press 1989

– *Fifth Business.* 1970. Markham: Penguin 1977

– *Leaven of Malice.* 1954. Toronto: Clarke Irwin 1964

– *The Lyre of Orpheus.* Toronto: Macmillan 1988

– *The Manticore.* 1972. Markham: Penguin 1976

– *A Mixture of Frailties.* 1958. Toronto: Macmillan 1968

– *Papers of Samuel Marchbanks* [new composite edition of *The Diary of Samuel Marchbanks* (1947), *The Table Talk of Samuel Marchbanks* (1949), and *Samuel Marchbanks' Almanack* (1967)]. 1985. Toronto: Totem Press 1987

– *The Rebel Angels.* Toronto: Macmillan 1981

– 'Stephen Leacock.' In *Our Living Tradition: Seven Canadians,* ed Claude Bissell, 128–49. Toronto: University of Toronto Press 1959

– *Stephen Leacock.* Toronto: McClelland and Stewart 1970

– *Tempest-Tost.* 1951. Toronto: Clarke Irwin 1965

– *What's Bred in the Bone.* Toronto: Macmillan 1985

– *World of Wonders.* 1975. Markham: Penguin 1977

Deacon, William Arthur. *The Four Jameses.* Ottawa: Graphic Press 1927

Dewdney, Christopher. *Predators of the Adoration.* Toronto: McClelland and Stewart 1983

– *Radiant Inventory.* Toronto: McClelland and Stewart 1988

Dickens, Charles. *American Notes.* 1842. *The Writings of Charles Dickens.* Vol. 11. Boston: Houghton Mifflin 1894

Dickson, Lovat. *Wilderness Man.* 1973. Scarborough: New American Library of Canada 1975

di Michele, Mary. *Bread and Chocolate* [published with Bronwen Wallace, *Marrying into the Family*]. Ottawa: Oberon Press 1980

– *Mimosa and Other Poems.* Oakville: Mosaic Press/Valley Editions 1981

Djwa, Sandra. *The Politics of the Imagination: A Life of F.R. Scott.* Toronto: McClelland and Stewart 1987

Dudek, Louis. *Selected Essays and Criticism.* Ottawa: Tecumseh Press 1978

Duncan, Sara Jeannette. *The Imperialist.* 1904. Toronto: McClelland and Stewart 1971

Dunlop, William. *Tiger Dunlop's Upper Canada.* Toronto: McClelland and Stewart 1967

Elliott, George. *The Kissing Man.* Toronto: Macmillan 1962

Engel, Marian. *The Glassy Sea.* Toronto: McClelland and Stewart 1978

– *Lunatic Villas.* Toronto: McClelland and Stewart 1981

Faessler, Shirley. *A Basket of Apples.* Toronto: McClelland and Stewart 1988

– *Everything in the Window.* 1979. Toronto: McClelland and Stewart n.d.

Findley, Timothy. *Dinner along the Amazon*. Markham: Penguin 1984
– *Stones*. Markham: Viking 1988
– *The Wars*. 1977. Markham: Penguin 1978
Finnigan, Joan. *Living Together*. Fredericton: Fiddlehead 1976
Forster, John. *The Life of Charles Dickens*. 1872–4. Ed. J.W. Ley. London: Palmer
    1928
Fowke, Edith, ed. *Lumbering Songs from the Northern Woods*. Austin: University of
    Texas Press (for American Folklore Society) 1970
– ed. *The Penguin Book of Canadian Folk Songs*. Harmondsworth: Penguin 1973
– ed. *Traditional Singers and Songs from Ontario*. Hatboro, PA: Folklore Associates;
    Don Mills: Burns and MacEachern 1965
Fraser, Sylvia. *Pandora*. 1972. Toronto: McClelland and Stewart 1976
Frye, Northrop. *The Bush Garden: Essays on the Canadian Imagination*. Toronto:
    Anansi 1971
Galt, John. *Bogle Corbet*. 1831. Toronto: McClelland and Stewart 1977
Garner, Hugh. *Cabbagetown*. Toronto: Ryerson Press 1968
– *The Intruders*. Toronto: McGraw Hill–Ryerson 1976
– 'One-Two-Three Little Indians.' In *Hugh Garner's Best Stories*, 243–54. Toronto:
    Ryerson Press 1963
– *The Silence on the Shore*. 1962. Toronto: Ryerson Press 1968
Gerson, Carole. *A Purer Taste: The Writing and Reading of Fiction in English in
    Nineteenth-Century Canada*. Toronto: University of Toronto Press 1989
Gibson, Graeme. *Eleven Canadian Novelists*. Toronto: Anansi 1973
Glazebrook, G.P. de T. *Life in Ontario: A Social History*. Toronto: University of
    Toronto Press 1968
Gordon, Charles William. *See* Connor, Ralph.
Grant, George M. *Ocean to Ocean: Sandford Fleming's Expedition through Canada in
    1872*. Toronto: Campbell 1873. Rpt Toronto: Coles 1979
Greenhill, Pauline. *True Poetry: Traditional and Popular Verse in Ontario*. Montréal
    and Kingston: McGill-Queen's University Press 1989
Grey Owl. *The Men of the Last Frontier*. 1931. Toronto: Macmillan 1972
– *Pilgrims of the Wild*. 1935. Toronto: Macmillan 1968
– *Tales of an Empty Cabin*. Toronto: Macmillan 1936
Grove, Frederick Philip. *A Search for America: The Odyssey of an Immigrant*. 1927.
    Toronto: McClelland and Stewart 1971
– *Two Generations: A Story of Present Day Ontario*. Toronto: Ryerson Press 1939
Gustafson, Ralph, ed. *The Penguin Book of Canadian Verse*. Harmondsworth: Penguin
    1958
Hall, Basil. *Travels in North America in the Years 1827 and 1828*. Edinburgh: Cadell
    1829. Rpt. Graz, Austria: Akademische Druck-u. Verlagsanstalt 1965
Head, George. *Forest Scenes and Incidents in the Wilds of North America*. London:
    Murray 1829. Rpt. Toronto: Coles 1980

Henry, Alexander. *Travels and Adventures in Canada and the Indian Territories between the Years 1760 and 1776*. 1809. Edmonton: Hurtig 1969

Heriot, George. *Travels through the Canadas*. 2 vols. London: Phillips 1807. Rpt. Toronto: Coles 1971

Hodgins, Jack. 'Invasions '79.' In *The Barclay Family Theatre*, 24–67. Toronto: Macmillan 1981

Hood, Hugh. *August Nights*. Toronto: Stoddart 1985

– *Black and White Keys*. Downsview: ECW Press 1982

– *Flying a Red Kite*. Toronto: Ryerson 1962

– *The Fruit Man, the Meat Man and the Manager*. Ottawa: Oberon Press 1971

– *The Governor's Bridge Is Closed*. Ottawa: Oberon Press 1973

– *The Motor Boys in Ottawa*. Toronto: Stoddart 1986

– *A New Athens*. Ottawa: Oberon Press 1977

– *None Genuine without This Signature*. Downsview: ECW Press 1980

– *Property and Value*. Toronto: Anansi 1990

– *Reservoir Ravine*. Ottawa: Oberon Press 1979

– *The Swing in the Garden*. Ottawa: Oberon Press 1975

– *Tony's Book*. Toronto: Stoddart 1988

Howison, John. *Sketches of Upper Canada*. Edinburgh: Oliver and Boyd 1821. Rpt. Wakefield, Yorks: S.R. Publishers; New York: Johnson Reprint Society 1965

Huggan, Isobel. *The Elizabeth Stories*. Ottawa: Oberon Press 1984

Jameson, Anna. *Winter Studies and Summer Rambles in Canada*. 3 vols. London: Saunders and Otley 1838. Rpt. Toronto: Coles 1872

Johnston, George. *Endeared by Dark: The Collected Poems*. Erin: Porcupine's Quill 1990

Jones, D.G. *Butterfly on Rock*. Toronto: University of Toronto Press 1970

– 'George Johnston.' *Canadian Literature*, no. 59 (Winter 1974), 81–7

Kane, Paul. *Wanderings of an Artist among the Indians of North America*. 1859. Edmonton: Hurtig 1974

Kilbourn, William, ed. *The Toronto Book*. Toronto: Macmillan 1976

King, Thomas, ed. *All My Relations: An Anthology of Contemporary Canadian Native Fiction*. Toronto: McClelland and Stewart 1990

Kirby, William. *The Golden Dog (Le Chien d'or)*. Montréal: Montreal News 1897

Klinck, Carl F. *Wilfred Campbell: A Study in Late Provincial Victorianism*. Toronto: Ryerson Press 1942

Knister, Raymond. *Collected Poems*. Ed. Dorothy Livesay. Toronto: Ryerson Press 1949

– *The First Day of Spring: Stories and Other Prose*. Ed. Peter Stevens. Toronto: University of Toronto Press 1976

– *Poems, Stories and Essays*. Ed. David Arnason et al. Montréal: Bellrock Press 1975

– *White Narcissus*. 1929. Toronto: McClelland and Stewart 1962

– *Windfalls for Cider*. Ed. Joy Kuropatwa. Windsor: Black Moss Press 1983

Kreisel, Henry. 'The Prairies: A State of Mind.' *Transactions of the Royal Society of Canada*, 6, series 4 (June 1968), 171–80

– *The Rich Man*. 1948. Toronto: McClelland and Stewart 1961

Laidlaw, Robert. *The McGregors: A Novel of an Ontario Pioneer Family*. Toronto: Macmillan 1979

Lambert, R.S. *Exploring the Supernatural: The Weird in Canadian Folklore*. Toronto: McClelland and Stewart 1955

Lampman, Archibald. *At the Long Sault and Other Poems*. Toronto: Ryerson Press 1943. Rpt. with *Poems*. Toronto: University of Toronto Press 1974

– (with Wilfred Campbell and Duncan Campbell Scott). *At the Mermaid Inn*. Ed. Barrie Davies. Toronto: University of Toronto Press 1979

– *Poems*. Ed. Duncan Campbell Scott. Toronto: Morang 1901. Rpt. with *At the Long Sault*. Toronto: University of Toronto Press 1974

Langton, Anne. *A Gentlewoman in Upper Canada: The Journals of Anne Langton*. Ed. H.H. Langton. Toronto: Clarke Irwin 1950

Langton, John. *Early Days in Upper Canada: Letters of John Langton*. Ed. W.A. Langton. Toronto: Macmilan 1926

Latham, David. 'McLachlan, Alexander (1818–96).' In *Oxford Companion to Canadian Literature*, ed. William Toye, 489–90. Toronto: Oxford University Press 1983

Layton, Irving. *A Red Carpet for the Sun*. Toronto: McClelland and Stewart 1958

Leacock, Stephen. *Arcadian Adventures with the Idle Rich*. 1914. Toronto: McClelland and Stewart 1969

– *The Boy I Left behind Me*. London: Bodley Head 1947

– *My Remarkable Uncle*. 1942. Toronto: McClelland and Stewart 1965

– *Sunshine Sketches of a Little Town*. 1912. Toronto: McClelland and Stewart 1970

Lee, Dennis. *Civil Elegies and Other Poems*. Enlarged ed. Toronto: Anansi 1972

Legate, David M. *Stephen Leacock: A Biography*. Toronto: Doubleday 1970

LePan, Douglas. *Weathering It: Complete Poems 1948–87*. Toronto: McClelland and Stewart 1987

Levine, Norman. *Canada Made Me*. 1958. Ottawa: Deneau and Greenberg 1979

– *One Way Ticket*. Toronto: McClelland and Stewart 1961

– *Thin Ice*. Ottawa: Deneau and Greenberg 1979

Lewis, Wyndham. *The Letters of Wyndham Lewis*. Ed. W.K. Rose. London: Methuen 1963

– *Self Condemned*. 1954. Toronto: McClelland and Stewart 1974

Livesay, Dorothy. Introduction to Raymond Knister, *Collected Poems*. Toronto: Ryerson Press 1949

Lochhead, Douglas. *The Full Furnace: Collected Poems*. Toronto: McGraw-Hill Ryerson 1975

Lower, A.R.M. *The North American Assault on the Canadian Forest*. Toronto: Ryerson Press 1938

Macklem, Michael. Untitled introduction to Raymond Souster, *Selected Poems*. Ottawa: Oberon Press 1972

MacLennan, Hugh. *Seven Rivers of Canada*. 1961. Toronto: Macmillan 1977

MacLulich, T.D. 'Mariposa Revisited.' *Studies in Canadian Literature*, 4 (Winter 1979), 167–76

Mair, Charles. *Tecumseh*. Toronto: Hunter Rose 1886

Marryat, Frederick. *Diary in America*. 1839. Ed. Jules Zanger. Bloomington: Indiana University Press 1960

McArthur, Peter. *The Best of Peter McArthur*. Ed. Alec Lucas. Toronto: Clarke Irwin 1967

McFadden, David. *A Trip around Lake Erie*. Toronto: Coach House 1980

McLachlan, Alexander. *Poetical Works*. 1900. Rpt. Toronto: University of Toronto Press 1974

Mitcham, Allison. *The Northern Imagination: A Study of Northern Canadian Literature*. Moonbeam: Penumbra Press 1983

Mitchell, John. *See* Slater, Patrick.

Moir, John S., ed. *Rhymes of Rebellion*. Toronto: Ryerson Press 1965

Moodie, Susanna. *Life in the Clearings*. 1853. Ed. Robert L. McDougall. Toronto: Macmillan 1976

– *Roughing It in the Bush*. 1852. Ed. Carl Ballstadt. Ottawa: Carleton University Press 1988

Munro, Alice. *Dance of the Happy Shades*. Toronto: Ryerson Press 1968

– *Friend of My Youth*. Toronto: McClelland and Stewart 1990

– *Lives of Girls and Women*. 1971. New York: New American Library 1974

– *The Moons of Jupiter*. 1982. Markham: Penguin 1983

– *The Progress of Love*. Toronto: McClelland and Stewart 1986

– *Something I've Been Meaning to Tell You*. 1974. Scarborough: New American Library of Canada 1975

– 'What Is Real?' In *Making It New: Contemporary Short Stories*, ed. John Metcalf, 223–6. Toronto: Methuen 1982

– *Who Do You Think You Are?* Toronto: Macmillan 1978

O'Brien, Mary. *The Journals of Mary O'Brien, 1828–1838*. Ed. Audrey Saunders Miller. Toronto: Macmillan 1968

Ondaatje, Michael. *In the Skin of a Lion*. Toronto: McClelland and Stewart 1987

Paci, F.G. *Black Madonna*. Ottawa: Oberon Press 1982

– *The Father*. Ottawa: Oberon Press 1984

– *The Italians*. Ottawa: Oberon Press 1978

Parker, Gilbert. *The Seats of the Mighty*. 1896. Ottawa: Tecumseh Press 1981

Pivato, Joseph. 'Cultura Canadese.' In *Roman Candles: An Anthology of Poems by Seventeen Italo-Canadian Poets*, ed. Pier Giorgio Di Cicco, 80–1. Toronto: Hounslow 1978

Pratt, E.J. *Collected Poems*. Ed. Sandra Djwa and R.G. Moyles. 2 vols. Toronto: University of Toronto Press 1989

Purdy, Al. *Collected Poems*. Ed. Russell Brown. Toronto: McClelland and Stewart 1986

– *In Search of Owen Roblin*. Toronto: McClelland and Stewart 1974
– *A Splinter in the Heart*. Toronto: McClelland and Stewart 1990
Radcliff, Thomas, ed. *Authentic Letters from Upper Canada*. 1833. Toronto: Macmillan 1953
Reaney, James. 'The Box Social.' In *Stories from Ontario*, ed. Germaine Warkentin, 149–51. Toronto: Macmillan 1974
– *Colours in the Dark*. Vancouver: Talonplays 1969
– *The Donnellys: A Trilogy*. Victoria: Press Porcepic 1983
– *Poems*. Ed. Germaine Warkentin. Toronto: New Press 1972
– (with C.H. Gervais). *Baldoon*. Erin: Porcupine's Quill 1976
Richardson, John. *The Canadian Brothers; or, The Prophecy Fulfilled: A Tale of the Late American War*. Montréal: Armour and Ramsay 1840. Rpt. Toronto: University of Toronto Press 1976
– *Wacousta or, The Prophecy: A Tale of the Canadas*. 1832. Ed. Douglas Cronk. Ottawa: Carleton University Press 1987
Roberts, Charles G.D. *The Heart of the Ancient Wood*. 1900. Toronto: McClelland and Stewart 1974
– *The Iceberg, and Other Poems*. Toronto: Ryerson Press 1934
Ross, W.W.E. *Shapes and Sounds: Poems of W.W.E. Ross*. Ed. Raymond Souster and John Robert Colombo. Toronto: Longmans 1968
Salutin, Rick. *A Man of Little Faith*. Toronto: McClelland and Stewart 1988
Sangster, Charles. *Hesperus and Other Poems and Lyrics*. Montréal: Lovell; Kingston: Creighton 1860. Rpt. with succeeding item. Toronto: University of Toronto Press 1972
– *The St. Lawrence and the Saguenay, and Other Poems*. Kingston: Creighton 1856. Rpt. with preceding item. Toronto: University of Toronto Press 1972
Scott, Duncan Campbell. *The Circle of Affection, and Other Pieces in Prose and Verse*. Toronto: McClelland and Stewart 1947
– *The Green Cloister: Later Poems*. Toronto: McClelland and Stewart 1935
– *The Poems of Duncan Campbell Scott*. Toronto: McClelland and Stewart 1926
– *The Witching of Elspie: A Book of Stories*. Toronto: McClelland and Stewart 1923
Scott, F.R. *Collected Poems*. Toronto: McClelland and Stewart 1981
Seton, Ernest Thompson. *Trail of an Artist-Naturalist*. New York: Scribner's 1940
– *Two Little Savages*. New York: Grosset and Dunlap 1911
– *Wild Animals I Have Known*. New York: Scribner's 1898
Shirreff, Patrick. *A Tour through North America*. Edinburgh: Oliver and Boyd 1835
Simcoe, Elizabeth. *Mrs. Simcoe's Diary*. Ed. Mary Quayle Innis. Toronto: Macmillan 1965
Sinclair, Lister. 'We All Hate Toronto.' In *A Play on Words and Other Radio Plays*, 255–78. Toronto: Dent 1948
Slater, Patrick. *The Yellow Briar*. Toronto: Thomas Allen 1933
Smith, A.J.M. *The Classic Shade*. Toronto: McClelland and Stewart 1978

– *Towards a View of Canadian Letters*. Vancouver: University of British Columbia
  Press 1973
Souster, Raymond. *Collected Poems*. 6 vols. Ottawa: Oberon Press 1980–8
– *A Local Pride*. Toronto: Contact Press 1962
– *Selected Poems*. Ottawa: Oberon Press 1972
Stewart, Frances. *Our Forest Home*. 1889. 2nd enlarged edition. Ed. E.S. Dunlop.
  Montréal: Gazette 1902
Strachan, James [=Strachan, John]. *A Visit to the Province of Upper Canada in 1819*.
  Aberdeen: James Strachan 1820. Rpt. Wakefield, Yorks: S.R. Publishers; New York:
  Johnson Reprint Corporation 1968
Strickland, Samuel. *Twenty-Seven Years in Canada West*. 1853. Rpt. (2 vols. in 1)
  Edmonton: Hurtig 1970
Struthers, J.R. (Tim). 'Alice Munro's Fictive Imagination.' In *The Art of Alice Munro:
  Saying the Unsayable*, ed. Judith Miller, 103–12. Waterloo: University of Waterloo
  Press 1984
– 'An Interview with Hugh Hood.' *Essays on Canadian Writing*, 13/14 (Winter/Spring
  1978–9), 21–99
Talbot, Edward Allen. *Five Years' Residence in the Canadas*. London: Longman 1824.
  Rpt. Wakefield, Yorks: S.R. Publishers; New York: Johnson Reprint Corporation 1968
Titley, E. Brian. *A Narrow Vision: Duncan Campbell Scott and the Administration of
  Indian Affairs in Canada*. Vancouver: University of British Columbia Press 1986
Traill, Catharine Parr. *The Backwoods of Canada*. London: Charles Knight 1836.
  Rpt. Toronto: Coles 1980
– *Canadian Crusoes: A Tale of the Rice Lake Plains*. 1852. Ed. Rupert Schieder.
  Ottawa: Carleton University Press 1986
– *Canadian Settler's Guide*. 1855. Toronto: McClelland and Stewart 1969
Trollope, Anthony. *North America*. New York: Harper 1862
Waddington, Miriam. *Collected Poems*. Toronto: Oxford University Press 1986
Wainwright, Andy. *Moving Outward*. Toronto: New Press 1970
Weaver, Robert. 'Introduction to the New Edition.' Morley Callaghan, *Strange
  Fugitive*. Edmonton: Hurtig 1970
– ed. *Canadian Short Stories*. Toronto: Oxford University Press 1960
West, Bruce. *Toronto*. Toronto: Doubleday 1967
White, Randall. *Ontario 1610–1985: A Political and Economic History*. Toronto:
  Dundurn Press 1985
Wiebe, Rudy. *First and Vital Candle*. Toronto: McClelland and Stewart 1966
Wilson, Sir Daniel. Review of Charles Sangster, *The St. Lawrence and the Saguenay*.
  1855. In *An Anthology of Canadian Literature in English, Volume 1*, ed. Russell
  Brown and Donna Bennett, 132–5. Toronto: Oxford University Press 1982
Woodcock, George. *Northern Spring: The Flowering of Canadian Literature*.
  Vancouver: Douglas and McIntyre 1987

Biographical Index

ATWOOD, MARGARET (b. 1939)

Novelist, poet, short-story writer, critic. Born in Ottawa, grew up in Toronto and, during summers, in the Ontario and Québec bush. One of the best-known Canadian writers at home and abroad.

BARR, ROBERT (1850–1912)

Born in Glasgow, brought to Canada West as a child. Trained as teacher, became journalist and author, eventually returning to England. Best known for *The Measure of the Rule* (1907).

BELANEY, ARCHIE. *See* Grey Owl.

BIRNEY, EARLE (b. 1904)

Poet and novelist. Born in Calgary, taught at Universities of Toronto and British Columbia. Best known for 'David' (1942). *Collected Poems* (2 vols.) appeared in 1975.

BLACKWOOD, ALGERNON (1869–1951)

English man of letters, well known as a writer of fiction involving the supernatural and the mysterious. Visited Canada in early 1890s.

BODSWORTH, FRED (b. 1918)

Writer, naturalist, journalist. His often exciting and always didactic fiction is invariably concerned with the relationship between human beings and the natural world.

BONNYCASTLE, SIR RICHARD (1791–1847)

Soldier, writer. Born in England, sent to Canada in 1826. Knighted 1840 for service during the Upper Canada Rebellion of 1837–8. Published *The Canadas in 1841* in 1842. Died in Kingston.

BOUCHETTE, JOSEPH (1774–1841)

Military surveyor. Born in Québec, present at the founding of York (Toronto) in 1793. Served in War of 1812. Published *The British Dominions of North America* in 1832. Died in Montréal.

BROOKE, RUPERT (1887–1915)

English poet, famous for 'The Old Vicarage, Grantchester' and 'The Soldier.'
Visited Canada and the U.S. in 1913. Died in Greece during First World War.

BULLARD, MARGARET

English writer. Lived in Toronto in 1940s while her husband taught physics at
University of Toronto. *Wedlock's the Devil* (1951) was her first novel.

BURWELL, ADAM HOOD (1790–1849)

Born near Fort Erie, Upper Canada. First an Anglican, then an Irvingite minister.
Best known as poet for 'The Talbot Road.'

CALLAGHAN, MORLEY (1903–90)

Born in Toronto, where he spent most of his life. Author of numerous novels and
short stories. Acquaintance of Hemingway and Fitzgerald in Paris in the 1920s.

CAMPBELL, WILFRED (1858–1918)

Born in Berlin (now Kitchener), Canada West. Poet best known for descriptive
poetry of the Lake Huron area. Later became an advocate of Imperialism.

CARVER, JONATHAN (1710–80)

Born in Massachusetts, served in army. Sent to explore northwestern American
territories in 1766. Later, moved to England, where he published *Travels through the
Interior Parts of North America* in 1768. Died in London.

CLARKE, AUSTIN (b. 1932)

Born in Barbados, immigrated to Canada in 1955. Novelist and short-story writer
best known for *The Meeting Point* (1967), *Storm of Fortune* (1973), and *The Bigger
Light* (1975).

COHEN, MATT (b. 1942)

Born in Kingston. Novelist and short-story writer, best known for his 'Salem'
tetralogy, especially *The Disinherited* (1974).

CONNOR, RALPH (1860–1937)

Pseudonym of Charles William Gordon. Born in Glengarry, Canada West. Presbyterian minister, author of once enormously popular moral-adventure stories,
especially *The Man from Glengarry* (1901).

CRAWFORD, ISABELLA VALANCY (1850–87)

Born in Dublin, came to Canada West as a child. Poet little recognized in her own
time, best known for 'Malcolm's Katie.'

DAVIES, ROBERTSON (b. 1913)

Born in Thamesville. Novelist, playwright, critic, and general man of letters, best
known for his 'Deptford Trilogy,' especially *Fifth Business* (1970).

DEWDNEY, CHRISTOPHER (b. 1951)

Poet, teacher, artist. Born in London, Ontario. Attempts to combine poetry and
science through verse and draws upon both intellect and imagination.

DICKENS, CHARLES (1812–70)

British novelist. Visited Canada as well as the U.S. in 1842 on the trip that resulted in
American Notes.

DI MICHELE, MARY (b. 1949)

Born in Italy, immigrated to Canada in 1955. Poet, frequently writing about Italian Canadians.

DUNCAN, SARA JEANNETTE (1861–1922)

Born in Brantford, Canada West. Journalist and novelist, who spent most of her later life with husband in India. Best known in Canada for *The Imperialist* (1904).

DUNLOP, DR WILLIAM 'TIGER' (1792–1848)

Born in Scotland. Soldier, doctor, sportsman, politician, eccentric, writer. Published *Statistical Sketches of Upper Canada* (1832) and *Recollections of the American War, 1812–14* (1847). Died in Lachine, Canada East.

ELLIOTT, GEORGE (b. 1923)

Born in London, Ontario, but drawing inspiration from the Strathroy area in *The Kissing Man* (1962). Also published *God's Big Acre: Life in 401 Country* (1986).

ENGEL, MARIAN (1933–85)

Née Passmore. Novelist and short-story writer, born in Toronto, married at one time to Howard Engel, the mystery writer. Best known for *The Honeyman Festival* (1970) and *Bear* (1976).

FAESSLER, SHIRLEY

Short-story writer, novelist. Born in Toronto of Jewish parentage. Writes mainly of Jewish life in Toronto.

FINDLEY, TIMOTHY (b. 1930)

Novelist, short-story writer, playwright, formerly actor. Born in Toronto. Best known for *The Wars* (1977), *Famous Last Words* (1981), and *Not Wanted on the Voyage* (1984).

FINNIGAN, JOAN (b. 1925)

Poet, journalist. Born in Ottawa, writes poetry and prose about the Ottawa Valley, as well as numerous other topics.

FRASER, SYLVIA (b. 1935)

Born in Hamilton. Novelist, journalist, best known for *Pandora* (1972) and *The Candy Factory* (1975).

GALT, JOHN (1779–1839)

Scots novelist best known for *The Annals of the Parish* (1821). In Upper Canada 1826-9 as secretary of the Canada Company. *Bogle Corbet* (1831) is set in the Huron Tract. Died in Scotland.

GARNER, HUGH (1913–79)

Born in England, brought to Canada as child. Became professional writer of novels and short stories, best known for *Cabbagetown* (1950, 1968).

GORDON, CHARLES WILLIAM. *See* CONNOR, RALPH.

GRANT, GEORGE M. (1835–1902)

Born in Nova Scotia. Principal of Queen's University, 1877–1902. Presbyterian leader, educator, writer. Remembered as author for *Ocean to Ocean* (1873).

GREY OWL (1888–1938)

Born Archie Belaney in Hastings, England. Immigrated to Canada in 1906, and eventually posed as an Indian. Wrote on frontier life, Indian attitudes, and ecological subjects.

GROVE, FREDERICK PHILIP (1879–1948)

Born Felix Paul Greve in West Prussia, of German parentage. Became author and translator, got into debt and was sentenced to prison (1903). Immigrated to North America in 1909, creating a new life as writer of prairie fiction. Moved to Ontario in 1929. *Two Generations* (1939) is his only novel set in Ontario.

HALL, BASIL (1788–1844)

Scots naval captain, author. Born in Edinburgh. Travelled through North America, 1827–8. Published *Travels in North America* in 1829. Died in Portsmouth.

HEAD, GEORGE (1782–1855)

Soldier, writer. Born in England, elder brother of Sir Francis Bond Head. Served in Canada c. 1814–21. Published *Forest Scenery and Incidents in the Wilds of North America* in 1829. Knighted in 1831.

HENRY, ALEXANDER (1739–1824)

Born in New Jersey, became a trader. Captured by Indians at Michilimackinac in 1763 and lived with them for three years. Author of *Travels and Adventures in Canada and the Indian Territories* (1809).

HERIOT, GEORGE (1759–1839)

Artist, postal official, writer. Born in Scotland, came to Canada in 1792, later returning to England. Wrote and illustrated *Travels through the Canadas* (1807). Died in London.

HODGINS, JACK (b. 1938)

British Columbia novelist and short-story writer, best known for *The Invention of the World* (1977). Spent some years teaching at the University of Ottawa.

HOOD, HUGH (b. 1928)

Born and brought up in Toronto, now lives and teaches in Montréal. Novelist, short-story writer, essayist, best known for his continuing *New Age* series begun in 1975, a twelve-novel sequence centred on Ontario.

HOWISON, JOHN (1797–1859)

Scots doctor and writer. Visited Upper and Lower Canada, 1818–20, publishing *Sketches of Upper Canada* in 1821. Worked for twenty years in India. Died in London.

HUGGAN, ISOBEL (b. 1943)

Writer, teacher, journalist, best known for *The Elizabeth Stories* (1984).

JAMESON, ANNA (1794–1860)

Née Murphy. Born in Dublin, educated in England. Versatile woman of letters, especially in areas of travel and art history. Important in Canadian literature for *Winter Studies and Summer Rambles in Canada* (1838).

JOHNSTON, GEORGE (b. 1913)

Born in Hamilton. Poet, translator, teacher. Best known for humorous poems of suburban life in *The Cruising Auk* (1959). Translates sagas from Old Norse. His collected poems, *Endeared by Dark*, appeared in 1990.

KANE, PAUL (1810–76)

Artist, born in Ireland. Well known for his paintings of Indians and Indian life. Died in Toronto.

KNISTER, RAYMOND (1899–1932)

Poet, short-story writer, novelist, editor. Came from an Ontarian farming background and wrote primarily of rural life. Died in a drowning accident.

KREISEL, HENRY (1922–91)

Novelist, short-story writer, teacher, administrator. Born in Austria, sent from England to Canada at opening of World War II. Taught at the University of Alberta.

LAIDLAW, ROBERT (1901–76)

Farmer in southwest Ontario. Father of Alice Munro. Wrote documentary novel, *The McGregors,* late in life.

LAMPMAN, ARCHIBALD (1861–99)

Poet. Born in Morpeth, worked as Post Office clerk in Ottawa, and wrote about the Ottawa valley. Often regarded as Canada's finest nineteenth-century poet.

LANGTON, ANNE (1804–93)

Settler, writer, artist. Sister of John Langton. Born in England, immigrated to Upper Canada with parents in 1837. Led uneventful life. Kept regular journal.

LANGTON, JOHN (1808–94)

Administrator, politician, brother of Anne Langton. Came to Upper Canada in 1833, eventually becoming auditor-general and deputy minister of finance. His valuable letters were published posthumously as *Early Days in Upper Canada* (1926).

LEACOCK, STEPHEN (1869–1944)

Humorist, teacher. Born in England, brought to Canada in 1876. Taught political economy at McGill, 1903–36. Best known for *Sunshine Sketches of a Little Town* (1912).

LEE, DENNIS (b. 1939)

Poet, editor, critic, publisher, teacher. Born in Toronto. Best known for *Civil Elegies* (1968, rev. 1972) and for his children's poetry, especially *Alligator Pie* (1974).

LEPAN, DOUGLAS (b. 1914)

Poet, novelist, teacher, civil servant, administrator. Born in Toronto, served in Canadian army in World War II, and later in Department of External Affairs. Poems collected in *Weathering It* (1987).

LEVINE, NORMAN (b. 1923)

Born in Ottawa of Jewish parentage. Novelist and poet, but best known as writer of short stories and for his critical memoir *Canada Made Me* (1958).

LEWIS, WYNDHAM (1884–1957)

English painter, writer, prominent in modernist circles in 1920s and 1930s, associate of Pound, Eliot, etc. Spent most of World War II in Canada; this led to writing of *Self Condemned* (1954).

LOCHHEAD, DOUGLAS (b. 1922)

Poet, librarian, teacher, bibliographer. Librarian at Massey College, University of Toronto, 1963–75. Born in Guelph but retired to New Brunswick. Best known for *The Full Furnace* (1975) and *High Marsh Road* (1980).

MAC LENNAN, HUGH (1907–90)

Novelist, essayist. Born in Cape Breton, taught at McGill. Wrote novels primarily about the Maritimes and Québec, emphasizing nationalistic and social issues.

MAGRATH FAMILY

Pioneer settlers. Eight family members immigrated to Upper Canada in 1829, settling in Erindale. Selections from their correspondence published as *Authentic Letters from Upper Canada* (ed. Thomas Radcliff) in 1833.

MARRYAT, CAPT. FREDERICK (1792–1848)

English sailor and novelist, who wrote adventures stories, generally about the sea, often for young people. Visited Canada and the U.S. in late 1830s.

MC ARTHUR, PETER (1866–1924)

Born in Middlesex County, Canada West. Journalist and writer on rural subjects, whose articles for the Toronto *Globe* and *The Farmer's Advocate* were subsequently collected in book form.

MC FADDEN, DAVID (b. 1940)

Born in Hamilton. Poet and writer of free-ranging travel books centred on the Great Lakes.

MC LACHLAN, ALEXANDER (1818–96)

Born in Scotland, immigrated to Upper Canada in 1840. Poet, farmer, teacher, mechanic. Best known for 'The Emigrant.' His *Collected Works* appeared in 1900.

MITCHELL, JOHN. *See* SLATER, PATRICK

MOODIE, SUSANNA (1803–85)

Née Strickland. Sister of Samuel Strickland and Catharine Parr Traill. Born in England, immigrated to Upper Canada in 1832. Writer of fiction and poetry, but best known for her memoirs, *Roughing It in the Bush* (1852) and *Life in the Clearings* (1853).

MUNRO, ALICE (b. 1931)

Née Laidlaw. Born in Wingham, best known for her fiction set in southwestern Ontario, including *Lives of Girls and Women* (1971) and *The Progress of Love* (1986).

O'BRIEN, MARY (1798–1876)

Née Gapper. Journal writer. Born in England, immigrated to Upper Canada in 1828. Lived in Thornhill and Richmond Hill area. Later settled near Lake Simcoe. Kept regular journal, 1828–38.

ONDAATJE, MICHAEL (b. 1943)

Poet, novelist, critic. Born in Ceylon (Sri Lanka), came to Canada in 1962. Much of

In the Skin of a Lion (1987), half documentary, half fantasy, is set in Toronto.

PACI, F.G. (b. 1948)

Born in Italy, brought to Canada in 1952. Writes novels about the Italian community in Sault Ste Marie, where he grew up.

PRATT, E.J. (1882–1964)

Poet, teacher. Born in Newfoundland, spent most of his adult life in Toronto. Generally regarded as Canada's leading narrative poet.

PURDY, AL (b. 1918)

Poet. Born in Wooler, settled in Ameliasburg. His *Collected Poems* appeared in 1986.

REANEY, JAMES (b. 1926)

Poet, playwright, teacher. Born near Stratford. Gained early reputation as poet: see *Poems* (1972). Later turned to stage best known as dramatist for *The Donnellys*, a trilogy (1975–7).

RICHARDSON, JOHN (1796–1852)

Novelist, poet, soldier. Born in Queenston, Upper Canada, served in War of 1812. Best known for *Wacousta* (1832). Died in New York.

ROSS, W.W.E. (1894–1966)

Poet, scientist. Born in Peterborough, worked as geophysicist. Wrote short imagistic poems, mainly about Canadian life and scenery.

SALUTIN, RICK (b. 1942)

Playwright, novelist, social commentator. Born in Toronto of Jewish parentage. Best known for his play *Les Canadiens* (1977). His novel, *A Man of Little Faith*, appeared in 1988.

SANGSTER, CHARLES (1822–93)

Poet. Born in Kingston. Worked as journalist and in post office. Best known for *The St. Lawrence and the Saguenay* (1856).

SCOTT, DUNCAN CAMPBELL (1862–1947)

Poet, civil servant, short-story writer. Born in Ottawa. Worked in Department of Indian Affairs, eventually becoming deputy superintendent-general. Friend of Archibald Lampman.

SCOTT, F.R. (1899–1985)

Poet, lawyer, politician. Born in Québec, taught law at McGill. Prominent in social and political issues. His *Collected Poems* appeared in 1981.

SETON, ERNEST THOMPSON (1860–1940)

Naturalist, writer, artist. Born in England, came to Canada in 1866. Well known for books on wildlife (both fiction and non-fiction) and for his championing of scouting and woodcraft organizations. Later moved to United States, where he died.

SHIRREFF, PATRICK

Little known about his life. Travelled in Canada in 1833. Scots farmer, businessman and author of a pamphlet on emigration. Patrick Shirreff published *A Tour through North America* (1835).

SIMCOE, ELIZABETH (1762–1850)

Née Gwillim. Diarist, painter. Born in England, came to Upper Canada when her husband was appointed first lieutenant-governor in 1792. Left in 1796.

SLATER, PATRICK (1880–1951)

Pseudonym of John Mitchell. Lawyer, writer. Practised law but was eventually disbarred for malpractice. Turned later to writing. Remembered only for his semi-fictional memoir *The Yellow Briar* (1933).

SMITH, A.J.M. (1902–80)

Poet, anthologist, teacher. Born in Montréal, taught mainly in United States. Well known for championing Canadian verse, especially in *The Book of Canadian Poetry* (1943), and for his own technically proficient poems.

SOUSTER, RAYMOND (b. 1921)

Poet. Born in Toronto, worked for most of his life in a bank. Well known for his championing of modern verse (as magazine-founder, editor, publisher), and for his prolific poetry, mainly about Toronto.

STEWART, FRANCES (1794–1872)

Born in Ireland, immigrated to Upper Canada in 1822, settling in Douro area. Her letters home became the basis for *Our Forest Home*, published posthumously (1889).

STRACHAN, JOHN (1778–1867)

Bishop, educator. Immigrated to Upper Canada in 1799, ordained 1803. Well known for educational organization and as defender of the Family Compact. Published *A Visit to the Province of Upper Canada in 1819* (1820) under the name of his brother James.

STRICKLAND, SAMUEL (1804–67)

Settler, writer, brother of Catharine Parr Traill and Susanna Moodie. Born in England, immigrated to Canada in 1825, settled in Douro. Published *Twenty-Seven Years in Canada West* in 1853.

TALBOT, EDWARD ALLEN (1796–1839)

Inventor, soldier, writer. Born in Ireland, immigrated to Canada in 1818. Published *Five Years' Residence in the Canadas* (1824). Involved in journalism and politics in the London area. Died in New York.

TRAILL, CATHARINE PARR (1802–99)

Writer, botanist, novelist. Née Strickland, sister of Samuel Strickland and Susanna Moodie. Born in England, immigrated to Upper Canada in 1832. Best known for *The Backwoods of Canada* (1836).

TROLLOPE, ANTHONY (1815–82)

English novelist, author of the famous Barsetshire novels. Published *North America* after a visit in 1862.

WADDINGTON, MIRIAM (b. 1917)

Poet. Née Dworkin. Born in Winnipeg of Jewish parentage. Became social worker and later university teacher. Her *Collected Poems* appeared in 1986.

WAINWRIGHT, ANDY (b. 1946)

Poet, short-story writer, teacher. Born in Toronto, professor of English at Dalhousie University.

WHITMAN, WALT (1819–92)

American poet, well known for *Leaves of Grass* (1855, much expanded later). Visited Canada in 1880.

WIEBE, RUDY (b. 1934)

Novelist, short-story writer. Born in Saskatchewan of Mennonite parentage, known for his novels about Mennonites, and about Indians and Métis in the nineteenth century. Only *First and Vital Candle* (1966) is set in Ontario.

WILSON, DANIEL (1816–92)

Scientist, historian, educator, writer. Born in Scotland, immigrated to Canada West in 1853. Distinguished writer on archaeology and ethnology. First president of the University of Toronto. Knighted in 1888.

Index

THE ONTARIO HISTORICAL STUDIES SERIES

Peter Oliver, *G. Howard Ferguson: Ontario Tory* (1977)

J.M.S. Careless, ed., *The Pre-Confederation Premiers: Ontario Government Leaders, 1841–1867* (1980)

Charles W. Humphries, *'Honest Enough to Be Bold': The Life and Times of Sir James Pliny Whitney* (1985)

Charles M. Johnston, *E.C. Drury: Agrarian Idealist* (1986)

A.K. McDougall, *John P. Robarts: His Life and Government* (1986)

Roger Graham, *Old Man Ontario: Leslie M. Frost* (1990)

John T. Saywell, *'Just call me Mitch': The Life of Mitchell F. Hepburn* (1991)

A. Margaret Evans, *Sir Oliver Mowat* (1992)

Joseph Schull, *Ontario since 1867* (McClelland and Stewart 1978)

Joseph Schull, *L'Ontario depuis 1867* (McClelland and Stewart 1987)

Olga B. Bishop, Barbara I. Irwin, Clara G. Miller, eds., *Bibliography of Ontario History, 1867–1976: Cultural, Economic, Political, Social* 2 volumes (1980)

Christopher Armstrong, *The Politics of Federalism: Ontario's Relations with the Federal Government, 1867–1942* (1981)

David Gagan, *Hopeful Travellers: Families, Land and Social Change in Mid-Victorian Peel County, Canada West* (1981)

Robert M. Stamp, *The Schools of Ontario, 1876–1976* (1982)

R. Louis Gentilcore and C. Grant Head, *Ontario's History in Maps* (1984)

K.J. Rea, *The Prosperous Years: The Economic History of Ontario, 1939–1975* (1985)

Ian M. Drummond, *Progress without Planning: The Economic History of Ontario from Confederation to the Second World War* (1987)

John Webster Grant, *A Profusion of Spires: Religion in Nineteenth-Century Ontario* (1988)

Susan E. Houston and Alison Prentice, *Schooling and Scholars in Nineteenth-Century Ontario* (1988)

Ann Saddlemyer, ed., *Early Stages: Theatre in Ontario, 1800–1914* (1990)

W.J. Keith, *Literary Images of Ontario* (1992)